TIMELESS CREEDS FOR WINNING

TIMELESS CREEDS FOR WINNING

VICTORY STRATEGIES FOR BUSINESS, WAR, POLITICS, AND LIFE

THAM TRONG MA

TIMELESS CREEDS FOR WINNING
Tham Trong Ma

All rights reserved
First Edition, 2023
© Tham Trong Ma, 2023

No part of this publication may be reproduced, or stored in a retrieval system, or transmitted in any form by means of electronic, mechanical, photocopying or otherwise, without prior written permission from the author.

Paperback ISBN: 978-1-954891-50-0
Hardback ISBN: 978-1-954891-51-7
ebook ISBN: 978-1-954891-49-4

Contents

Introduction 1

The Writings of Miyamoto Musashi (宮本 武 蔵) 13

The Five Spheres 五輪の書 15
    Introduction 29
    Scroll 1 – Earth 地 31
    Scroll 2 – Water 水 47
    Scroll 3 – Fire 火 67
    Scroll 4 – Wind 風 89
    Scroll 5 – Emptiness 空 103
    The Thirty-Five Articles About Sword Strategy
    剣 戦 略 に 関 する35の 記 事 105
      1. On Using Two Swords
      2. Understanding the Way of Strategy
      3. On Holding the Sword
      4. On Positioning
      5. On Footsteps
      6. On Gazing
      7. On Timing
      8. On Mindset
      9. The High, Middle, and Low Levels of Strategy
      10. The Measuring Cord
      11. The Path of the Sword
      12. Hitting and Cutting
      13. The Three Initiatives

14. Crossing the Ford
15. The Body Replacing Sword
16. The Two Feet
17. Pressing Down the Sword
18. Loosened Shadow
19. The Moving Shadow
20. Loosening the Bowstring
21. The Small Comb
22. The Rhythm Interval
23. Pressing Down the Pillow
24. Understanding the Situation
25. On Becoming the Opponent
26. Maintaining and Releasing the Mind
27. On Attacking as an Opportunity
28. The Lacquer Adhesion
29. The Body of an Autumn Monkey
30. Comparing Heights
31. The Hinge Body
32. The General and The Army
33. Defensive – Not Defensive
34. The Body of a Rock
35. On Understanding Moments

The Way Of Walking Alone – Dokkōdō 獨行道

The Writing of Sun Vu (孫武)..................125
The Law Of War 兵法 127
Chapter 1 – Planning 始計 139
Chapter 2 – Combating 作戰 143
Chapter 3 – Offensive Strategy 謀攻 147
Chapter 4 – Military Disposition 軍形 151
Chapter 5 – Military Force 兵勢 155
Chapter 6 – Real and Unreal 虛實 159
Chapter 7 – Maneuvering 軍爭 163
Chapter 8 – Nine Changes 九變 167
Chapter 9 – Marching 行軍 169
Chapter 10 – Terrain 地形 175

Chapter 11 – Nine Ground Positions 九 地............. 179
Chapter 12 – Fire Attack 火 攻..................... 187
Chapter 13 – Using Spy 用 間 189

The Writing of Niccolò Machiavelli 193
The Prince..195
Chapter 1 - Of Different Country Types And
How To Acquire Them 207
Chapter 2 - About The Hereditary Monarchy 209
Chapter 3 - About Mixed Monarchy 211
Chapter 4 - Why the Kingdom Of Darius10 Conquered By Alexander The Great11 Did Not Rebel Against
The Successors Of Alexander The Great After His Death......221
Chapter 5 - About How To Govern Cities Or Countries
That Live Under Their Laws Before They Were annexed......225
Chapter 6 - About New Countries Acquired With
Your Own Abilities 227
Chapter 7 - About Newly Acquired Territorial Lands
Either By Arms Of Others Or By Luck....................233
Chapter 8 - Of Countries Captured By Wickedness......243
Chapter 9 - About Civil Monarchy..........................249
Chapter 10 - About The Way Of Measuring
The Strength of Nations..255
Chapter 11 - About The Church Nations.................259
Chapter 12 - About Soldiery Types And The Mercenaries 263
Chapter 13 - About The Auxiliary Army, The Mixed
Army, And The Private Army..................................271
Chapter 14 - Of The Prince On The Art Of War.....277
Chapter 15 - Involving Men Things, Especially
Prince About Praising Or Blaming..........................281
Chapter 16 - Of Generosity And Miserliness 283
Chapter 17 - Of Ruthlessness and Mercy, And
Whether Love Is Better Than Fear 287
Chapter 18 - About How Prince Keeps His Promise......291
Chapter 19 - Of Avoiding Being Scorned And Hated............295

Chapter 20 - Whether Citadels And Many Other Things
The Prince Used Are Useful Or Useless 309
Chapter 21 - How The Prince Must Behave To Be Famous ...315
Chapter 22 - Of The Prince's Personal Staff............................321
Chapter 23 - How To Avoid Flatterers 323
Chapter 24 - Why The Italian Princes Lost The States...........327
Chapter 25 - Effects Of Human Fate And How To Fight It....329
Chapter 26 - An Exhortation To Free Italy From
The Barbarians...333

The Writing of Lao Tzu (老子)...**349**
　The Book of Ethics 道德经
　Part I - The Way 道 (Chapter 1 to Chapter 37).......................353
　Part II - The Virtue 德 (Chapter 38 to Chapter 81).................377

Notes..**405**

Further Readings **447**

Introduction

Vietnam's history cannot be chronicled without mentioning China's influence and domination. China dominated Vietnam for 1000 years (from 111 BC to 938 AD) till Vietnam broke free. Vietnam's independence lasted from 938 AD – 1407 AD, and China retook control. This time, China's dominance was brief, lasting till 1428 AD, when Vietnam overthrew them and declared independence.

For decades, Vietnam has fought to wriggle free from Chinese dominance, yet communist China has not stopped its scheme of occupying our small territory until present day. They want to turn Vietnam into a province of China. In addition, the malevolent aggression of communist China does not end in our country. They consider themselves as the "only son of God 神 的 獨 生 子," so they must own and rule the world. To do this, they (in)directly encroach or violently invade the lands of countries they share borders with.

Throughout Vietnam's five thousand years as a nation, the truth of its history has been robbed and distorted by Chinese invaders. That is not to mention the devastation caused by the Viet Cong or the Vietnamese Communist Party (VCP).

They burned books, erased cultural traditions, and destroyed religions of the Vietnamese people. They represented the China Communist Party (CCP) and worked to fulfill the agenda of the CCP, which was to suppress the Vietnamese people and control the world with their dictatorship.

They supplanted our original stories with distorted, single versions written and told by them. It is for this reason that I selected and translated some outstanding, timeless, and practical books. These books include The Writings of Miyamoto Musashi (*The Five Spheres*, *The Thirty-Five Articles About Sword Strategy*, and *The Way of Walking Alone*), Sun Vu's *The Law of War*, Niccolo Machiavelli's *The Prince*, and Lao Tzu's *The Book of Ethics*. These books, free from Chinese adulterations, retain the cultural essence of the Vietnamese people. They expose us to the truth and goodness of the outside world so that we can cultivate our own truths, harness our goodness, and proudly walk at the same pace as the rest of the world.

If we, like the Vietnamese, must expand and connect our minds to today's vast and complex society, then we need to embrace our roots. The tenets of Vietnamese culture do not undermine humanity; rather, they uphold core values (such as respect, kindness, and unity) that oil the wheel of humanity. I expect that in these six books, the Vietnamese reader will find a portal that connects him back to his roots. The books in this anthology are thematically different, yet they drive the reader towards one goal: cultivating and harnessing human virtues.

The Five Spheres trains the human body and spirit — to present to the world a complete individual with an inviolable exterior *and* an invincible core, two qualities that defined its author, Miyamoto Musashi. Between age 13 and 29, Musashi fought sixty to-the-death duels and lost none. But when he turned 30, he looked back at his past — his battles, his wins — and realized that his victories were not because of his great swordsmanship. He figured that they were probably due to innate gifts, divine predestination, or the inferior swordsmanship of his opponents. However, after much study and introspection, he discovered that his victories could be attributed to what he called The Way of the Warrior or The Way of Strategy, or simply The Way.

The Five Spheres sections its discourse on The Way of the Warrior into five scrolls: Earth, Water, Fire, Wind, and Emptiness. Each scroll teaches the warrior the various strategies to employ in a battle.

The Earth or Ground scroll compares the Way to carpentry. Like a carpenter building a house, the warrior must fight the enemy methodically to gain victory. He must understand perception and timing because, without them, his stance and gaze when facing the enemy may yield nothing.

The Water scroll guides the warrior on sword fighting by teaching him the right gaze and posture to assume when facing the enemy. For Musashi, The Way should be part and parcel of the warrior to the point where one cannot tell his daily posture from his fighting posture. The Water scroll also emphasizes the importance of vision. "Your vision must be wide and broad," Musashi writes. There are two types of vision: perception and sight. "With perception, you look to feel; with sight, you look to see. Perception is strong; sight is weak."

Armed with perception and timing coupled with the right gaze and posture, the warrior can easily exploit his opponent's weaknesses and take the victory. This is what the Fire scroll teaches. Musashi likens a battle to a fire. A battle is where a warrior risks his lives, where he dances between life and death, learns the sword's strategy, and understands the strengths and adversaries of his adversary's sword.

The Five Spheres does not only show the warrior how to be invincible; it also explains why other warriors are not. In the Wind scroll, Musashi criticizes the techniques of other schools of swordsmanship. They channeled their art of swordsmanship towards monetary gains. Their fighting strategy was theatrical and lacked the depth to understand and achieve victory.

Musashi aimed to show the warrior the path to victory, to teach the warrior all he, Musashi, knew. However, in the Emptiness scroll, otherwise known as the Scroll of the Void, he instructs the warrior to be flexible with knowledge. The warrior should see all the knowledge gained as nothing, empty, void. Because "the more knowledge we gain, the more we realize how little we know."

Musashi's principles of swordsmanship were so wide in scope that they spanned into another book, *The Thirty-Five Articles About Sword Strategy*.

The Thirty-Five Articles About Sword Strategy is a short compilation of the practices and strategies Musashi used as standards to train himself and master the use of the sword. In it, he leaves the warrior with valuable fighting philosophies that could apply in other aspects of life. For instance, Musashi writes that strength grows, so a warrior should carry a sword that suits his body and matches his strength.

Since the warrior's strength lies in his body, the whole body should be treated as one. Every part should receive equal attention — from head to toe. The warrior's body should exist in balance and oneness, just as his mind should be calm and fearless. He shouldn't be distracted by fear. "Develop a large mind — a mind like water. Depending on the situation, the mind should be flexible like water. Water can be dark blue. It can be a drop or a vast ocean," Musashi says.

The Thirty-Five Articles About Sword Strategy reiterates perception and sight. But it is one thing to see or perceive, and it is another thing to see at the right moment. Seeing and acting at the right moment guarantees victory no matter the warrior's position. Knowing the right moment is not only important in striking the opponent; it is also important for the warrior's escape. The warrior should understand fast and slow moments; moments for escape, and moments when escape is impossible.

Musashi further writes about another key strategy of swordsmanship: the warrior should think of himself — his body — as the opponent. That way, the warrior would gain insight into the opponent's mind and predict his weakness, even if the opponent is big, protected, or versed in strategy. Of this strategy, Musashi writes, "If you are not aware of the enemy's mind, you may mistake a weak person for a strong one, a person with no skills for one that is competent, and a small opponent for a dangerous one. The enemy may capitalize on this mistake." In these writings about swordsmanship, Musashi emphasized the need for the warrior to attain a strong body through consistent training and a solid spirit that is thoroughly forged.

Musashi not only guided the warrior on swordsmanship, but he also showed the warrior a different perspective for living. In his treatise, *Dokkodo*, which translates to *The Way of Walking Alone*, Musashi penned down 21 precepts to guide the warrior's path. Through these precepts, Musashi wanted the warrior to embrace certain virtues such as honesty (Precept 18: Do not try to own anything illegal or from political bribes), humility (Precept 4: Downplay yourself and think deeply about people), contentment (Precept 5: Do not be greedy or be malicious in life), and honor (Precept 20: One may abandon one's body but must preserve one's honor). In the latter days of his life, Musashi gave himself to asceticism, which was obvious in some of his precepts. Precept 2: Do not seek pleasure for its own sake; Precept 10: Do not direct your thoughts to sensuality; Precept 11: Do not over-enjoy anything in life; Precept 12: Be indifferent to where to live, and Precept 13: Do not pursue a taste for delicious food.

From Musashi's *The Way of Walking Alone*, this anthology takes the reader to Sun Vu's *The Law of War*. For thousands of years, war generals and military strategists have relied on *The Law of War*. Asides from the proven military principles, the book has stood out over time because of the ethos of its author. As a military strategist and general, Sun Vu *never* lost a battle. Like Musashi, Vu did not attribute his conquests to military might or skill; he understood that every battle is unique and should be approached differently.

Vu and Musashi had similar ideologies about warfare. They believed battles transcended weapons; thus, they never aligned with conventional schools of thought regarding battles. For them, a soldier or warrior can only be victorious when they understand that battles are as mental as they are physical. This ideology was parallel to the military ideologies obtainable in their days. For instance, military generals in Sun Vu's days would interpret battle readiness as preparing soldiers to take up arms and march to the battlefield. However, Vu thought differently: battle readiness meant having a perfect strategy, being enigmatic, being unpredictable. Unconventional, yet it's a principle that led to countless victories for Vu and other generals who used it.

In the *Law of War*, Sun Vu addressed important aspects of warfare, including weapons, strategy, espionage, and discipline. Chaptered into thirteen sections, each chapter treats the various stages and strategies of war — from planning and combating to military disposition and spies.

Vu pointed out that planning is one of the essential elements in warfare. It is only after having a perfect plan that the general can combat the enemy easily. However, Vu wanted the soldier to realize that sometimes, combat can be more physiological than physical. A soldier who understands this has a broader strategy than the enemy. Such a soldier can take the enemy by surprise. For instance, instead of clashing weapons, the soldier could gain victory by removing the enemy's comfort, making them miserable and powerless.

The book also explained the importance of arriving early at the battleground, especially before the enemy troop. This allows the general to survey the terrain and know how to use it to his advantage. These principles guide the general to victory, no matter his military might. But before victory can be assured, the general must make proper use of his soldiers. He must also be flexible to improvise since war situations can change. There could be changes in the weather, terrain, weapons, or even soldiers.

Soldiers, the key elements of a battle, must be tough to withstand the rigors of the terrain. Vu also emphasized another key element of warfare: spies. He advised the general to use spies and endeavor to discover enemy spies to use them to his advantage.

The beauty of *The Law of War* is that its principles do not apply to the military alone; they apply to other aspects of life like business, law, sports, daily interactions, and parenting. Life itself is like a war front. We can only confront the challenges thrown to us on our life's journey if we arm ourselves with the right knowledge. It is important to state that these principles formed the framework for my book, *The Entrepreneur's Battle Plan*. A book where I revealed strategies for standing out from the crowd in a ruthlessly competitive business world; although with milder principles, *The Entrepreneur's Battle Plan* is to business and what *The Prince* is to politics.

Nicolo Machiavelli's *The Prince* is a politician's guidebook. In a world defined by never-ending political tussles, we constantly see the central theme of *The Prince* — the end justifies the means — manifest in power-hungry leaders. *The Prince* gives a guide on how to obtain *and* maintain power. First, it exposes the reader to the different leadership systems and how leaders through history acquired countries. Then, like *The Law of War*, it takes the reader on a military exposition — the different types of armies, how to manage them, and how to conduct oneself as a military leader. It further shows the reader how a prince should conduct himself and secure his kingdom for a long time.

The name, Machiavelli or its coined adjective, "Machiavellian," is often associated with cunning and devious schemes. This is because many believe that *The Prince* is rooted in evil. This belief is quite accurate yet unfair. While the book might have presented politics as a dirty game, it is important to point out that it was written in a time when people lived and died by the sword. So what Machiavelli simply did was to expose the political realities he had observed and studied. If we stick to the general assumption that he validated the devious paths to political might, then it would have been hypocritical of him to entreat for the deliverance of Italy.

Machiavelli did not praise vices such as foolishness, greed, corruption, and moral decadence as useful political tools; he exposed them for what they actually are — sociopolitical pathologies. Unfortunately, these vices are still present in the global political scene, and unscrupulous political actors use them to validate Machiavelli's saying of the end justifying the means. While these actors cling to this saying, they forget that Machiavelli also admonished leaders to have goodwill; to avoid being hated by the people, because being hated leads to downfall.

The Prince does not lead politicians down an evil path; instead, what we see in the various political systems of the world are leaders who have chosen to blind themselves to scruples and goodwill. Leaders who have chosen to be hated but forestall their downfall through more schemes and wickedness - they do not care about the world or its people. They deliberately upturn systems for their selfish gains. The result of their misdeeds is a chaotic world where the hearts of many quake. But thankfully, through Lao Tzu's *The Book of Ethics*, people can seek ways to find peace in a chaotic world.

A chaotic world is the product of the imbalance between good and evil, right and wrong. So what Lao Tzu aimed to achieve with this book was to bring ethics into every aspect of human life, including politics. These ethics were based on philosophies birthed from his spiritual experiences. In fact, *The Book of Ethics* is considered a fundamental text for philosophical and religious Taoism. However, its precept spans beyond the boundaries of religion, philosophy, and politics. Professionals like poets, artists, calligraphers, and gardeners have read and applied principles from the book to their professions.

Divided into two parts, The Way and The Virtue, Lao Tzu taught principles bordering on living in harmony with nature and the universe. He advised people to transform themselves, and, like Musashi, he taught them to embrace asceticism by giving up their desires. "If people and things were in harmony, they would all be inanimate and desireless, so there would be no need to fight and conquer. Therefore, humans will have peace, wellbeing, and happiness," he explained. And this is the sole objective of this anthology — to show the path of peace and fulfillment in a world where they are lacking.

The volumes in this anthology contain the basic principles to guide one through the path of cultivating oneself, family ruling, nation ruling, and world peace. The ideas in each volume can also be applied to other aspects of life — from the big things like war, politics, and business to the little things that influence your personal life. Implementing these principles is up to you, but one thing is certain — they will guide you into making the right choices. Reading and applying the ideas of these books will broaden your perspectives and increase your resilience towards life.

Tham Trong Ma
Colorado 2020

The Writings of
Miyamoto Musashi
宮 本 武 蔵

THE FIVE SPHERES AND OTHER WRITINGS

*Japanese Classic Strategic Principles For Success
In War, Business And Life*

Written by
Miyamoto Musashi
宮本武蔵

Translated by
Tham Trong Ma

A Few Words

The Hồng Bàng Dynasty marked the beginning of ancient Vietnam. It all began when the tribal chief, Prince Lộc Tục (c. 2919 – 2792 BC) took the throne, proclaimed himself as Kinh Dương Vương, and founded the state of Xích Quỷ, based in Phong Châu. The capital of the state was Ngàn Hống in the Red River Delta. To create Xích Quỷ, Kinh Dương amalgamated the then Vietnamese tribes that occupied modern territories of China down to the Hồng River.

Legend has that Kinh Dương was a sea dragon who married Long Nữ, a mountain god. Long Nữ and Kinh Dương had a son, Sùng Lãm who succeeded his father. Sùng Lãm was popularly known in the kingdom as Lạc Long Quân, meaning the "Dragon Lord of Lạc".

Lạc Long Quân, as king, he ruled over the Lạc-Việt tribe, and to forge an alliance with the northern tribe ruled by Đế Lai, Lạc Long Quân married Đế Lai's daughter, Âu Cơ. Their union birthed 100 identical sons, and to determine Lạc Long Quân's heir, lots were drawn and Hùng Lang became the legal successor.

When the children came of age, Lạc Long Quân suggested to Âu Cơ that they go their separate ways — him to the lowlands, rivers and seas; her to the highlands and mountains. She agreed and departed with 50 of their sons, while he departed with 49. Hùng Lang, the legal heir, remained in Xích Quỷ to rule over the entire kingdom.

Hùng Lang renamed the country Văn Lang and took up the title of Hùng Quốc Vương. At that time, Văn Lang was bordered north to Động Đình lake, south to Hồ Tôn country, west to Ba Thục country, and east to the Pacific Ocean. The land mass[1] of ancient Vietnam at the time of founding the nation was 2,900,000 km^2. But today, the territory of Vietnam is only 331,212 km^2. This means nearly ninety percent of Vietnamese territory has been taken away by China during the past five thousand years.

Vietnam's history cannot be chronicled without mentioning China's influence and domination. For 1000 years (111 BC – 938 AD), China dominated Vietnam till the latter broke free. Vietnam's independence lasted for almost five centuries (938 AD – 1407 AD) before China retook control. Although Chinese dominance was brief this time (lasted for 21 years), it was long enough to wreak havoc on the cultural narratives of Vietnam. This is why the book series, *The Successful Way*[2] or I renamed later as *Timeless Creeds for Winning* was born.[3]

Timeless Creeds for Winning series consists of four volumes: *The Five Spheres and Other Writings* by Miyamoto Musashi of Japan, *The Law of War* by Sun Tzu of Qi territory (belong to ancient Vietnamese land[4]), *The Prince* by Niccolò Machiavelli of Italy, and *The Book of Ethics* by Lao Tzu from Kinh Sở (also belong to ancient Vietnamese land[5]). I will publish these books in the order mentioned above, first in Vietnamese and then in English.

Each book has its unique characteristics. For example, *The Five Spheres and Other Writings* by Miyamoto Musashi trains your body and spirit, and shapes you into an individual with "inviolable exterior and inner invincibility"[6]. It is a guide to "cultivate yourself".

The Law of War by Sun Vu, the second book in the series, teaches you everything about warfare — benefits, disasters, strategies, and tactics. The principles in this book are not restricted to the military alone, as they can also be applied to business, sports, law, daily interactions with others, and even parenting. You can think of it as a "family ruling" guide.

Niccolò Machiavelli's *The Prince* will follow after *The Law of War*. The book clearly outlines the superficial nature of humanity. You are to understand the workings of the human mind and infer what your opponent may likely do. So while Socrates says, "Know thyself," Machiavelli adds, "Know other people." *The Prince* can be considered as a "nation ruling" guide.

The last book in the series, Lao Tzu's *The Book of Ethics* is an exposition on how to remain at peace in a world filled with temptation and confusion. It highlights the need to stand above good and evil, and acts as a guide to "world peace".

These volumes contain the basic principles to guide one through the path of cultivating oneself, family building, nation ruling, and world peace[7]. Thus, these ideas apply to other aspects of life such as politics, warfare, business, and personal development. They are sure to broaden your perspective and guide you into making right choices.

Of all the books written on "The Art of War" and related subjects from ancient times till today, I selected these four outstanding, timeless and practical books to translate into Vietnamese. I tried to translate them in a way that would be easy to read and understand, but equally applicable to everyone — whether male or female, young or old, religious or non-religious. While translating, I was always concerned about maintaining the meaning, essence, and profundity of the author's ideas because they were important to the writer's heart and he wanted to communicate them as best as he could to the reader. Of course, all errors or mistakes during translation are my own.

As for *The Five Spheres and Other Writings* that you hold in your hand, I really wanted to write a few words to introduce the quintessential principles in the author's book. But I decided against that because I don't want to give you a preconceived standard to measure the book. Such a move will box you into my thoughts and deprive you of the ability to analyze the concepts of the book by and for yourself. I believe you'd have vaster vision, better perspective, and more holistic thoughts if you read and digest the book all by yourself. That way, you will reap more results from it.

I chose to translate these foreign volumes instead of books by Vietnamese writers because the narratives by these writers have been infiltrated by the Chinese, thus, they cannot be trusted.

Also, the Viet Cong[8] or the Vietnamese Communist Party (VCP) burned books, erased cultural traditions, and destroyed the religions of the Vietnamese people. They represented the China Communist Party (CCP) and worked to fulfill the agenda of the CCP which was to suppress the Vietnamese people and control the world with their dictatorship.

Besides, we also need to learn as well as cultivate the truth and goodness of the outside world so that we can proudly walk alongside humanity today. Today's society is vast and complex, and to utilize the lessons handed down to us by our ancestors[12] after five thousand years, we must expand and connect our minds to the rest of the world, else it would be difficult to achieve our ambitions as individuals and collectively as a nation.

Our ancestors taught that people have never been born geniuses, and must cultivate diligently to become talented. Thus, we must learn and ponder. This is the reason for this series. You will learn to believe in love and giving, in every action you take as you live, and ultimately, in yourself. This is what I wish for.

Tham Trong Ma

About Miyamoto Musashi

Miyamoto Musashi 宮本武蔵 was born on March 12, 1584, in Miyamoto-Sanomo village, Harima province, Japan and died at 61[1] in Higo province, Japan on June 13, 1645. The Japanese people respect him as a *Kensei*, a sword saint of Japan because he fought in more than 60 to-the-death sword fights against other samurai masters and was undefeated in all.

Miyamoto Musashi's father, Hirata Munisai (honored as Shinmen Munisai 新免無二斎) was an expert using the sword and the jitte. His father — Musashi's grandfather — was Hirata Shogen 平田将監, a vassal of Shinmen Iga no Kami, the lord of Takayama castle in Yoshino district of Mimasaka Province. Since he was favored by Lord Shinmen, he was allowed to use the title of Shinmen.

Miyamoto's full name and title was Shinmen Musashi-no-Kami Fujiwara no Harunobu. Musashi no Kami was a court title that made him the nominal governor of the province of Musashi, while Fujiwara was the lineage that he claimed to have descended from.

At the age of seven, Miyamoto Musashi was raised by his uncle, Dorinbo in Shoreian Temple. There, he learned to read, write, and study the Zen Buddhist texts. It is said that he learned martial arts from his father as a child, and from his uncle after the age of seven.

At thirteen, Miyamoto Musashi fought his first match against Arima Kihei of the Shinto sect, whom he defeated Arima Kihei. At the age of sixteen, he struck down the high master Akiyama of Tajima. When he was twenty-one, his fame spread through Japan as he defeated three members of the Yoshioka family, which were the instructors of House of Shogun, an official swordsman school. In this duel, it was recorded that Musashi fought against 60 opponents at the same time, all armed with swords, muskets, spears, bows and arrows. After that, he traveled and competed with many masters in one-on-one duels. Between thirteen and twenty-nine years old, Musashi fought 60 matches and lost none.

When Miyamoto Musashi turned thirty, he was determined to train himself every day in order to gain deeper principles of swordsmanship. Practicing hard until the age of fifty, he discovered the Way of the Warrior[4], and applied it to everything he did without ever needing a teacher.

In 1642, Miyamoto Musashi suffered neuralgic attacks and secluded himself in the *Reigandō* cave to write *The Five Spheres* and *The Way of Walking Alone*. He wrote in *The Five Spheres* that he was a warrior, but he was more than that — he was a samurai, strategist, painter, and sculptor.

Miyamoto Musashi founded the school of swordsmanship of Hyōhō Niten Ichi-ryū (二天 一流). He completed *The Five*

Spheres (*Go Rin No Sho* 五輪の書) in February 1645 and *The Way of Walking Alone* (*Dokkōdō* 獨行道) in June 1645. *The Five Spheres* transmits the practice and strategic significance of his martial art. *The Way of Walking Alone* shares his philosophy of life in 21 short proverbs. It is said that he handed these two volumes to his disciple, Terao Magonojō, seven days before his death. Musashi was also the author[2] of *The Thirty Five Articles About Sword Strategy* (*Ken Senryaku Ni Kansuru 35 No Kiji* 剣戦略に関する35の記事) which he completed on a lucky day[3] in February 1641 and gave to the nobleman, Hosokawa Tadatoshi. This volume contains the practices and strategies he used as standards to train himself and master the use of the sword.

He died in 1645 from what was believed to be lung cancer. It is said that at the time of his death, he stood up by himself, tightened his belt, and inserted his sword into it. He knelt with one knee upright, holding the sword in his left hand and a walking stick in his right hand, and died in this position.

Tham Trong Ma

THE FIVE SPHERES
五輪の書

GO RIN NO SHO

Introduction

I trained for many years in the "Warrior Way"[1] known as "Two Heaven Unifications"[2] and now I think I will explain it in writing for the first time. It is the first ten days of October 1643[3]. I have climbed Mount Iwato in Higo, Kyushu to make offerings to Heaven and Earth. I have knelt down in front of Guan Yin Buddha[4] and bowed to Shakymuni Buddha[5]. I am a warrior born in Harima, and named Shinmen Musashi no kami Fujiwara no Genshin. I am sixty years old.

From my childhood, I devoted myself to the warrior path. I had my first match at the age of thirteen. My opponent was Arima Kihei from the Shinto sect and I defeated him. At sixteen, I struck down a powerful fighter Akiyama of Tajima. When I was twenty-one, I went to the capital, where I fought many famous swordsmen. Despite participating in many duels, I have never failed to achieve victory. After that, I went to various regions to compete with swordsmen of different sects. And I never lost even though I competed in sixty duels. All these fights happened between when I was thirteen and twenty-eight or twenty-nine.

When I turned thirty, I looked back at my past and realized that I didn't win all of those matches because I had great sword skills. It might have been because I had innate gifts or was predestined to win from heaven, or my opponents' swordsmanship and strategy were inferior. I studied morning and evening, training myself, and searching for deeper principles. This was how I discovered the Warrior Way. I was fifty years old.

Since then I have never needed to follow a particular Way, neither do I require a teacher to teach me anything. I only apply the principles of my Warrior Way to practice various arts. So while writing this book, I didn't need to borrow old Buddhist or Confucius teachings, nor did I need military chronicles or comments on war techniques to convey the true essence of "Unification". I simply took the path of nirvana and bodhisattva[6] as a mirror and guide.

On the tenth night of the tenth month, at the hour of the tiger[7], I take the pen and begin to write.

Scroll 1
Earth 地

Military strategy[1] is the profession of the military class. The commanders must know how to apply it and the soldiers must understand its path. In today's world, no soldier can say that he fully understands the Way of Strategy. There are different Ways if we think about this issue. Buddhism is the Way to save people. Confucianism is the Way to guide people to learning. The doctor practices the Way of curing illness. A poet teaches the Way of words. There are also tea connoisseurs, archers and practitioners of many other arts and skills, and they all act when they see fit and follow their own personality.

Only few people follow the Way of the Warrior. A soldier must have interest in and pursue both literary and martial arts. Even if he has an awkward appearance and is not suitable for this road, he has to get rid of that thought and practice diligently in the Way of the Warrior.

For a warrior from any of the famous sects, the Way of the warrior means the willing and resolute acceptance of death.

However, warriors aren't the only ones known to readily accept death in the cause of duty; monks, women, farmers and peasants have also been known to die readily out of responsibility or shame - theirs is no different case.

Practicing military strategy is the Way of the soldier. A soldier must win his opponent at all cost, whether it is a duel or a battle with many opponents to gain fame for his lord[2] or honor for him. This is his virtue. Some people think that even if they learned the methods of the Way of the warrior, it would not be usable at the time of its existence.

However, it is important to bear in mind that strategy is effective at any time and useful in everything. That is the truth of the Way of the Warrior.

On the Way of Strategy
From China to Japan, followers of the Way are known as "experts of strategy". A warrior who doesn't learn this Way is not worth classifying as a warrior.

Nowadays there are people who call themselves warriors or strategists, but they only know swordsmanship. In Hitachi prefecture, the priests of Kashima and Kantori temples claimed to have received direct instruction from gods. They established schools and traveled from region to region to educate people. This is the recent meaning of strategy. In the days of old, strategy was listed among the "Ten Skills" and "Seven Arts" as an advantageous practice, but it was not limited to swordsmanship. Without the "Ten Skills" and "Seven Arts" what is achieved is only superficial. Thus, it would be hard to understand swordsmanship and, of course, we won't realize the true principles of military strategy.

Looking around the world, we see arts sold as goods. People even put themselves up as goods for sale. Every equipment they make is a merchandise to be sold. This is like separating the flower from the seed, with the seed having lesser value than the flower. This is also seen in the martial arts where only the showy colors of the technique are displayed. People talk about this school or that school, and teach one way or the other with the hope of making profit.

There is a saying that "immature martial art is the source of great harm". And this is absolutely right.

Usually, people follow one of the four paths in life: the path of the farmer, merchant, warrior or craftsman.

First is the Way of the farmer. The farmer uses his agricultural tools and carefully tracks changes in the four seasons — spring, summer, autumn and winter — from year to year.

Second is the Way of the merchant. For example, the sa-ke (wine) brewer collects necessary ingredients, blends them together, and profits from the quality of alcohol — this is the way he makes his living. Whatever the business, all merchants make a living from the profits of selling their goods. This is the Way of business.

Third is the Way of the warrior. He must prepare weapons and understand the specific characteristics of each. This is the Way of Warrior. Without using and mastering a weapon, a warrior cannot realize its benefits.

Fourth is the Way of craftsmanship. Consider the carpenter's method: he must be familiar with all types of tools and understand the utility of each. He must understand how to create the perfect shape from his designs drawn on paper. This is how he lives through life.

Above are the four Ways of the farmer, merchant, warrior and craftsman.

Comparing The Carpenter's Way to Strategy
Houses can be used to compare military strategy to the carpenter's way. There are aristocratic houses, houses of warriors, the four houses[3], and so on. We also consider the survival or development of these houses, their traditions, and their names. To build a house, the carpenter uses the master plan of the building. This is similar to the Way of Strategy in which the warrior uses a plan for his fight. In addition, the word "carpenter[4]" is composed of the words "noble" and "talented". The Way of the Warrior is one of nobility and talent. If you want to learn the art of war practice, use this book to guide your thoughts. The master is as a needle, the disciple is as a thread, thus you have to practice consistently.

A carpenter foreman understands measurements, studies the topography of land and water, and knows the construction measures for the house.

He must know how to use his ruler to measure and arrange temples, pagodas and monasteries, and also understand the plans of palaces, manor houses, towers, and fortresses. While building a house, he employs the skills of different people. The Way of the carpenter foreman is the same as the Way of a commander of a warrior clan[5].

In the construction of a house, wood must be allocated. A straight, unknotted wood with good appearance is used for the outer pillars. Wood that is slightly knotted but straight and strong can be used for inner pillars. An unknotted wood that is a bit weak but with a fine appearance can be used for different things like sills, bars, doors or partitions. A wood that is knotted, rough and hard can be used in constructing the solid parts of a house, provided that those parts are carefully analyzed and the stability of the house is ensured without the possibility of collapse. If the wood is knotted, deformed and weak, it can be used in scaffolding and then as firewood.

The carpenter foreman must know the abilities of his men and assign roles according to their ability. For example, skillful men would make wall niches, others sliding doors, some lintels, another ceilings, and so on. Those who are less skillful could lay out floor wedges, while those that are unskillful could cut the wedges and do other miscellaneous tasks. If the carpenter foreman knows how to allocate duties to his workers, the job will be done well and on time.

The carpenter foreman must be determined, effective, pay attention to details, and understand the form and function of his tools. He should also know the capacity and morale of his workers, and encourage them when necessary. These are the principles of the carpenter, and also the principles of strategy.

The Way of Strategy

Like a foot soldier, the carpenter hones his tools, assembles them, puts them in a toolbox, and comes to the place where the carpenter foreman had been appointed. He makes pillars and beams with an ax and smoothens floors and shelves with a plane. He does these with finesse and precision, using his craftsmanship to the tiniest detail. This is the practice of carpentry. By learning the techniques of carpentry and understanding designs and measures, the carpenter can later become a foreman.

As a carpenter, it is important to have tools for cutting and sharpening. These tools are used to make shrines, bookshelves, lanterns, chopping boards, or pot lids. These are the specialties of the carpenter and he must strive to be a professional at them. Just like a soldier, you should ponder on this. The work of a carpenter should not be twisted, the corners should fit squarely together so they don't detach afterwards. This is essential. If you want to learn military strategy, you should read what is written in this book. Pay attention to every detail and practice them.

An Overview of Military Strategy in Five Scrolls

I have divided the principles of strategy into five Ways with a scroll for each way. The five scrolls are: Earth, Water, Fire, Wind and Emptiness.

The Earth scroll explains the general ideas of the Way of Strategy from my viewpoint. It is difficult to understand the Way of Strategy only through swordsmanship. To understand the big and deep things, you must first understand the small and shallow things. Like a straight line drawn on the ground, the first scroll is named the Earth scroll.

Second is the Water scroll. Taking water as a foundation, the mind becomes like water. Water takes the shape of whatever container it is poured in, whether angled or round. It is sometimes a drop or a vast ocean. Water has a blue color. It is pure. And with its purity as a model, I write to explain my personal sect in this scroll. When you understand the fundamentals of swordsmanship and you freely defeat one opponent, then you can defeat anyone in the world, because the spirit that defeats one enemy is the same spirit that would defeat a thousand or ten thousand. The general's strategy progresses from the small things into the big things. It is like taking a small woodwork model and sculpting a giant Buddha statue from it.

The truth is, it is difficult to explain this in detail, but the basic principle of military strategy is to use one information to deduce ten thousand. I write about my own sect in this Water scroll.

Third is the Fire scroll. In this scroll, I specifically write about battles. Fire, whether big or small, has a fierce spirit, and so do battles.

The Way of battle applies to all kinds of battles — from a one-on-one fight to a battle of ten thousand. You have to understand that your mind is elastic; sometimes it can expand and become big, other times it can contract and become small. What is big is easy to see, while what is small is difficult to perceive. In a battle, it is easy to predict the movement of a large number of soldiers because they cannot easily change directions at the same time. But the movement of an individual is difficult to predict since he has only one mind and can change position quickly. You must understand and appreciate this, for this is the essence of the Fire scroll. Because of the immediate nature of battles, you must practice daily. Think of battles everyday so you can ready yourself and build a solid spirit. This is important in military strategy. Thus, I wrote about battles and hand-to-hand combats in the Fire scroll.

The fourth is the Wind scroll. In this scroll, I do not discuss my own sect. Instead, I write about other schools of strategy. When we talk about the wind, we talk about the styles or traditions of strategy of old sects, current sects, or families.

Understanding the strategies of others is important because if you do not know others, you cannot know yourself. To every path, there are smaller, divergent paths — sidetracks. So you could be doing your best to train your sword daily, yet your mind would deviate from the Way. This may look like a good path but when you view it objectively, you'd discover that it is not the true Way. A little divergence from the true way may later become a large one. You must understand this.

The strategies of other schools of martial art are often limited to swordsmanship, and this is understandable. However, my own strategy follows different principles and techniques. I have explained what strategy means to other sects in the Wind scroll.

The fifth is the Emptiness scroll. In this scroll, I talk about emptiness — that with no beginning or end, that with no depths or shallows, nothingness. This means that once you understand principles of the Way, you'd have to let go of them. As a warrior, you'd become free and gain extraordinary strength. You'd understand the right rhythm for any moment, and spontaneously attack and hit your opponent. This is the Way of Emptiness. Through emptiness, people naturally enter the right path.

On Naming The Two Heaven Unifications
Here, we talk about two swords[6]. Warriors, from generals to soldiers, have two swords attached to their belt. In the past they were called the long sword and the short sword, now they are called the sword and the companion sword. There is no need to write extensively about these two swords. You just have to know that here in our country, for whatever reason, carrying two swords is the Way of the Warrior. In order to show the basic principles of these two swords, I call this "The Two Heaven Unifications".

We will not talk about the spear and the halberd, although they are part of the warrior's weapons. The specialty of this sect that teaches the Two Heaven Unifications is that even beginners must practice with both long and short swords, one in each hand, to achieve mastery.

Here is the truth: when you accept to sacrifice your life, you must make maximum use of all your weapons. It is an anomaly to die with your sword still in its scabbard.

If you hold something, say a sword, with both hands, it would be difficult to wield it freely to the right or to the left. So it is best to carry your sword in one hand. This does not apply to large weapons like spears or halberds, but to swords and companion swords. It is burdensome to hold a sword with both hands when you are on a horseback or running through a swamp, a wet rice field, a stony terrain or in a crowd of people. Holding the sword in both hands is not the right way, because when you are holding a bow or spear or any other weapon in your left hand, you have just one hand free to hold the sword. However, in a case where it is difficult to cut down an opponent with one hand, you must use both hands.

To learn how to wield a sword with one hand, you'd have to practice with two swords, one in each hand. This would be difficult at the start; the sword is heavy and difficult to swing around, but all things are difficult at the beginning. The bow is hard to draw, the sword is hard to wield. But as you understand and familiarize yourself with the weapon, gradually it becomes easy for you to draw a strong bow. As you become used to wielding the long sword, you will understand the power of the Way of the sword and the sword becomes easy to use.

Swinging the sword in a fast manner is not the way of the long sword. I will explain this in the Water scroll. The long sword is for large spaces, while the short sword is for confined spaces. This is the foremost and most important to know. This is also the basic idea in this Way. In this style, you win with the long sword as well as the short sword. Therefore, there is no need to be concerned about the length or size of the sword. All you have to do is to set your mind on winning at any cost.

There are times when it is better to fight with two swords than one - for instance, if you are fighting a crowd, or you want to take hostages. These things cannot be explained in detail. So from one information, know ten thousand. When you practice and achieve the Way of the Warrior, then there is nothing you cannot see. You must research extensively.

The Usefulness of Strategy
Speaking of this Way, those who are able to use swords are called military strategists. In the Way of martial arts, a person who knows how to shoot a bow is called an archer. One who has mastered the use of the gun is called a gunner. A person who masters the spear is called a spearman. A master of the halberd is called a halberdier. However, a person who has mastered the use of the sword is neither called a long swordsman nor a companion swordsman. All bows, guns, spears and halberds are the tools of the warrior and each of them is a part of the Way of the Warrior. However, there is a reason why a special sword school is mentioned when people talk about military strategy. By virtue of the sword, man restrains himself and the world is also restrained. Thus, the sword is the basis of military strategy.

By grasping the virtue of the sword, one man can beat ten. And if one person can beat ten, then a hundred can beat a thousand, and a thousand can beat ten thousand. In my strategy, one person is the same as ten thousand. This means that this is a complete strategy for a warrior's practice.

The Way of the Warrior is not the way of Confucianists, Buddhists, teachers, priests, and dancers. But even when

I say they don't belong to this Way, if you understand the Way broadly, you will find it in everything. Each one must carefully hone their own Way. It is essential.

The Benefits of Weapons in Strategy
When you know the purpose of weapons, you'd be able to use each weapon appropriately, at the right time and place. A short sword is best used in a confined space, or when you are close to the opponent. The long sword is effective in any situation. The halberd is used on the battlefield and seems inferior to the spear. The spear is for attacking, while the halberd is for defense. In the hands of two warriors with equal level of practice, the spear gives a little extra advantage, but this depends on the situation. Both the spear and the halberd are not beneficial in a confined space. They cannot also be used for capturing prisoners. They are only essential weapons on the battlefield.

If you study the principles of weapons that can only be applied indoors or in your home[7], your focus would be limited and you'd forget about the true Way, thus you'd face difficulties in actual battles.

Crossbows, when combined with a spear or used together with other weapons, are suitable for advancing towards or retreating from an opponent. Because crossbows can be shot quickly, they are good for battles in open field. They are not useful in sieges or when the enemy is farther than twenty "ken[8]".

For this reason, crossbows and all other arts have lots of flowers but few seeds in today's world. That is, the skill is of little importance nowadays.

From inside a castle or other fortresses, no other weapon compares with the musket[9]. Before the battle begins, the musket is supreme, but once the battle begins and swords are drawn, it becomes less effective. One of the advantages of the bow is that you can see the arrow when it is in flight, but a bullet from a gun cannot be seen. You should study the meaning of this.

As for horses, it is important for them to be strong, enduring and free of defects. Horses must gallop strongly, while swords and companion swords must cut strongly. Spears and halberds must be able to thrust violently. Bows and guns must be strong and durable.

You should not have a favorite weapon. Being over-familiar with a weapon is as bad as not knowing how to use it well.

Don't imitate others. Choose weapons that fit your size and shape, weapons you can handle easily. It is bad for generals or soldiers to have likes and dislikes. It is important to be flexible, adaptable and creative.

Rhythm in Strategy
There is rhythm in everything. Rhythm in strategy requires meticulous training to master. Rhythm is expressed in the world in things like dancing and the music of wind and strings instruments. In these, there is a harmonious and peaceful rhythm. In martial arts, there is rhythm and timing in archery, shooting guns and riding horses. In all skills and abilities, rhythm is vital. In addition, there is rhythm in emptiness.

There is rhythm in the life of a warrior. There is a rhythm that strives to serve his master, a rhythm that does not look out for self-interest, and rhythm for both expected and unexpected events. There is also rhythm in the Way of business. There is the rhythm of becoming rich and the rhythm of becoming poor. Different rhythms exist in each Way. In everything, there is a thriving rhythm and there is a falling rhythm. You should carefully distinguish them.

There is a wide range of rhythms in the Way of strategy. From the outset, you have to distinguish between appropriate and inappropriate rhythm, and between slow and fast rhythm. Understand the right rhythm at the right time, and the wrong rhythm at the wrong time. These are the most important things in the Way of strategy. Without knowing the rhythm of the opposition, your strategy will never be certain.

In a battle, understand the opponent's rhythm and launch rhythms that the opponent cannot predict. The emptiness rhythm comes from the rhythm of skill, and with it victory will come.

The five scrolls are centered on rhythm. Study them and train rigorously.

I practice the Way of the Warrior every morning and every night, especially the strategies discussed above. My thoughts are broadened and I know how to apply the Way of Strategy on a large or small scale. Now, I pass these thoughts to people by putting them in writing for the first time in five scrolls: Earth scroll, Water scroll, Fire scroll, Wind scroll and Emptiness scroll.

TIMELESS CREEDS FOR WINNING

For those who want to learn my strategy, there are rules for practicing the Way:

1. Don't think dishonestly.
2. The Way is in diligently practice.
3. Familiarize yourself with all the arts.
4. Understand the Way of all professions.
5. Distinguish the pros and cons in everything.
6. Expand your judgment and understanding for everything.
7. Recognize the unseen.
8. Pay attention to detail, even in the smallest thing.
9. Do not do things that have no use.

Keep these broad principles in mind and diligently practice the Way of the Warrior. In this Way, if you do not have a broad perspective of issues, you can hardly become a master strategist. However, if you study and understand these laws, you can beat up twenty or thirty opponents even if you are alone.

If you constantly pay attention to the Way and develop the culture of hard work, you will not only master your technique but also defeat your opponent by looking into their eyes. Also, by training in the way, you'd have complete control and freedom of your body, and use your body to defeat an opponent. You would also gain the spirit of practicing the Way and defeat others with this spirit. When you get to this level, can you be defeated by anyone?

Moreover, on a large scale, one wins by using a large number of talented people, treating himself correctly, governing his country, cultivating the people, and implementing the laws of the nation.

In any given path, know how not to lose to others, know how to help yourself, and know how to build a reputation for yourself. This is the Way of the Warrior.

May 12, 1645.
Shinmen Musashi

Scroll 2
Water 水

The spirit of the Two Heaven Unifications is the mind relies on water to put it into practice a method in order to gain advantages. In writing the Water scroll, I recorded the handling of the sword in this style.

Language poses a barrier to explain this Way in detail without diluting its meaning. However, you can grasp it intuitively to understand the profound principles for yourself.

Study what is written in this scroll, and reflect on it word for word. If you think about it only at a surface level, there are many things you will misunderstand about this Way.

The strategic principles I have written about here are peculiar to one-on-one combat. You would need broader insights to understand the principles of a battle of ten thousand against ten thousand.

In following this Way, if you are lost or misled, even a little, you will fall into the wrong path. Reading these documents aren't enough to understand the Way of the Warrior. You have to understand what is written therein. Do not just read, learn or imitate what is in them, but research thoroughly and practice them daily so that these principles would flow naturally you're your heart.

The Mind of Strategy
In the Way of the Warrior, the mind should not be different from the spirit of your daily life. Let your mind be always calm and upright both in your normal life and in moments of battle. Do not change, not even a little. Do not be uptight, yet do not live recklessly. Be focused and keep your mind from wavering. Give yourself to frequent introspection until your mind achieves and maintains a symphony that shouldn't stop, even for a second.

At quiet times, let your mind not be quiet. And in moments of haste, let your mind be calm and unrushed. The mind should not be affected by the body, neither should the body be affected by the mind.

Pay attention to the state of your mind and worry less about the body. Fill up what your mind lacks, but don't it let go overboard.

While relaxing the mind from the environment, make sure the depth of your mind (your inner self) is strong. Do not allow others to influence your mind.

Understand that a person may have a small stature yet have a large mind, while another may have a huge stature yet have a small mind. Therefore it is the key not to allow the mind to be controlled by the body.

Be open-minded. Look at things from a wide perspective, and in this vastness, cultivate wisdom. This is the most important way to polish your wisdom and also your mind.

By polishing your mind and intellect, you will be able to distinguish between right and wrong, and also know the Ways of different arts and skills. At this level of wisdom, you cannot be fooled by anyone in the world. That is the center of wisdom in the strategy.

In the Way of the Warrior, the mind is different from other elements. You should extensively research and refine the principles of the Way so that even when the battle is chaotic, your mind would remain steadfast.

The Posture in Strategy
When you stand, your head should be straight, it should not tilt or droop or look up. Do not frown or widen your eyes. Do not frown but create a wrinkle between your eyebrows to avoid blinking or moving your eyebrows. Squint your eyes a bit and soften your look discreetly. Your nasal passages should be straight with a slight shift on the chin. Straighten the tendons on the rear of your neck and instil vigor into your hairline.

The body — from the shoulders down to the toes — is one piece. Lower your shoulders, straighten your back without your butt sticking out, and extend energy to your legs, from your knees to the tips of the feet. To avoid bending at your hips, extend your belly and push it a bit forward. There is a technique called "wedging in" — you wedge your companion sword into your lower abdomen to prevent your belt from sagging.

In general, it is necessary to maintain your fighting posture in your daily life and maintain your daily posture as your fighting posture. You must study this carefully.

The Gaze in Strategy
Your vision must be wide and broad. There are two types of vision: perception and sight. With perception, you look to feel; with sight, you look to see. Perception is strong, sight is weak. In strategy, it is important to see distant things as if they were near, and close things as if they were far.

It is important in strategy that you know your opponent's sword by just looking at it. This must be taken seriously. Vision is the same both in single combats and big battles.

It is crucial that you should be able to see both flanks without moving your eyeballs. This is hard to master especially under pressure. Learn what is written here and practice it daily. You should practice this carefully until your gaze does not change in any situation.

Holding the Sword
When holding the sword, hold with a comfortable feeling in the thumb and forefinger, with the middle finger neither tight nor slack, and with the last two fingers tight. A loose grip on a sword is bad.

When drawing the sword, think of it only as an object to cut down an opponent. As you cut down your opponent, do not change your grip. Hold the sword in such a way that the hand is not weakened.

In times when you block, parry, hit, or press down an opponent's sword, just change the thumb and index finger, although even then it feels a little bit different. In any case, always hold the sword with the intent of cutting down an opponent. The grip for sword-testing[1] and for combat is the same when learning "how to handle swords to cut people". That has not changed.

In general, I don't like the sword to be fixed to my hand. Being fixed means dead hands, but flexibility means a living hand. You must keep this in mind.

Footwork
To move your feet[2], walk slightly on the tip of your toes, you should walk firmly on your heels. Depending on the circumstances, there are long, short, slow or fast steps. But irrespective of the circumstance, the feet should move just like the way you walk normally. I don't like these three types of footsteps: flying feet, floating feet and fixed feet. These steps should be avoided.

In our Way, it is very important to mention the yin and yang footsteps. In these, there is no moving of only one foot. This means that as you cut, reverse or attack, the yin and yang footsteps are always changing; your feet move right-left and left-right. Do not move several times on the same foot. This is something to study carefully.

The Five Positions
The five positions are upper, middle, lower, left and right. Although there are five divisions, they are all aimed at cutting down the opponent. There is nothing but these five positions.

Whatever position you find yourself, don't think about it; only think of cutting down the opponent. Whether your position is big or small depends on the situation.

The upper, middle and lower positions are solid positions; while the left and right are flexible positions. The left and right positions are for cases where there is an obstruction above or on one side. The decision to use either the left or right position depends on the terrain.

In order to understand positions, you have to thoroughly understand the middle position. Middle is the focus of all positions. Looking at strategy on a large scale, you would see that the middle is the place of commander, while the other four positions follow the commander. You must appreciate this.

The Way of the Sword
This talks about the way to understand the long sword that we often carry. If we know the path[3] of the sword, we can swing the long sword with two fingers and use it easily.

If you try to swing the long sword quickly, the sword will resist, thus making it difficult to wield. For good use, the sword should be swung calmly. Trying to swing the sword like a fan or a dagger designed to move quickly, would make it difficult to wield. This is called "cutting a dagger". And you cannot cut a person with a sword this way.

When cutting down, lift the sword straight upwards. When cutting horizontally, return the sword along the horizontal path and always widen your elbows to cut strongly. This is the Way of the sword.

If you learn how to use the five approaches of my strategy, you will be able to wield the sword well. You must practice continuously.

The Five Approaches[4]

First Approach
First approach is the middle attitude. Point the sword at your opponent's face. As you and the opponent approach each other and he attacks, move his sword to the right and crush it with your long sword. When the opponent tries to strike again, rotate your sword and cut his down, then keep your sword there. When the opponent attempts to strike again, cut his hand from below. This is the first approach.

The five approaches are similar. You must constantly practice with the long sword to learn them. When you master the Way of the long sword, you would be able to control and defend any attack from your opponent. I assure you, there is no other way than this.

Second Approach
In the second approach, the sword is held in the upper position. In this position, you cut down the opponent just when he is about to attack. If you miss, keep the sword there, and when he tries to attack again, cut him by picking up the sword from below. If he tries to attack again, you can repeat this move.

In this approach there are many changes in rhythm and spirit. If you practice in this style and understand the five approaches of sword very accurately, you will win in any situation. You have to practice constantly.

Third Approach

As for the third approach, you hold the sword in a lower position, and when the opponent attacks, you cut his hand from below. When the opponent tries to hit down your sword while it touches his hand, raise your sword to the rhythm of the forest (just as if you want to cut trees in the forest) after he swings the sword with the intention of cutting across your upper arm.

The lower approach is all about attack. You attack the enemy the instant he attacks you. This approach is often used in the Way of the sword, doesn't matter whether you're moving fast or moving slowly. Using the sword, you must practice with discipline.

Fourth Approach

In this approach, you stand with the sword on the left, then hit the opponent's hand from below when he attacks. If the opponent tries to block your rising blow, run along his sword with the feeling of slashing his hand, then cut diagonally across his shoulder. This is the Way of the sword. When faced with an opponent, understanding the opponent's long sword is the way to win. You should practice how to handle swords effectively.

Fifth Approach

For the fifth approach, you stand with your sword on the right. By the time you realize your opponent is about to strike, swing your long sword from that angle (the opponent's strike position) and from up cut straight down.

This method is essential for knowing the Way of the sword. If you use this technique, you would know how to wield a heavy sword freely.

It is impossible to write down these five approaches in detail. The purpose of this style is basically to understand the Way of the sword, to learn general rhythms, and to understand the opponent's sword.

Use these five approaches from the outset and practice them endlessly. Also when fighting your opponent, understand the Way of the sword, read his intentions, use different rhythms and win by all means. You must consider this carefully.

The "Position – No Position" Teaching

Position – no position means that there is no such thing as sword positions. However, since they can be labelled according to the five methods, there are also five positions. No matter the opponent's approach, the terrain, the circumstances, or sword, always have the intention of cutting down the opponent easily.

When in the upper position, you can gently lower your sword and adopt the middle posture. Also, when in the middle posture, you can move up a bit and adopt the upper position. In the lower position, you could move up a bit and take up the middle position. Depending on the condition, if you are on the left or right side and you move towards the center, it basically becomes the middle or lower position.

This is the principle of position no-position.

Above all, no matter how you hold the sword, your intention must be to cut down the opponent.

Although there are techniques like parrying, blocking, hitting, clinging or touching an opponent's sword, you must understand that they are all aimed at cutting down the opponent. If your thought is only to parry, block, hit, cling to, or touch the opponent's sword, then you will not be able to cut him down. It is important to see every moment as an opportunity to cut down your opponent. Research this thoroughly.

For large-scale strategy consisting of many people, there are also different positions. And they are all aimed at winning the battle.

In any situation, don't be rigid or fixed. This is bad. Always bear this in mind.

One-Beat Cut
In the rhythms of attacking an opponent, there is a something called the one-beat cut. When you and the opponent are in a fighting position, you have to find the moment when he's unable to counter, then attack him without moving your body and with no discomfort in your spirit. This is an extremely fast and direct rhythm when you are on the offensive.

The rhythm hits the opponent before he can think of drawing his sword, moving, or even attacking. This is a one-beat cut.

Practice this rhythm until you are adept. Also practice attacking quickly in the blink of an eye.

Two-Beat Cut
When you attack the opponent and he backs away to avoid the attack, act as if you want to hit him, as he tries to back away again or parry your blow, strike him down at that moment. This move is called the two-beat cut.

It is extremely difficult for you to use this attack just by reading what is written here. Therefore, you must train to be able to use it.

No Form
When the enemy is about to attack and you also decide to attack, attack both with your body and spirit, then spring your strike from nowhere quickly and powerfully. This is called no form. It is a critical attack and it is frequently used. Be diligent in your study and practice consistently.

The Flowing Water Cut
The flowing water cut is used when you are close to the enemy and he tries to retreat quickly or let go or tries to parry the long sword aside. You fight both with your body and your will with the long sword and use your best technique. The sword's path flows smoothly like water in a dam. Strike full and strong! When you learn and understand this strategy, you can attack and cut down your opponent with certainty. You must recognize the opponent's strategy.

The Continuous Cut
When you attack your opponent and he tries to block or move aside, attack his head, arms and legs all at the same time with a single swing of the long sword, and cut continuously

anywhere. This is called continuous cutting. Understand and practice this fighting method. It is a blow that can be used at any time. To understand the essence of this move, you need to be in combat to analyze it.

The Flint Cut

Flint cut is used when the opponent's sword and your sword clash together. You cut as hard as you can without lifting your sword even a little. This blow is powerful when you attack with your legs, body and arms. Unless you practice this method consistently, it is very difficult to do. If you practice well, you will be able to attack strongly.

The Autumn Leaves Cut

With the autumn leaves cut, you knock down the opponent's sword from his hand. When the opponent stands in front of you and tries to attack, cut his sword forcefully using the "no form" or "flint cut", then attack immediately with the aim of knocking off his sword. Keep attacking until the tip of your sword drops, the opponent's sword will surely drop. This attack, if practiced well, makes it easy to knock off the opponent's sword from his hand. You should practice this technique carefully.

Using the Body to Replace the Sword

This technique is also known as "the sword in place of the body". Generally when attacking an opponent, you do not attack with the sword and the body at the same time. When an opponent is within your range, you charge with your body first, then cut down with your sword. There are cases where you attack with the sword first without moving your body. But usually the body moves first, then the sword follows. You should research this technique extensively while practicing your attack.

The Cut and Slash

Cutting and slashing are two different things. Cutting, in whatever form, is done with a resolute and excellent spirit; while slashing just touches the opponent anywhere. Even if you slash strongly and the opponent dies immediately, it is still called slashing. Cutting is performed with purpose. Always remember this.

Whether you slash an opponent's arm or leg, it is still a slash. Slashing only helps you make a powerful attack afterwards. Slashing actually feels like touching. If you practice well, you would be able to distinguish the two. You should do this.

The Monkey Body

Monkey body[5] is about not stretching out your arms. The trick is to move your body quickly when getting close to the opponent, without extending your arms, before the opponent cuts.

If you think to approach with your arms, your body will definitely stay far away. So you need to focus on moving quickly with your body close to the opponent. If you are at a distance that you can reach the opponent with your arm, you can easily go into the opponent with your body. Try this for yourself.

The Lacquer Body

Lacquer body[6] means when you stick your body to your opponent with the intention of not being separated. When you stand right next to your opponent, cling to him firmly with your face, body and feet. Everyone tends to cling fast with their face and feet, but allow their body to lag behind. Stick your body to your opponent's body firmly. Do not allow even the smallest space between the two bodies. This is something that needs to be thoroughly researched.

Comparing Height
Comparing height is a way to approach and size up your opponent without allowing your body to contract. You stretch your legs, stretch your body, and stretch your neck face to face with him. Think of it as comparing height with your opponent to prove that you are taller. This is important to bulk up your height and give you a strong movement. You should study this hard.

The Sticky Sword
When the opponent attacks and you also attack with the long sword, stick your long sword to the enemy's sword as you try to block his blow. Sticking the sword makes it difficult for the opponent to move and draw the sword. However, do not try to put too much strength into it.

As you apply the sticky sword to the opponent's sword, do it as calmly as possible without difficulty.

There is the sticky sword and there is the entangling sword. The sticky sword is strong, while the entangling sword is weak. You need to distinguish these things.

The Body Strike

Body strike is when you stand beside an opponent and attack him with your body. You turn your face to the side a bit and use your left shoulder to strike the opponent in the chest. Make the blow as strong and quick as possible, with a sense of pushing the opponent away. If you do this, the strike will be so strong that you can knock the opponent four or five yards away. The strike from this technique is also strong enough to kill your opponent. You should practice this strike very well.

The Three Parries

Here, I talk about the three parries.

The first is when you are close to your opponent and he attacks with a long sword. To block his attack, act as if you would stab him in the eye with your long sword, then deflect his sword to your right.

Next is what I call the thrusting parry. Here, you block your opponent's attack by his right eye with the feeling of cutting open his throat.

For the third parry: when the opponent attacks, you enter inside the attack with your short sword without worrying about the opponent's sword, move in and try to punch his face with your left hand.

These are the three parries. Think of them like clenching your left hand into a fist and punching your opponent in the face. This is a technique you should practice carefully.

The Face Stabbing
Face stabbing means having the intention to stab the opponent in the face with the tip of your sword when you are confronting him.

If you are determined to stab the opponent in the face, he will try to protect both his face and body from your sword. When he tries to avoid your attack, you have various opportunities to win. You must specialize in this technique. In battle, if the opponent's mind is only focused on protecting his body from your sword, then you have already won.

For this reason, you should never forget the technique I call face stabbing. Whenever you are practicing martial arts, you should follow this principle and practice it.

The Heart Stabbing
Heart stabbing is when you are constrained and have obstructions in the midst of battle such as from above or at the side, thus making it difficult to cut the enemy in any direction. What you need to do is to stab the opponent without allowing your sword slip. You point the long sword at the opponent, pull it back without allowing the tip to rotate, and push the sword into the opponent's chest.

Understand that this this technique is useful in times when you are very tired and when your sword will not cut. You need to understand the application of this technique.

The Shouting and Screaming
Shouting and screaming are used whenever you attack the opponent. When you move to attack and the opponent tries to

counterattack, raise the sword from below as if you want to cut the opponent with the sword, then rotate the sword and cut back with a superfast rhythm.

Raising your sword up is shouting, while the actual cutting down is screaming. These two rhythms should be used whenever exchanging attacks. The way to practice shouting is to enter with the feeling of lifting your sword as if you want to stab the opponent and in the same beat as you lift and cut. You should practice this technique diligently.

The Tilting Parry
Tilting parry is when you are exchanging swords with your opponent and in situations that fall into the regular rhythm of back and forth. You parry his strikes and cut him with your long sword. This technique is neither a strong blow nor a strong support. You predict opponent's sword path, tilt it aside and immediately attack opponent. Tilting and cutting should be proactive. This is an important point.

If you tilt in time, no matter how strong the opponent's sword is, your sword tip will not be knocked down, even a little. You should study well and try it.

The Beating Crowd
Beating crowd[7] is when you are in a fight against a large group of people. You use both the sword and the companion sword. Stretch your swords to the left and right positions. The goal of this is to chase the opponents in one direction even if they attack from all four directions.

Determine the order in which the opponent is about to attack and quickly beat those who advance first. Keep your vision wide. When you realize that an opponent is about to attack, swing both swords left, right and back at the same time. Waiting is bad.

Quickly return to standing position with the swords on both sides. When you are approaching, cut violently as the opponent moves forward and crush him. If you do so and the opponent still advances, attack in that same direction and cut him down. That is the idea.

As much as you can, put your opponents in a row and chase them around like you are chasing a school of fish. If you see them piling up, cut them down immediately without giving them the opportunity to pause. Cut them down strongly.

If the opponent advances and you chase them around in a group, it would be very difficult to fight them. On the other hand, by thinking of the direction each enemy will come from, you fall into the trap of waiting, and this wouldn't help your fight either.

Recognize the opponent's rhythm and understand where they would disperse. You will win.

Sometimes you should practice with a large group of colleagues. Fight with them to understand this. You will feel fight one, ten or even twenty opponents with ease. You should practice hard and discover this.

The Battle Principles
The battle principles are a way of understanding how to use strategy to achieve victory using swords. They are not written in detail. You must learn to win by practicing thoroughly.

Basically, the Way of the Warrior was revealed through the sword.

One Strike

One strike[8] is just like its name. If you pay attention to it, you will definitely achieve victory. It is very difficult to attain this if you are not trained in strategy.

If you train hard to master the skill of this technique, you will know how to automatically concentrate on strategy. In this way, you can win as you like. You must constantly practice.

The Direct Transmission

The focus of direct transmission is to receive and hand down the true Way of the Two Heaven Unifications. Training hard and applying this strategy is very important.

What I did in this scroll is to document my style of sword techniques in a general and easy way for future reference.

Strategy is to learn how to use swords and to win people over. The first step towards understanding strategy is by knowing the five basic positions. By understanding these five approaches, you learn the natural way of the sword. Your whole body becomes flexible. Your mind will also become sharpened, and you will understand the rhythm of the Way. Both you and the sword will exist in a harmony of sharpness and clarity. When you can move your body and legs as freely as you like, you can defeat any opponent, whether they are one or two. Then you will understand what is good and what is bad in strategy.

Practice what is written here one by one. As you fight with different opponents, you will gradually grasp the principles of the Way. Put your mind to this nonstop. Do not rush. Whenever the opportunity arises, pick up your sword and learn its virtues so that you can fight with anyone and learn their minds.

A road of a thousand miles has to be taken one step at a time. Do not rush. Practice this regularly and remember that it is a warrior's responsibility.

Have the spirit of a warrior: Today I will beat who I was yesterday, tomorrow I will defeat the less skilled, and then later I will defeat the one that is more skilled. Follow the instructions in these articles and do not allow your mind to be distracted. No matter how many opponents you can overcome, if you don't practice and apply what you've learnt, then it is not the true Way.

You have to practice hard until you understand basic principles and they automatically come to your mind. This mindset allows you to overcome dozens of opponents alone. After achieving that, you will understand strategy both on a large and small scale.

Train yourself with a thousand days of practice and refine yourself with ten thousand days of practice. This is something you need to think through.

May 12, 1645.
Shinmen Musashi

Scroll 3
Fire 火

In the strategy of Two Heaven Unifications, I think of battles as fire. I studied battles and one-on-one combats in order to write this scroll.

In the first place, how people understand the principles of strategy is limited. If it involves fingers, they can only use one finger slang[1] of strength on their wrists. Or if using a hand fan[2], they try to find a way to win with their forearms or with something like a bamboo sword[3]. They try to learn to take advantage of a bit of speed, try to hone their limbs, and take advantage of these small differences in speed.

Battles are where we risk our lives. As we fight many times between duels, we distinguish the principles of life and death, learn the sword's strategy, and understand the strengths and weaknesses of the opponent's sword. Distinguish the different directions of the sword and practice to be able to cut down the opponent. So you can't bother thinking about things that are inconsequential especially when you're wearing a full set of armor[4]. You are fighting for your life so you don't have time to think about trivialities. You are fighting alone against five or even ten people; hence you must devise a way to win. That is the Way of the Warrior. Whether one person defeats ten people or one thousand people defeat ten thousand people, is there any difference? You should ponder this.

By holding a sword alone, you evaluate the competencies of each opponent — their strengths and weaknesses. You will have the wisdom and strategy to perfect the way to win against ten thousand people. You will become a master of this Way.

The true Way of the Warrior is for someone in the world to be able to understand, practice, and advance the technique by oneself. Workout from morning to night, once the martial arts strategy has been polished to perfection, you will gain freedom. Naturally, you have a miraculous ability and mysterious power. This is the ideal spirit of a warrior.

The Topography
This means examining the nature of your terrain or environment. To do this, you have to use what is called "sun shouldering". This means you stand in such a way that the sun is behind you. In a situation where the sun can't be behind you, position yourself in a way that it is at your right. This applies also when you are indoors — let the light be at your back or your right. Try not to have an obstruction behind, have a free space on your left, and keep off the enemy from your right flank. To be able to see the opponent at night, keep the fire behind you or on your right. Never forget to put yourself in these positions.

It is also better to "look down on the opponent". Try to stand at a position slightly higher than your surroundings. If indoors, think of revered places[5] as the high ground.

At the beginning of the battle, as you chase your opponent around, try to chase him to your left. It is essential that you chase your opponents such that the tough terrains would be behind him. In any situation, always try to put him in unfavorable terrain.

When in a dangerous place, we say "don't let your opponent see this place". This means you should not give the opponent a single moment to look around his surroundings. This also applies to when you corner the opponent to a threshold, curtain, sliding door, corridor or pillar — "don't let the opponent see this place".

Any time you chase an opponent, focus on getting him to dangerous terrain or places full of obstacles on either side. In any case, use the features of the terrain to your advantage and make sure to "win by topography". Research broadly. This is what you should practice.

The Three Initiatives
There are three types of initiative. First is when you take the initiative to attack. This is called "advance initiative". Second is when the opponent takes the initiative to attack. This is called "postponed initiative". The third is when you and the opponent take initiative to attack at the same time. This is called a "simultaneous initiative". These are the three types of initiative.

Every battle begins with one of these three types of initiative. Because these initiatives can determine the winner from the beginning, taking an initiative is the most important thing in the strategy.

Of course, the details of these types of initiatives vary, so you have to evaluate each type of initiative accordingly. Read the opponent's intentions, use your mind, and take advantage of our strategy to win. No need to write down details here.

Advance Initiative
First is the advance initiative. When you want to attack, stay calm, and then attack suddenly using this initiative. About this initiative, be quick and strong outwardly but always have calm thoughts. Move forward with an extremely strong spirit, with your steps a little faster than usual. When approaching the opponent, attack quickly with this initiative. Also, have calm thoughts and maintain this in the beginning, during and end of completely dominating the opponent. Make the most of your mental strength and win.

Postponed Initiative
The second is the postponed initiative. When the opponent advances to attack, do not worry at all, just pretend to be weak. Then when he attacks, you explode and suddenly show your strength. Act as if you want to jump on him, when he falters a little, seize the moment immediately to win. One thing you should do is to advance stronger as the opponent moves forward. Try to find a loophole as the opponent changes his rhythm and capitalizes on this to win. These are the techniques for the postponed initiative.

Simultaneous Initiative
The third is the simultaneous initiative. When the opponent advances quickly, you approach him calmly but strongly. When he approaches you, explode. Use your best technique. The moment the opponent relaxes, strike directly and forcefully and take the victory on the spot. On the other hand, when the opponent is moving calmly, approach him quickly with a slight "floating" feeling. When he approaches, you approach him once to test your sword, then adjust your attack according to his condition and cut violently to win.

I am unable to write down all the techniques in detail, you have to deduce the rest from this writing. When using these three types of initiative, watch out for opportunities, and follow principles. You may not always be the first to attack. Try to move the opponent around as you like.

In any type of initiative, you should always use the wisdom of strategy and intend to win at all costs. You have to practice continuously.

The Pressing Down a Pillow
Pressing down a pillow means that you don't allow the opponent to lift his head, specifically in one-on-one combat. Letting your opponent move you around and putting you on the defensive is bad. At all times, aim to move your opponent around freely.

Of course, the opponent would think the same because he has the same intention. It is difficult to constantly adapt to what others do, so don't get distracted. In strategy, you must stop the opponent before he attacks, strike the opponent before he hits, and pull the opponent out of his strategy before he can strike you back.

Once you have grasped the true Way of pressing down a pillow, you would realize the intention of your opponent when he attacks, and you won't allow him to do that. Preventing the opponent's attack at the syllable "s" sound and not allowing him to continue. This is the nature of pressing the pillow down. Similarly, if your opponent thinks about an attack, stop him at the "ah" sound. If he jumps, cut him at the "j" sound. If he wants to cut then restrain him at the "c" sound. These are all tactics that come from the same spirit.

When your opponent tries to use these techniques against you, allow him to do the useless things and prevent him from doing useful things. Do not allow him to continue. This is one of the most important elements of strategy.

If you continually think of "pressing him down", you will be on the defensive. Regardless of the situation, trust in the Way to guide your techniques. When the opponent tries to attack, stop his attack right from his mind. Do not allow him to do anything useful; move him around as you like. This is a sign of a talented strategist that has given himself to continuous training and practice. You should deeply consider the principle of "pressing down the pillow".

Crossing the Ford
We talk about "crossing at a ford" when, for example, you are crossing a sea of forty or fifty nautical miles[6] where there are

narrow spaces and long stretches at the channels. Through the course of one's life, there are many cases where you'd have to "cross the ford".

When you are about to journey at sea, you need to know the location of the places you want to go, understand the capacity of a boat, and consider the weather carefully. Even without a compass, you must be able to adjust to the changes of the wind at each time; sometimes you can use the tail wind or favorable wind to sail. If the wind changes within two or three nautical miles to your destination, you may need to use the oars or a pair of paddles for the rest of the journey. With the determination to reach the harbor, continue to propel the boat, and in this way, you would cross the sea.

Apply this to your everyday life. When you are striving towards a goal, you should have the same determination like you are "crossing the ford".

In strategy, "crossing the ford" during battle is very important. Know your opponent's situation and understand your own abilities. Use the principle of "crossing the ford" to overcome. Be like a master captain when crossing the sea. Once you've "crossed the ford", you can rest again.

"Crossing the ford" basically means weakening the opponent and taking the initiative to ensure victory right there. Whether you are applying strategy on a large or small scale, it is important to have the spirit of "crossing the ford". You should consider this deeply.

Understanding the Situation
Understanding the situation in large-scale strategy means perceiving more of the enemy's weakness or strength. Understand the intention of the enemy's soldiers, their terrain, their disposition, and how to deploy your soldiers accordingly. Using this information, fight the battle with the principles of strategy to ensure victory.

In a one-on-one battle, you must recognize the opponent's style and distinguish his strengths and weaknesses. Your actions should counter his own. Understand any adjustment he makes, capture the loophole in his rhythm, and from there take the initiative. All of these are very important.

If your intellectual capacity is high, you can completely read the situation.

When you understand strategy, you become a completely free person. You will be able to recognize the opponent's intention. This will give you many opportunities to win. You must study this.

To Tread Down The Sword
To "tread down the sword" has a special meaning in strategy. First of all, in large-scale strategy, allow the enemy to attack with all they have with their bows and guns, then attack them immediately they are through and trying to reload their guns with gunpowder or nocking their bows. As you do this, it becomes difficult for them to advance.

When dealing with bows and guns, it is important to attack quickly while the enemy is firing. When you attack them like a storm, it becomes difficult for the enemy to load their bows or reload and shoot their guns. So every time the enemy tries to reload, attack before they have to chance to (re)load their weapons. Win by smashing everything the enemy is doing.

Similarly in individual strategy, if you attack the opponent after he has launched a blow, you cannot win. Instead, you attack your opponent with the feeling of holding his sword down when he attacks. Make sure the opponent doesn't have a second chance to attack.

"Treading" is not limited to the feet but to the whole body. Tread with your spirit and, of course, tread with your sword. Determine not to give the enemy a second chance to attack. This means that you should be proactive in every situation. This does not mean you should run towards the enemy to attack at the same time that he attacks. You should begin your attack immediately after his. You must study deeply.

The Collapse
Everything has a tendency to collapse. A house can collapse, a body can collapse, and an enemy can collapse when the time comes and their rhythm becomes chaotic.

The same goes for large-scale strategy. When you sense the chaotic rhythm of the enemy and their consequent collapse, it is essential you knock them down without allowing the opportunity to slip by. If you fail to make use of the opportunity, the enemy may have a chance to recover.

This is similar to the strategy for single combat. In the middle of the battle, attack the opponent when he loses his rhythm and he starts to collapse. If you falter and let this moment pass, your opponent may recover and be on the defensive thereafter. It is very important to note this. You have to attack and decisively defeat the opponent in that moment of his initial downfall so that he cannot recover.

When chasing the enemy, be direct and vigorous. Smash the enemy to pieces so he cannot recover. You should carefully consider what I call "smashing into debris". If you don't smash him into pieces, he can still persevere and recover. Hence, you must completely cut down the enemy.

Becoming The Enemy
"Becoming the enemy" means that you should think of yourself as your opponent. Looking around the world, you see bandits carrying out a robbery. Now, when bandits are trapped in the house, they are considered as strong opponents. However, if you put yourself in the position of the bandit, you would feel like the world is against you, you'd feel desperate and probably hopeless.

The one trapped in the house is a pheasant and the one who comes in to cut him down is a hawk. Please ponder this thoroughly.

In large-scale strategy, if you feel that the enemy is strong, you would find it difficult to attack them. However, if you have good warriors and understand the principles of strategy, you would surely defeat the enemy. You have nothing to worry about.

Similarly in individual strategy, you should picture yourself as your opponent. If you understand the strategy and master the profound principles, the Way will be clearly shown. Any opponent who encounters a person who has mastered the Warrior Way, firmly believes that he has already lost. You should think seriously about this.

Releasing Four Hands

Releasing four hands[7] is a situation where you and your opponent have the same intention as you fight and there is no clear winner. You cannot advance in battles like this. If you think there is going to be a deadlock, give up your intention immediately and use some other advantageous tactics to win.

In large-scale strategy, if you sense a deadlock, that is, the spirit of "four hands", do not try to advance as that would make you lose many of your men. Quickly re-strategize and achieve victory using tactics that the enemy cannot think of. This is extremely important.

Similarly, in a hand-to-hand combat, if you think you will fall into a "four-hand" stalemate, change your approach immediately. It is important that you improve the way you assess your opponent's attitude. Use a completely different tactic to win. You must be able to judge this.

Moving the Shade

What we call "moving the shade[8]" applies when we do not understand the enemy's intention clearly.

In large-scale strategy, when you do not know the intention of the enemy, pretend as if you want to attack strongly. Then you would see the intention of the enemy. Having seen the opponent's approach, you would easily win by changing your tactics.

Similarly in individual strategy, when the opponent takes a stance like having his sword behind or by his side, make a feint attack, and what the opponent is thinking will be revealed when he shows his sword. When that is revealed and understood, instantly realize where your advantage lies. At this point, you will be able to assess how to achieve victory. If you let your guard down, the rhythm will pass. You should evaluate carefully.

Shade Choking
Shade choking is a technique used when we see an enemy's intention to attack.

In large-scale strategy, "choke" the enemy just at the time they are about to make a move. Use all your strength to attack as well as defend when the enemy makes a move. The enemy will be inhibited by that power and will change their approach. You would also alter your approach, then using the "emptiness" strategy, take initiative, and win.

The same applies in single combat, when the enemy attacks strongly; stop him with a suitable rhythm. While the enemy stopped, take initiative and win. You have to work hard at this.

The Contagious
Many things are contagious. For example, drowsiness is contagious, yawning is contagious. Time can also be transferred.

In large-scale strategy, when the enemy is agitated and in a hurry to act, do not allow your side to suffer even a little. If you show the enemy that you are calm, they will be taken by this and also relax, thus their will to attack will be reduced. When you notice that the enemy has been "infected" with this feeling of calmness, attack quickly and strongly with an "empty" mindset. You will achieve victory.

In single combat, relax your body and mind, and then capitalize on the moment when the opponent relaxes too. Attack strongly and quickly, and take the initiative to win there. This is very important. So to weaken your opponent, infect him with melancholic feeling, then hopelessness, and lastly weakness. You have to work hard at this.

The Confused Opponent
There is confusion in everything. One reason for this is the immediate sense of danger. The other is a sense of failure, and the third is, surprise. You should study these.

In large-scale strategy, confusion is very important. Attack the enemy, the moment they least expect without giving them space to think or strategize. While they are thinking of the next move, take advantage of their confusion, take initiative, and win. This is very necessary.

Also in single combat, pretend to be relaxed, then suddenly put all your energy into a strong attack. Do not allow the opponent to have space to recover from this mental turmoil or to realize any advantage he might have. It is important to understand how to win this way. You must study this matter thoroughly.

To Frighten
Fright is commonplace. People are frightened by the things that they never expected to happen.

Your utmost aim in large-scale strategy is to cause the enemy to be frightened. You can frighten them through a loud sound, or by making a small army seem large, or by threatening from the flank without warning. These would make the enemy frightened. Seize this frightened rhythm and use it to your advantage. You will achieve victory.

The same applies in a duel. The key is to frighten the opponent with your body, your sword, or your voice. Frighten the opponent with things he doesn't expect. Cause the enemy to be frightened, and take advantage of this moment of fear to win. Think about this.

Soaking in
"Soaking in" is when you and the enemy grapple each other and are fighting hard. If you find yourself unable to advance, immediately "soak in" or merge with the enemy. When you merge with the enemy, you need to use that advantage to win.

Whether in a large or small scale strategy, if you separate yourself from the opponent, you will not win. The only way to win is to mutually entangle you with the opponent. Apply wisdom in this situation. Understand how to win under these conditions and win powerfully. You must understand this.

The Hurting Corners
It is difficult to move big things by direct pushing, so you should "hurt the corners". In large-scale strategy, you have the

advantage when you attack the corners of the enemy. If the corners were overthrown, the spirit of the whole body would also be overthrown. To defeat the enemy, you must follow up with the attack when the corners have fallen.

In an individual strategy, you can easily win once the opponent collapses. This happens when you hurt the "corners" of the opponent's body, thus weakening him. It is important to know how to do this. So you have to study deeply.

The Unstable

This means making the enemy lose determination. In large-scale strategy, you can use your army to confuse the enemy on the battlefield. Observe the spirit of the enemy and make them think "Here? That? Like this? Like that? Slow? Quick?" You will definitely win when the enemy is caught up in confusion.

In single combat, you can confuse the enemy by attacking with different techniques when the opportunity arises. Create tension with a stab or a cut. Or confuse your enemies to think that you are not going to make any important move. When he is confused, then you can easily win. This is the nature of battle. You must study deeply.

The Three Shouts

The three shouts are divided like this: before, during, and after. Shout according to the situation. Voice is a quality of life. We shout against fire, against the wind, against waves, and so on. Voice shows strength.

In large-scale strategy, we shout at the beginning of the battle as loudly as we can. During the battle, the voice is low, and we shout as we attack. After the battle, we shout in the wake of victory. These are three shouts.

In single combat, you act as if to make a cut and then shout "Ei!" at the same time to disturb the enemy. Then after the shout, cut the opponent with the long sword. Then you shout after cutting the enemy. This is to announce victory. This is called before and after voice. You do not shout at the same time as when you are drawing the sword. You shout to get into the rhythm of the fight. You must examine this deeply.

To Mingle
When confronting the army in battle, we attack the strong point of the enemy. When you see that they have been defeated, quickly separate, and attack another strong point within the perimeter of the enemy force. The spirit of this is like a winding mountain path. This is an important fighting method when one person faces many people. Hit the enemy in one quarter and force them back. Then seize the time and strike further strong points to the right and to the left as if on a winding mountain path. You need to consider the arrangement of the enemies. When you know the enemy's level, attack them aggressively without showing signs of retreating.

In a single combat too, use this style to match the strength of the enemy. To mingle means to move forward to engage the enemy and not retreating even a step. You must understand this.

To Crush
This is meant to crush weak enemies.

We use this in large-scale strategy either when we see that the enemies are few, or if they are many but are mentally weak and confused. We knock the hat over their eyes and crush them completely. If we crush them lightly, they can recover. You must learn the spirit of crushing as if with a fist.

In a single strategy, crush your opponent immediately if he is less skillful than yourself, or if his rhythms are not organized, or if he withdraws or becomes elusive. Do not care about his presence and do not give him space to breathe. It is essential to crush the opponent at once. Your main aim should be not to let the opponent recover their stance even a little. You have to understand this.

The Mountain-Sea Transformation

The "mountain-sea transformation" means that it is bad to repeat an action in the midst of a battle with an enemy. Sometimes you have to do the same thing twice, but that should be only when it is inevitable. Make sure you don't repeat it the third time.

When you launch a blow against an opponent and it fails the first time, you can try again, but if it doesn't work, then you should do something completely different. If this technique isn't favorable, then you have to try another form of attack.

So the point of this is: when the opponent thinks of the "mountain" then you attack with "sea". But if he thinks of the "sea" then you attack with the "mountain". That is the Way of the Warrior. You must research this.

Pulling the Bottom Out

I call it "pulling the bottom out" because when you are fighting with the enemy, even when you see that you can win on the surface using the principles of the Way of the Warrior, make sure the spirit of the opponent is defeated, else he may be defeated on the surface but his spirit remains undefeated.

So with the principle of "pulling the bottom out", change your approach suddenly. You have to silence the enemy's spirit by pulling his heart out from below and watch until he knows that he is completely defeated. This is important. "Pulling the bottom out" can be done with the sword or with your body. You can even do it with your spirit. You cannot understand how to do this just at a glance.

Once the opponent collapses at the root, you do not need to pay attention to him anymore. If you pay attention to him, he may recover.

In both large and small scale strategy, you should carefully practice this "pulling the bottom out" tactic.

To Renew

Renew is when you feel that there is no way the fight between you and your opponent can be resolved. You would have to start all over, think about the situation from a new perspective, and understand how to win by capturing a fresh rhythm.

Renew is what can be done whenever you realize that you and your opponent have reached a deadlock. You would have to change your and use a completely different tactic to win.

It is also important to understand how to renew in large-scale strategy. When you are skilled in strategy, you will able to see how immediately. You should consider this deeply.

The Rat Head - Ox Neck

The "rat head - ox neck" happens during a fight when you and the enemy focus on minor details and become confused. Whenever you become preoccupied with small details, remember that the Way of the Warrior is always a "rat head - ox neck, rat head - ox neck". Whenever you think of small details, you must suddenly change into a large spirit, swapping large with small. This is one of the essences of strategy. In everyday life, you should also think of the "rat head - ox neck ". That is the necessity of a warrior.

You must not depart from this spirit whether in large-scale strategy or in single combat. This is something you should consider daily.

The General Knows His Troop

This is how to engage in any battle when you have mastered the strategy of the Way. Continually implement this strategy to capture its essence. In this strategy, think of your opponents like your own army. When you do this, you would be able to bend them to your will and move them around freely. You are the general. The enemy is your army. You must master this.

To Let Go the Hilt

The phrase "let go the hilt" has different meanings. There is the idea that you don't need a sword to gain victory. Then there is also another idea that it is impossible to win without a sword. The methods are different so we cannot express them in writing. You must train well.

The Body of a Rock

You have the body of a rock[9] when you attain the Way of the Warrior. You suddenly become a giant rock — you cannot be moved. Ten thousand things cannot touch you. This is the body of a rock.

Afterword

What is recorded above is what I have pondered consistently concerning my swordsmanship style. I have decided to put these thoughts down in writing, and this is the first time I am writing these principles. While writing, I felt that there was no logical flow to my words as I put the last points first and vice versa. It's hard to explain everything in detail. However, for those who want to learn the Way of the Warrior, what I have written here is a spiritual guide.

Since my youthful years, I have focused on the Way of the Warrior. I basically devoted time to learning swordsmanship. I diligently trained my hands and body and attaining the right mindsets. I went out and saw many different sects. All of them were only interested in discussing theories or skillful hands techniques. Although they boasted about their skills, they had no true spirit. Of course, if you learn something like this and you are mainly focused on training your body or broadening your mind, it would become an obstacle to the Way. And this will be hard to get rid of. It is for this reason the Way of the Warrior is actually falling apart and abandoned in the world.

TIMELESS CREEDS FOR WINNING

The true Way in terms of swordsmanship means fighting with the opponent and winning. This is not replaceable. If you thoroughly grasp the essence of my strategy and put it into practice correctly, you would have no doubt that you will win.

May 12, 1645
Shinmen Musashi

Scroll 4
Wind 風

It is important in strategy to understand the ways of other sects. So I write about different sects in the "wind" scroll. If you do not know the ways of other sects, you will certainly have difficulty understanding the truth of my sect.

Looking at other schools of martial arts, we see that there are some schools that use extra-long swords and emphasize physical strength to perform their techniques. On the contrary, there are schools that call themselves the "short sword[1]" school and use very short swords to practice their way. Then there are the sects that teach countless techniques and postures of the sword. Some of them are called "surface[2]" techniques and others are called "interior[3]" techniques. None of these is the true Way.

In this scroll, I will write about these sects clearly. I will explain what is good and bad about them, their natural principles, and how my style (that reflects the Way of the Warrior) is different from theirs.

Other sects created and developed the art of fighting so that they could use their achievements to make a living. They created and developed the art of fighting for monetary gains, so how can they be the true Way?

Moreover, most people see strategy from a narrow perspective and limit it only to swordsmanship. They only teach how to swing the sword, move the body effectively, or focus on how to control the hands. Do they really understand how to achieve victory?

The sects do not focus on the essence of the Way.

I will record the shortcomings of other sects in this scroll. If you study deeply, you will understand the advantages of Two Heaven Unifications.

Other Sects Using Extra-Long Swords
Some schools have a practice of carrying an extra-long sword. From my own perspective of what strategy should be, I consider this a weak style.

This is because they do not understand the principles of defeating an opponent under any conditions. They think of the sword's length as an advantage that would allow them to defeat enemies from afar. This is the only logical explanation of why they prefer extra-long swords.

Many people say "more than an inch gives an advantage", but this is a statement made by people who do not understand strategy. They are unable to grasp the principles of strategy because they feel it takes a lot of time, hence they prefer to depend on the length of their sword for victory. This shows a weakness of the spirit, therefore, it should be considered a weak strategy.

If the enemy is close, like so close that you can grapple him, a long sword would make it difficult for you to cut him. The sword becomes useless. You are restricted by the sword and even worse than a person with a short sword or someone without a weapon.

There are different personal reasons why people like an extra-long sword. But when viewed from the perspective of the true Way, there is no reason in this world for this practice. Without carrying a long sword, would someone with a short sword lose? In the event that a person is confronted above, below, on either side, or other situations, carrying an extra-long sword would be a question of strategy, and therefore it becomes a bad idea.

Some people are physically weaker and for such people having a long sword is useless.

It has long been said that "Great and small go together". So I am not saying you should avoid the long sword, but do not be dependent on it.

In large-scale strategy, a large army is like a long sword, while a small army is like a short sword. Don't small armies meet large armies during a battle? A small army can defeat a large one if they take advantage of military strategy. There have been so many examples in the past where a small army won a large one.

According to our sect, these types of biased and narrow-minded ideas should be avoided. You need to study carefully.

The Strong Long Sword of Other Sects
In swords, there shouldn't be "strong swords" or "weak swords". Trying to swing a sword strongly is a bad thing, and it is difficult to win with such a rough technique. Also, when you try to cut a person too hard because you feel you have a "strong sword", you will not cut anything. It is also bad to try to cut forcefully when you are testing your sword.

Do not think about anyone when swinging the sword to cut the enemy. When you think about cutting a person and killing them, you should not cut too hard and, of course, you should not cut too weakly. The only thing you should think of is that your cutting should be enough for the enemy to die.

Striking too hard or too weakly at the opponent's sword may be disadvantageous, so apply just enough energy to cut opponent. If you hit too hard on the opponent's sword, you may shatter your own sword.

For these reasons, things like "strong swords" do not exist.

In large-scale strategy, if you and the enemy are relying on the strength of your strong armies to win, the battle will be fierce. And without the right principles, the battle will not be won.

The spirit of my style is to win through the wisdom of strategy without paying attention to trifles. Study this well.

Other Sects Using Short Sword
The thought of winning using a short sword is not the true Way. Long and short swords have been clearly explained in ancient times. But they do not matter, all that matters is taking advantage of the situation.

In the world, those with superior power can wield a long sword lightly, so there is no need to force oneself to like a short sword. They can also use other weapons like spears and halberds.

Some people try to use a short sword with the intention of jumping in and catching the opponent off-guard in that moment when the opponent swings his long sword. Relying on such an idea is bad. Moreover, aiming for the opponent's unguarded moment is a defensive strategy and cannot be used when the enemy is close to you. If you use something small, then try to enter the opponent or capture, or steal the enemy's weapon. When you're in the middle of a lot of rivals, this idea is not helpful.

Those who specialize in wielding the short sword think they can block the hits from many attackers by freely jumping and turning. But all these actions are defensive actions, and it is not a smart way to fight.

In such a situation, it is better to make your body straight and strong, while chasing the enemies around, causing them to jump and creating chaos. This is the way to guarantee victory.

In large-scale strategy, the same principle applies. Your army should focus on repelling the enemy. They should attack the enemy fiercely and immediately crush them. This is an important idea in strategy.

Most people study strategy and learn how to parry, dodge, escape, bend over, or things like that. Then their minds become divided by these techniques so much so that they are easily manipulated by others.

The Way of the Warrior is straight and true. So adhere to the principles — push your enemies around and control them as you like. That's the most important thing. You must study this deeply.

The Sword Techniques of Other Sects
Inventing a large number of sword techniques and teaching them to people is just a way to turn the Way of the Warrior into a commodity for sale. By doing this, beginners start to think they have learned and understood a lot of techniques. Thinking about strategy this way should be avoided.

This should be avoided because when you think about all the different ways to cut a person down, you may feel lost. In fact, when it comes to cutting down a person, there is no special way to do that. Whether someone is knowledgeable or ignorant, whether it is a woman or a child attacking, all it takes is stabbing or cutting. There are not many ways to do this. As for other things, you can talk about stabbing or cutting but other than these, there is nothing else. The way to win is to cut first, and not pay attention to small details.

However, depending on the terrain and the situation, there are times when you have to parry on the top, on the side or similar angles. Since it is true that you cannot hold yourself at will, we have five positions; one for each method. The positions of other sects such as hand twists, body twists, jumps, dodges are ways to cut a person down. But this is not the true Way.

When aiming to cut down the enemy, if you twist your hand, you cannot cut. If you twist your body, you cannot cut. If you jump, you cannot cut. None of these can be used in any situation.

According to my strategy, you make both your posture and spirit straight. As for the opponent, make him weak and fall. You win by distorting his spirit — throw him into confusion and terrify him. This is important. You should study this diligently.

The Special Sword Positions of Other Sects

It is a mistake to emphasize special positions to take when wielding a sword. The only time to use the "defensive" position is when there is really no opponent.

These special positions have been drawn from long-standing customs and have been made and coded into rules today. They have no place in a one-on-one battle. You have to think of putting your opponent in a disadvantaged situation.

Having a "defense stance" means trying to use immobility to your advantage. Whether it is defending a castle or lining up the ranks, the goal is to be strong and not to move even when attacked by the enemy. This is common sense.

When fighting in the Way of the Warrior, always have the intention to take the initiative; always be proactive. When you are on the defensive, it means you are waiting for others to take the initiative. You should completely avoid doing this.

When you fight in the Way of the Warrior, try to make others move their position. Do things that the enemy cannot imagine — confuse the enemy, disturb the enemy, or threaten the enemy in order to catch him when his rhythm wavers. To win, you must avoid ideas like being on the defensive.

It is because of this we say in the Way of the Warrior, "Position - No position". This means that although we know what might happen when we take a certain position, we decide not to take that position.

In large-scale strategy, understand the enemy's forces. Be aware of the natural terrain of the battlefield. And know the strength of your military force. Weaken the advantages of the enemy and capitalize on their disadvantages. Then prepare your troops and begin the fight. These are necessary elements to note to participate in combat. From the moment the enemy takes the initiative against you to the moment you take the initiative, the changes in the situation become double.

Taking a good sword position and skillfully deflecting or defeating the opponent's attack is like using spears and halberds to make a fence. Then when you want to attack the enemy, pull out the fence and use them as spears and halberds. You should consider this deeply.

Gazing in Other Sects

When it comes to gazing, different sects have different opinions. There are sects that focus on the opponent's sword, while there are others that focus on the opponent's arm. There is also a sect that advocates focusing on the face, or on the feet, etc. Focusing on separate things can cause a distraction, and this is considered blindness in strategy.

An example of this is a soccer[4] player. The soccer player doesn't have to look at the ball[5] closely before he kicks or performs other skills with the ball. They are accustomed to kicking the ball, so there is no need to look at the ball closely.

The acrobat masters have their perching doors on the tip of their nose. They juggle many swords without looking, yet they do not make mistakes. They are accustomed to juggling, so it comes to them naturally.

The same goes for large-scale strategy when you get used to facing enemies. You will be able to see the burden of the enemy's mind. Once you have trained and grasped the Way of the Warrior, you will also be able to see the distance and speed of any sword.

Fixing the eyes in strategy means gazing at the opponent's mind.

In large-scale strategy, it means gazing or watching the strength of the enemy's forces.

There are two ways to see: Perception and Sight. Perception means concentrating strongly on the opponent's mind and terrain of the battle place. It also involves observing the situation of the battle and seeing how the advantage changes. That is the way to win.

In small- and large-scale strategy, there is no reason to gaze on minute things. As I mentioned before, if you focus closely on specifics, you would forget the big things. You would lose your perspective and victory would elude you.

Carefully study these principles and practice them.

Use of the Feet in Other Sects
There are various ways of using the feet: floating feet, flying feet, shrugging feet, climbing feet, and crowing feet. From the standpoint of my strategy, all of these methods are unsatisfactory.

For instance, avoid the floating step because when used during a fight, it would appear as if you are galloping. So it is best you use firm footsteps so you would tread as firmly as possible.

You should also avoid the flying feet. It encourages the habit of jumping. And there is no benefit in jumping or flying around all the time. So the flying feet are bad.

Also, avoid the shrugging feet. This makes you indecisive and you won't be able to attack.

The climbing feet are the "waiting feet", so they should also be avoided.

Besides these, there are a number of quick steps like the crow feet, etc.

When you fight an opponent in the swamp, in the field, on the mountains, in a river, in a rocky beach, or on a narrow road, there are situations where you cannot jump around or walk quickly.

In our strategy, nothing changes about the footstep. The step should be the same as for a normal walk. You should move according to the rhythm of the opponent. Whether you are moving quickly or slowly, maintain the same attitude and posture. Do not move too fast or too slow and your steps should not falter.

If you walk slowly, you may miss the opportunity when the enemy begins to collapse and the chance of victory will slip through, thus you would be unable to finish the fight quickly.

When you clearly see a moment of disruption and collapse, it is your time for you to claim your victory. Do not allow the enemy to recover even a little bit. You should practice and execute this carefully.

Speed in Other Sects
Speed is not a true Way of the Warrior. With speed, you lose coordination and the flow of your rhythm. From custom/tradition, everything in life is grouped as either "fast" or "slow". When you master the Way of the Warrior, you would not be in a hurry. There are people called "express courier[6]". They can move forty or fifty miles in a day, but that doesn't mean they ran continuously from morning till night like that. Novice runners, on the other, may run all day, yet may not go far.

In dance dramas, the expert singer can sing while dancing but when the beginner tries this, he feels he is lagging and must hurry to catch up. Also, when an expert drummer beats the melody of "The Old Pine[7]" on a drum, the melody is tranquil, but a less skilled drummer would fall behind the rhythm and try to get ahead. "High Sand[8]" has a fast rhythm but it would be wrong to play it fast. Being too fast or too slow in anything is bad.

When talented people do something, they seem to be calm and never miss a beat. Also, when an expert does a thing, he is never in a hurry. From these examples, you should understand the principles of the Way of the Warrior.

In the Way of the Warrior, trying to be fast is bad. The reason for this is that depending on the terrain, swamps, and moors, it would be difficult to move both the feet and body quickly. For the sword, cutting quickly is bad. If you try to cut quickly, you won't be able to cut at all because the sword is not like a fan or a knife. You must learn to distinguish this clearly.

The same goes for large-scale strategy. The feeling of hurrying is bad. If you maintain the idea of "pressing the pillow down" you will never be slow even for a moment. Moreover, in situations where the opponent is too fast, it is necessary for you to do the opposite — be slow, calm, and not allow yourself to be drawn in. You have to practice hard to get this spirit.

"Interior" and "Surface" in Other Sects
There is neither "deep" nor "surface" in strategy. Artistic achievements often claim inner meanings and traditional

secrets are either deep inner thoughts or at the gate. But in combat there is no such thing as surface combat or cutting with depth. When teaching the Way of the Warrior, I first teach it through easy technical training for students to understand; an easy doctrine. I gradually try to explain deep principles — points that are difficult to understand — according to the students' progress. In any case, the way to understand is through experience. I am not talking about "deep" or "gateway".

In this world, if you go into the mountains and decide to go deeper when you go deeper, you will appear at the gate. Every Way has "profoundness" and that is sometimes a good thing to point out. In strategy, we cannot say what is hidden and what is revealed. Therefore, I do not pass my Way of the Warrior through written commitments and regulations. Recognizing the abilities of my students, I teach them directly, eliminate the bad influence of other schools, and gradually introduce them to the true Way of the Warrior. My method of teaching strategy is with the spirit of trust, with a free mind that is free from doubt. You must train thoroughly.

Afterword

Above, I have laid out nine sections on the strategy of other sects and have written them down in this "Wind" scroll. Perhaps I should write about them in detail, giving specific accounts of each school section by section, from "gateway" to "deep" teachings. But I deliberately didn't mention the names of these sects, neither did I mention important points about any of them. The reason for this is that even if I point out individuals in each sect and write about their ways, each individual has their own way of thinking and interpreting the doctrines of the sect. Even within the same school, ideas change from time to time. So I will have to constantly write periodic updates for each sect.

I have divided the general idea of the other sects into nine parts. If you look at the techniques of people around the world in general, you would see that some prefer long swords, while others say that short swords are more favorable. Some tend to use "strong" or "rough" or "correct" techniques during battle. All of these are ways of creating prejudice, therefore I did not discuss everything about the "gate" and "depth" of other sects. Everyone should understand.

According to my sect, the sword does not have "depth" or "entrance" nor does it have a "supreme" posture. You only need your mind, and you also need to perfect the attitude of the sword. This is the nature of strategy.

May 12, 1645
Shinmen Musashi

Scroll 5

Emptiness 空

I wrote about the Way of The Warrior of the Two Heaven Unifications in this "Emptiness" scroll.

What is called the spirit of the void is a place of nothing. It is not included in human knowledge. Of course, the void is nothingness. By knowing things that exist, you can know what does not exist. That is "emptiness".

In the world, if you see things the wrong way, you cannot understand things like "emptiness." We don't see it physically but it is there in existence.

Also, the Way of the Warrior is like an enforcement warrior. That you don't understand the reality of a warrior doesn't mean it is "void" of existence. Every thought that exists in the mind also exists in reality.

As a member of the warrior class, you should learn the Way properly and practice the strategy of other sects[1]. Never let the Way of the Warrior we practice to become tainted or obscured, not even a little bit. Your mind must never be lost. Never skip workouts every morning or at any other time. Polish the twofold spirit of your mind and your will.²

Train the eyes to perceive and see. There are no small clouds. You must understand that when the illusion clouds dissipate, then that is true "emptiness".

Unless you know the true Way of the Warrior, whether through the law of Buddhism or the law of the human world, you would think that all things are right and good. However, from the standpoint of the true Way of the Warrior, the great models and standards in the world are recognized as prejudices of the mind and based on these distortions, they go against the true Way of the Warrior.

Understand this idea. Choose the true Way of the Warrior. Develop the true heart³ of the Way of the Warrior for yourself and train in the Way. Take "emptiness" like the Way, then you will see the Way as emptiness.

Think accurately and clearly. Think big. Develop the "empty" nature in your strategy. Then you will see the Way of the Warrior as emptiness.

In emptiness is virtue and there is no evil. In emptiness, intellect exists. Principle exists. The Way exists. And the spirit is nothingness.

May 12, 1645
Shinmen Musashi

THIRTY-FIVE ARTICLES ABOUT SWORD STRATEGY

Ken Senryaku Ni Kansuru 35 No Kiji
剣戦略に関する35の記事

Thirty-Five Articles About Sword Strategy
Ken Senryaku Ni Kansuru 35 No Kiji
剣戦略に関する35の記事

I have many years of training under the Two Heaven Unifications. Now I put brush on paper to write about these things for the first time and humbly send it. With your great authority, this humble effort is not enough and it is very difficult to deliver what I want to say. But these are the techniques that I use as a standard to train and understand the use of swords in strategy. I humbly write down the general ideas on what I have learned.

1. On Using Two Swords
The Way of the "Two Heaven" is to train to hold two swords[1]. Do not hold in the left hand. This would help one learn how to wield the sword in one hand. Holding the sword in one hand is advantageous in battles, on horseback, in rivers and streams, on narrow streets, and in capturing prisoners. Similarly, when one has to hold a weapon or another object while in some difficult positions, one has to hold the sword with one hand. When people hold the sword in one hand, at first it feels heavy

but then later it becomes possible to wield the sword freely without difficulty. For example, through training, people learn and develop the necessary strength to shoot a bow and also to ride a horse. Also, in rowing a boat every day, people train and learn how to hold onto the oars with power. With consistency, the farmer holds his shovel and hoe and becomes perfect with using them. The same goes for the sword. If people pick up the sword and train, they will develop the necessary strength required to wield it with one hand. Strength is something that grows. That said, it is important that everyone should carry a sword that suits their body and matches their strength or weakness.

2. Understanding the Way of Strategy
In the Way of the Warrior, the large-scale and one-on-one strategy are the same. Both should be viewed the same way. For example in what is written here about personal strategy, the mind can be thought of as a general[2], the hands and feet[3] as ministers, and the body as like soldiers and peasants. The administration of a nation and the training of the body, whether big or small, are the same in the Way of the Warrior, as well as in the training in the Way of strategy. The whole body should be thought of completely as one and no part should be excluded at all. Pay equal attention to the entire body from head to toe — not too much and not too little, not too strongly and not too weakly, so that the body exists in oneness. Such training must be practiced.

3. On Holding the Sword
When holding the sword, the thumb and index finger should "float" or hold lightly, the middle finger should hold with

medium strength, while the ring finger and little finger should hold firmly. Just like with the sword, there is life and death in the hand. When taking a stance, striking or stopping, the hand that forgets to cut and becomes rigid is called a "dead hand". The "living hand" moves at any time with the sword without being stiff and cuts easily. Do not twist your wrists, do not stretch your elbows or bend them excessively. Hold the sword with the upper muscle of the arm relaxed and the lower muscle strong or tensed. This needs to be thoroughly researched.

4. On Positioning
In positioning, the face is neither tilted nor too far upwards. Shoulders should not be raised or twisted and should not be puffed up. Push your belly forward and don't bend your hips. Do not stiffen your knees but make your body straight and spread horizontally. The idea is to make your everyday posture the same as your fighting posture. This must be fully studied.

5. On Footsteps
Your footstep depends on the situation. While steps may be big or small, fast or slow, your footsteps should be the same as when you are walking normally. Among the steps to avoid are "flying feet[4]", "floating feet[5]", "climbing feet[6]", "withdraw feet[7]" and "back-forth feet[8]". These footsteps are unsuitable. Whatever the difficult terrain, your step should be firm. This will become more understandable based on what will be written later.

6. On Gazing
There have been many ideas on the subject of "eye-attachment[9]". There is an idea called "muscle mass[10]" that

is now commonly referred to as "to look in the face". When gazing during combat, your look should be soft by narrowing your eyes a bit more than usual. Do not move the eyeballs when the enemy is approaching. No matter how close the enemy is, see the enemy as if he is far away. With this type of gaze, you don't just perceive the opponent's techniques, but you can also see both sides.

There are two types of gaze: the gaze of perceiving and the gaze of seeing. The "gaze of perceiving[11]" is strong, while the "gaze of seeing[12]" is weak. You can also convey your intentions to the enemy through your gaze. For this reason, your gaze should reveal only your will, but not your mind and thoughts. This requires careful research.

7. On Timing

The right time in strategy involves the existence of the mind and the body in one place. Now I would say that there should not be such a mind. No matter the Way a person follows, if he is familiar with this then he can be understood. Do not get distracted; use the power of the now. Generally, when your sword is close enough to hit the opponent, know that the opponent's sword is also close enough to hit you. If you are going to attack the opponent then you have to forget about your body. You have to do this rigorously.

8. On Mindset

As for the state of the mind, it should not be agitated or weakened but be calm and fearless. Try not to be distracted by fear. Develop a large mind — a mind like water. Depending on the situation, the mind should be flexible like water. Water can be dark blue. It can be a drop or a vast ocean. This needs to be deeply studied.

9. The High, Middle, and Low Levels of Strategy
In strategy, body postures that display different sword positions and appear slow, close, or fast are known as low-level positions. Those that express techniques as complex and rhythmic, and try to make the individual look impressive are called middle-level positions. The high-level position is neither strong nor weak, nor obtrusive, nor fast. It does not attempt to impress, yet does not present the body in a bad light. The strategy appears large, frank, calm, and peaceful. This is the highest level. This needs to be thoroughly researched.

10. The Measuring Cord
Always have a measuring cord or yardstick in mind for all opponents. Use this cord to measure their strengths, weaknesses, upright places, cramped places, points where they are stressed, and points where they are relaxed. Use your mind as a measure to perceive the intention of the opponent. With the measuring cord, measure what it is round and angular, long and short, twisted, and straight in the opponent so that you can have a holistic understanding of the opponent. This should be practiced.

11. The Path of the Sword
If the path of the sword[13] is not well understood, it would be difficult to swing it according to one's will. Moreover, do not try to misuse the ridge and flat surface of the blade, or try to use the sword as a small knife. Similarly, if the sword is handled like a sickle, it would be difficult to cut the enemy

with it. Keep learning the path of the sword. Hold the sword calmly as if it were heavy and train to cut the opponent.

12. Hitting and Cutting

Hitting and cutting involve the use of swords. Have a definite target in mind to cut. Then just like hitting, when you can't see a decisive blow, you can hit anywhere. Even if your blow is strong, it is not cutting. Whenever you hit an enemy on his body or his sword, even if you miss, your attempt is not pointless. In fact, hitting can precede cutting especially if your hands and feet do not betray your movement. This needs to be diligently trained.

13. The Three Initiatives

The three initiatives are: one, when you actively attack the enemy; two, when the enemy actively attacks you; and three, when you and the enemy actively attack each other simultaneously. There are no possible initiatives besides these three. The best posture when you attack first is to use your body as weapon of attack. Keep your mind and your feet focused, and don't collapse or stretch to deceive the enemy. This is a proactive attack.

Next is when the enemy comes to attack. You do away with every intention to attack. When the enemy is quite close, let your mind free, observe his movements, and immediately take the initiative.

The final initiative is when you and the enemy attack simultaneously. Your body should be kept upright, straight, and strong. The initiative should be seized with the sword, the body, the legs and the mind. This way you are proactive. Seizing the initiative is of utmost importance.

14. Crossing the Ford
When faced with two enemies and you are close enough to attack with your sword, but you think attacking would give the enemy the advantage, then you have to close the right flank with your body and legs. This way, if you cross the ford, you have nothing to worry about. To understand this, you must carefully analyze what I wrote earlier about initiative.

15. The Body Replacing Sword
The body replacing the sword is when the body serves as a representative of the sword during an attack and then the sword follows. This attack is carried out from the "empty" mind. When you are about to attack, the sword, the body, and the mind should not attack at the same time. Only focus on the mind and the body. They must be studied diligently.

16. The Two Feet
The two feet means using both feet to move when attacking with the sword. When pressing down the opponent's sword with yours, or evading it, or when stepping forward or backward, use two feet. Use the two feet in harmony. Attacking with the sword with only one foot would make you become rigid or fixed to a spot. Think of the feet like a couple, and they should move together just like when you walk normally. This requires comprehensive research.

17. Pressing Down the Sword
This is the idea of stepping on the tip of the sword with your foot. The moment you cut the opponent down, you can

suddenly press down his sword with your left foot. With his sword pressed down, take the initiative with your sword, your body and your mind. If you do this, you will be in a winning position no matter what. But without this initiative, you would just fight back and forth and this is a very bad thing. However, there are times when you should rest your feet because pressing down the sword is not something that can be done at all times. This must be studied carefully.

18. Loosened Shadow

The loosened shadow[14] or the negative shadow[15] is a method used to attack the opponent's weak point according to your prediction. If you study your opponent closely, you would see the areas he pays attention to as well as the areas he does not notice. If you notice the area where the opponent pays attention to and at the same time, before the opponent moves, aim the tip of your sword at the shadow of the areas where he doesn't pay sufficient attention, he would lose the rhythm, and then you can defeat him easily. However, the important thing is to maintain the spirit and never forget the real goal — cutting the opponent. This requires subtlety to perform.

19. The Moving Shadow[16]

Here, the shadow is visible. A positive shadow[17] means the opponent holds the sword behind and exposes the body. Then you prohibit the attack of the enemy when his sword is out and in position. The idea is to stop the enemy's sword and make your own body empty. If you attack with your sword right at the protruding part of the enemy's body, his body will definitely move. And if he moves then you will easily win. This theory did not exist before. You should attack the protruding part of his body to avoid stiffening of the mind. This should be tried carefully.

20. Loosening the Bowstring

Loosening the bowstring is a time when both the enemy's mind and yours are stretched and you have to release yourself from the deadlock. It is important to quickly relax your body, sword, legs, and mind. Let go when the opponent is least expecting. This needs to be practiced.

21. The Small Comb

The spirit of the small comb[18] dissolves confusion. Keep a small comb in your mind. When the enemy tries to confuse you through whatever means, your aim is to untangle yourself from the confusion. Tying and untying are the same, but untying has a strong spirit while tying has a weak spirit. This needs to be extensively studied.

22. The Rhythm Interval

Understanding the time interval in the rhythm depends on the opponent; some are fast, while some are slow. Rhythm depends on the opponent. When crossing swords with an opponent with a slow spirit, don't move your body and don't let the opponent predict your next move. Quickly attack into the void. This is a beat. For enemies with a quick spirit, attack with both your body and mind. Wait till the enemy makes his move before you attack. This is called the "two beats". Also, there is what is called "heartless, invisible". With this technique, you expose the body as if you don't want to attack. Then at the same time, put your mind and sword together, combine your power with your enemies and strike hard at the void. This is "heartless, invisible". Moreover, as it relates to the "slow beat" when the opponent tries to parry or deflect your sword, you become extremely slow as if you don't want to attack, then when your enemy is deceived, attack at that moment. This is called "slow beat". This should be practiced thoroughly.

23. Pressing Down the Pillow
Pressing down the pillow means crushing the enemy's intention to attack without the enemy expecting or predicting the move. To suppress the enemy's attack, use your spirit, body, and sword. When you understand this technique, you can use it to attack the enemy to gain the upper hand, to retreat, or to hold the initiative. It is a method that can be used in any situation. This is important in training.

24. Understanding the Situation
To understand the situation, it is necessary to grasp and understand the conditions of the terrain and the condition of the enemy. Understand if the conditions are floating or sinking, shallow or deep, strong or weak. By continuously practicing with the "measuring cord", the situation can be assessed on the spot. See and act at the right moment, and you would win whether at the front or at the rear. This needs to be deeply considered.

25. On Becoming the Opponent
You should think of your body as the opponent. Whether you are dealing with someone who has retreated into a protected place, or a very large opponent, or someone who is well versed in strategy, you should think about the weakness in his mind. If you are not aware of the enemy's mind, you may mistake a weak person for a strong one, a person with no skills for one that is competent, and a small opponent for a dangerous

one. The enemy may capitalize on this mistake. So become the opponent! You should analyze this carefully.

26. Maintaining and Releasing the Mind
Maintaining the mind or releasing the mind is something that depends on the situation and time. When you hold a sword, often the will of the mind[19] is liberated, and that spirit[20] is maintained. On the other hand, when you decisively attack the enemy, your spirit is relaxed and your willpower is maintained. There are many ways to look at maintaining or releasing the mind. This needs to be investigated in depth.

27. On Attacking as an Opportunity
What is called "attacking as an opportunity[21]" is when the enemy comes near and cuts you with his sword, then you use your sword to knock away his sword, or parry or even strike the opponent. Whether knocking away, parrying or striking, the opponent's sword should be considered an opportunity to take off, slip or stick. If this is all the purpose of attack, then your body, mind, and sword must have the same intention of attack. You need to study this carefully.

28. The Lacquer Adhesion
The lacquer adhesion[22] means to fight with the opponent in close quarters so that you stick to him from your feet to your hips to your head, leaving nothing open. You stick completely to him like how things stick together with lacquer glue. If there is a space between both bodies, then the opponent has the chance to use different techniques. The rhythm of sticking with the opponent should have a calm spirit like "pressing the pillow down".

29. The Body of an Autumn Monkey
The body of an autumn monkey[23] means clinging to the enemy's body as if you have no hands. Keeping your body separate from that of the opponent is bad. If the hand is loosened further, the body tends to retract. Although the left shoulder to the forearm is helpful, the extra hand is not. The rhythm of clinging to the opponent is the same as before.

30. Comparing Heights
In comparing heights, you stand right next to the enemy as if comparing height with him. You expand your body to give a feeling that you are taller. The rhythm of standing next to the opponent is the same as other rhythms of clinging or sticking discussed above. This needs to be studied carefully.

31. The Hinge Body
The hinge body[24] means that when you stick to the opponent, you first make the body wider and straight as if trying to hide the sword and the body of the opponent. Stick in a way that does not leave any space between your body and that of the opponent. Then when the opponent turns to the side, slam your shoulder into the opponent's chest. This is the way to defeat the opponent. This should be practiced.

32. The General and The Army
The general and the army[25] mean likening your body to a large-scale strategy. See the opponent as your army and you as the general. Do not give the opponent the slightest freedom and do not let him swing the sword or cut. Realize that everything done must be according to your will. You should make it impossible for the opponent to even have a strategy in his mind. This is essential.

33. Defensive – Not Defensive

Defensive – not defensive[26] is what happens in the body when you hold a sword. No matter what the body is in a position. If you intend to "occupy position" then both the sword and the body become fixed. Take action according to the terrain and the situation. While you always have a sword, there is no need to think of taking a position in the head for the sword to match the enemy. There are three ways to raise the sword high. In the middle and low there are also three different ideas, similarly for the left and the right. Even when you are standing, the idea is not to make the body become static. This should be studied diligently.

34. The Body of a Rock

The body of a rock[27] should be attained through non-stop training along with a solid spirit that is strong and thoroughly forged. A body that has realized the whole truth of strategy is extremely powerful. Everything in the world voluntarily tries to avoid the body. Even lifeless grasses and natural trees avoid spreading their roots. Even the rain and the wind have the same tendency in his presence. You must be eager to strive to train this body.

35. On Understanding Moments

Understanding moments mean having the ability to understand fast moments and slow moments. Understand the moments when you can escape and understand the moments when escaping is impossible. In this technique, there is a profound principle called "direct transmission". The details of this principle are handed down orally.

Epilogue

I have humbly written countless ideas concerning my principle. But it is only on "Emptiness" that I couldn't write. So it's best if you can please reflect on this for yourself. For the thirty-five techniques written above, I tried to humbly write down a general outline of strategic thinking and how they should be considered. If in some places I have failed to provide some points, know that the ideas are similar to what was written before. In addition, individuals train and absorb this style, hence, the specifics of the sword's movements and other ideas are transmitted orally. There's no need to write them here. Moreover, if you are confused about any idea, it is best if you allow me to humbly explain to you directly.

Lucky Day, February 1645
Shinmen Musashi

THE WAY OF WALKING ALONE

Dokkōdō
獨行道

The Way Of Walking Alone[1]
Dokkōdō 獨行道

Do not ignore the Way in the world.
Do not seek pleasure for its own sake.
Do not rely on anything.
Downplay yourself and think deeply about people.
Do not be greedy or be malicious in life.
Do not regret personal matters.
Never be jealous of others.
Do not be upset when being separated on any Path.
Do not complain or blame yourself or others.
Do not direct your thoughts to sensuality.
Do not over-enjoy anything in life.
Be indifferent to where to live.
Do not pursue a taste for delicious food.
Do not keep things that you no longer need.
Do not act following customary superstition.
Do not collect or train with weapons beyond usefulness.
Do not fear death.
Do not try to own anything illegal or from political bribes.
Respect the Buddha and the gods but don't request them.
One may abandon one's body but must preserve one's honor.
Never stray from the Way.

May 2nd, 1645
Shinmen Musashi

The Writing of

Sun Vu
孫 武

THE LAW OF WAR
兵法

The Art Of Competition Benefits In War, Business, And Life

Written by
Sun Vu
孫武

Translated by
Tham Trong Ma

A Few Words

The Law of War is one of the old Chinese writings that have been around as far back as the 5th century BC. This book is composed of thirteen chapters, and it is said to have been composed by the popular war strategist of that time named Sun Vu (who, of course, is now globally known as Sun Tzu – the author of the equally popular treatise called The Art of War). In a way, it seems like Sun and his work suffered a change in name over times. While his original name was Sun Vu, he became popular with Sun Tzu. Similarly, his work The Law of War, after many years, became The Art of War.

Each chapter of this book (The Law of War) focuses on a particular situation of warfare and its relation to the strategy and tactics inherent in military affairs, especially ones that deal with battle of every aspect – either land or water. The lessons therein have been adopted by various war generals for hundreds of years, and it is still a relevant work even today, as I have no doubt it will continue to be for hundreds of more years to come. For about 1,500 years, The Law of War, has remained the leading work in a collection of ancient works that became formalized as the by Emperor Shenzong of Song in 1080. He listed The Law of War as one of the

Seven Military Classics of ancient times. This incredible work has maintained the reputation of not only being the most influential text about strategy in warfare in East Asia, but has also influenced the lifestyle, legal strategy, business tactics and military organization in both the East and the West.

Arguably, no other book about the analysis of the Chinese military is as detailed as The Law of War. It touches on very important areas as the use of weapons, the application of strategy during battle, and the process of discipline. It also highlights how necessary it is to make use of intelligent operatives and espionage to increase the chance of success during battle and every other aspect of warfare. Indeed, it is safe to say that most of the modern military cultures of today have their origin from The Law of War. This is why the lessons taught in this book will continue to be relevant for many generations to come; it has formed the basis of military trainings of today all over the world and it shall continue to be for more thousands of years.

While this particular book has been translated into various languages, including Vietnamese, it was partially translated to English by British officer Everard Ferguson Calthrop in the early 20th century; and it came with the title The Book of War, but the translation was completed five years later by Lionel Giles.

Many have drawn inspiration from the lessons in The Law of War; some of these people include political and military leaders all over the world – American military general Norman Schwarzkopf Jr., Vietnamese general Ngô Quang Trưởng, Japanese daimyō Takeda Shingen, amongst a lot of other powerful people of the world.

Cao Cao, the poet, warlord and strategist wrote the earliest known commentary about Sun Vu's work during the early 3rd century AD; his writing was reportedly the earliest known commentary about the book. Cao Cao himself admitted in his preface that he removed certain passages from the original, and he also changed many words. So it was not really clear how much of a change he made to the original work. Also, in the early 20th century, about the time the work was being translated to English by Calthrop and Giles, the Chinese writer and reformer Liang Qichao explained that the texts of The Law of War were actually written in the 4th century BC by the descendant of Sun Vu – the name of this descendant was Sun Bin.

Over the years, the thirteen chapters contained in the work have also suffered a change in titles. For chapter 1, it was titled Laying Plans by Lionel Giles in 1910, The Calculations by R.L. Wing in 1988, and Initial Estimation by Ralph D. Sawyer in 1996. Different changes also occurred in the subsequent thirteen chapters. This book, also, has peculiar titles for each of the thirteen chapters it contains. Planning, Combating, Offensive Strategy, Military Disposition, Military Force, Real and Unreal, Maneuvering, Nine Changes, Marching, Terrain, Nine Ground Positions, Fire Attack, and Using Spy.

The first chapter illustrates all that is required to understand the nature of war, and planning for the war is one of the most important elements of the tactics and strategy of warfare. The second chapter directly goes into the art of combating enemy during battle; it explains the entire angles one must consider before deciding to engage enemy in combat. Sometimes, combat can be more of psychological than physical. The third chapter introduces the strategy of taking enemy by surprise and showing that one has broader strategy than the enemy. Chapter four observes the method of making the enemy troop miserable by doing everything possible to take the comfort off of them and rendering them totally powerless. Chapter five explains the principles that guide the control of military forces, either a large force or a small one. It shows that the same principle guides whatever number the force might be. Chapter six stresses the benefit of arriving early at the battle ground, especially before the enemy troop – it shows the advantage of being the first troop to occupy the ground. The seventh chapter is all about maneuvering against the enemy by making proper use of the soldiers. In most cases, it is better to improvise, depending on the situation of the war. The eighth chapter highlights all the changes that may affect the result of a war. Some of these changes could be the road, the weather, the weapons, or even the soldiers. Chapter nine explains the process of moving soldiers to the battlefield, and surviving the rigors of the terrains. Chapter ten further assesses the terrains of war; it observes all the grounds and points, then how to bear responsibility as a war general. Chapter eleven introduces the nine ground positions and how to manage each of them, depending on the nature of the war and the application of military power. The twelfth chapter teaches how to make use of fire to attack the enemy; it explains the five ways one can make use of the fire to decimate the enemy and render the troop powerless. And lastly, the thirteenth chapter emphasizes the importance of making use of spies during war. It does not only talk about the use of one's spies but also discovering enemy spies and making use of them to one's advantage. All these thirteen chapters are necessary for a war general who aspires to emerge victorious during war.

The Law of War is not only applicable to military strategy alone, it is also applicable to life. For in a way, life itself is like a warfront, and one must be ready to fight the battles it brings and come out victorious in the end. Life comes with many challenges, and only a man armed with the necessary knowledge of war and knows the right application of tactics would not be defeated.

In East Asia, The Law of War has become a part of the syllabus for candidates of military service examinations. Takeda Shingen was invincible in battle because he read the works of Sun Vu which gave him great inspiration against the battle of Fūrinkazan. Some South Vietnamese officers during the Vietnam War extensively studied The Law of War so much that they could recite every passage of the book from their heads.

Generally, The Law of War teaches how to outsmart one's opponent without having to engage in physical combat or battle, as the case may be.

Tham trong Ma

About Sun Vu

Sun Vu, popularly known as Sun Tzu, was born in 545 BC and died in 470 BC; he was 75 years old – this was during the period known as 'The Spring and Autumn Period of China'. Vu, who is also believed to have authored the globally acclaimed book The Art of War, was a military expert, a general and a philosopher. His book is one of the best books that deal with strategies and theories of the warfare. Only few people in the West may know that his original name is Sun Vu, and that the Tzu only means 'Master', which, of course, is a title of respect, especially in ancient Chinese.

A lot of details about Sun Vu are sketchy, and most of what we know today comes from Ssu-ma Ch'ien's Shi Chi. According to the Grand Historian records, Sun Vu was born in the State of Qi. But there was further controversy about his birth; the Spring and Autumn Annals of Wu and Yueh maintained that he was born in Wu. It is hard to really determine Sun Wu's true origin since it's a very long time ago that he existed; records are sometimes bound to contradict themselves.

Even details about Sun Vu's early life are blurry. All that is known is that Vu grew up in a military family and he studied military science. The only fact that stands out is that Sun Vu, at some point in his life, became a great strategist and general in the military. In fact, he was a general for King Helü of Wu where it was recorded that he won many wars, especially the ones most people already thought he would lose. With hi strategic thinking and brilliant maneuvering, he was able to conquer a lot of enemies.

Sun won his battles in various unique manners. Most times, he would win without actually fighting his enemies. He was known to always analyze battles and decide whether it was necessary to fight or not. Instead of picking up arms and charging head-on toward his enemies, Sun Vu would rather make use of spies to discover the chink in the enemies' armors. Sun Vu was one of the earliest generals to make use of spies. And whenever it was necessary for him to fight, he would also attack in manners the enemies never saw coming because he understood warfare strategies better than a lot of his opponents. And when the battle was over, he would not only win but also have the least number of casualties – he rarely lost his men.

Also according to historical reports, Sun Vu was believed to be the victor during the Battle of Boju in 506 BC. Sima Qian (145/135 – 86 BC), who authored the Shiji regarded Sun Vu as an outstanding strategist; he explained that Vu was not only a flexible commanded but also had an unlimited surprises for his enemies. His opponents were always quaking in their boots whenever they discovered that Sun Vu was the opposing general, for they never knew what Sun Vu's point of attack would be, or method as the case would be. In almost 40 years as a general, Vu never lost a war or battle – he kept a clean sheet all through his life.

The Art of War, written by Sun Tzu, was originally titled The Law of War; but for some reasons The Law of War became The Art of War in the West. This book was one of the earliest books that explained the concept of warfare. As one of the most influential books ever, it has been read by kings and commanders for over two thousand years; and it has successfully influenced a lot of battles historically. According to an historical report, it was written on bamboo slats that were joined together by a twine; it became a widely popular book even in the western world, and it wasn't translated into English until the 20th century.

In the times of Sun Vu, war was seen as a form of chivalry, and it was considered the sport of rich people of noble backgrounds. But Vu refused to see any nobility, chivalry or sport in war. To him, war was a brutal battle between two opposing forces that ultimately leads to deaths and destruction – and if you want to play the game, you should as well know how to play it right; hence his decision to write the book. So Sun Vu used the Taoist principles to further his warfare strategies; and in no time he became a force to reckon with in the battle field. By merging the principles with war strategies, Sun Vu succeeded in changing the rules of war - which, of course, were conventional at the time. He came up with sure methods that won him a lot of battles.

Many historians agreed that Sun Vu's mind worked differently from others in his rank. Unlike other generals who fancied long campaigns and the systematic dance around the bush, Vu knew that war was a serious business which should not be handled with levity. You must strike when the iron is hot, and you must strike very hard. It is the first blow that will determine how the fight will end. He believed that as soon as war started, the ultimate goal was to defeat the enemy. With this knowledge, Sun Vu knew that he must not follow the conventional method of warfare; he must carve out his own path, create his own niche. He didn't follow the basic wisdom that ruled the art of war in his time. So when it was time for battle, the other generals were always simply unprepared for Sun Vu's tactics.

Because of him, basic military concepts were changed and improved for thousands of years. Even in the Gulf War, American generals Norman Schwarzkopf, Jr and Colin Powell applied the principles inherent in The Art of War.

Today, Sun Vu's name remains on the tongues of most army generals of the world.

Tham Trong Ma

Chapter 1
Planning[1] 始 計

Understanding the nature of war is a nationally important task. War is the point where life and death meet. It is the path to destruction or survival. So war must be scrutinized. War has five determinants that we must plan. We must understand their correlations. One is righteousness.[2] Two is atmosphere. Three is terrain. Four is the general. Five is martial law.

Righteousness is a way of making people willing to join with the king, to make them unite and join forces, to live and die with courage. Atmosphere is the night or day, hotness or coldness, and change of four seasons. Terrain is high or low ground, near or far distance, easy or difficult roads, plains or canyons and the conditions of survival. The general must be strategic, trustworthy, kind, courageous and strict. Martial law means the organization, management of soldiers and expenditures in the military.

The general must know all the five determinants explained above because if he knows, he will win and if he doesn't know, he will lose. So he has to calculate carefully in planning and find out their actual correlations. Therefore, the general must compare the following seven situations:

1. Which party has the righteous king?
2. Which party has the talented general?
3. Which party benefits more from the atmosphere and terrain?
4. Which party abides by martial law?
5. Which party owns the better more sophisticated weapons?
6. Which party's soldiers train more frequently?
7. Which party rewards and punishes more fairly?

Based on the answers to these questions, we know which party will win and which party will fail.

We should keep the generals who obey the instructions given above because they will win. We should get rid of the generals who do not obey the instructions given above because they will fail.

When planning for advantage according to the advice above, act on the situation and take advantage of factors outside that common rule. To act according to the situation is to take advantage by adjusting the plan that flexibly, improvably[3], and firmly grasps the initiatives.

War tactics should follow the principle of deception. So when one has the power, appear powerless. When one deploys, appear not use soldiers. When one wants to fight near, seem to want to fight faraway. When one wants to get close, seem to be backing away. When enemy tries to find an advantage then

TIMELESS CREEDS FOR WINNING

one uses small benefits to lure them. When enemy disorders, one advances. If the enemy is strong enough, one can guard against them. If the enemy is lithe and strong then one will temporarily avoid them. If the enemy is aggressive, one harasses. If enemy is guarded and cautious, one makes them arrogant. If the enemy is rested, one disturbs them. If enemy is united, one wants to divide them. If the enemy does not defend, one will surprisingly attack them. Attack where enemy is not prepared, appears where enemy least expects. So we can see that in war, surprise is the key to victory.

Those are the basic strategies of the generals to harvest successfully. It must be flexible but improvised, not guided or anticipated.

Before fighting, the right calculation[4] and proper planning[5] will result in victory, whereas incomplete planning before the battle will not bring victory. So to ensure complete victory, complete planning is the condition that must be met. If the plan is sketchy and there are only few winning conditions, such a plan is bound to end in failure. So based on this analysis, it will be easy to determine who will win and who will be defeated.

Chapter 2

Combating 作 戰

During combat, we usually mobilize an army[1] of one thousand light chariots[2], one thousand heavy chariots[3], and hundred thousand armored soldiers[4]. Food must travel thousands of "li"[5] along with forward and backward costs. The reception of guests, expenses such as materials for making weapons, repairing chariots, weapons, etc. cost thousands of taels[6] of gold every day. All these must be ready before marching a hundred thousand soldiers to the battlefield.

With such an army in the battlefield, quick victory must be achieved. Being on the battlefield for too long is not ideal. Delay in combat will make the weapons rust and soldiers will begin to lose their morale; and if the enemy discovers this weakness, an attack will be inevitable. There is no better moment to attack than when the enemy is weary and seems hopeless.

Although I have heard about reckless combat, I have never seen a delay in combat that is considered wise. Using soldiers to fight a battle for an unnecessarily long time is really unprecedented. Only someone who understands the danger that comes from such a careless strategy will understand the resulting effect.

A person who is good at using soldiers does not recruit soldiers twice and does not transport food three times. A good general uses domestic weapons but uses the enemy's food to feed the troops, so the soldiers are well fed.

When the military has to travel a very long distance to fight the battle, the national treasury is often left empty and the citizens suffer the effect. It is highly expensive to maintain the financial cost of war. Close to the garrison, the price is expensive. Whenever prices go up, the national treasure runs the risk of running out; and if the treasure is exhausted, taxes will have to be raised to keep up. Hundred of the citizens suffer this for when the tax is raised, a lot of them run out of money. The longer the soldiers stay on the battlefield, the more it costs the people. Yet, there is no certainty of victory. The weary soldiers are decreasing on the battle front and the people remain poor at home. An average wealth of ten is depleted to seven. More expenses on the battlefield such as damaged chariots, lame horses, additional weapons, armor, large buffalo, heavy chariots, etc of ten are depleted by six.

Those are the reasons why a wise general always forages food from enemy. Eating one "bushel"[8] of enemy's food will save us the rigor of bringing along twenty. Using one "picul"[9] of haulm and grass will help us to cut twenty picul of haulm and grass to raise horses.

For our soldiers, anger must be the impetus to destroy the enemy and the reward must be the stimulus to defeat the enemy. If one wants brave army to fight, one must encourage morale. If one wants soldiers to forage enemy food, one must reward them. Therefore, in the chariots battle, out of ten or more chariots won, the soldiers who won the first chariot were rewarded. After that, we added our flag and then mixed into our army. We treated the surrendered soldiers well and used them. By convincing the surrendered army to join us, we have strategically increased our strength.

Therefore, we see that in combat only the quick victory matters and there is no reward for extending a campaign. A general who truly understands warfare controls the fate of the people and is a master of national security.

Chapter 3
Offensive Strategy 謀 攻

In military maneuvering, the supreme art of war is to keep our nation intact as a superior policy; taking over an undamaged enemy nation is more appropriately than breaking it. Keeping our army[1] whole is the best policy, capturing all the enemy troops is better than killing them. Keeping an entire brigade[2] of our own is superior, capturing an entire brigade of the enemy is better than breaking them. Keeping an entire regiment[3] of our own is superior, capturing an entire regiment of the enemy is better than breaking them. Keeping an entire battalion[4] of our own is superior, capturing an entire battalion of the enemy is better than breaking them. By applying this principle, we can understand that winning a hundred times in a hundred battles is not the ultimate achievement. The ultimate achievement is subduing the enemy without fighting.

Therefore, the highest form of war is having broader strategy[5] than the enemy, followed by breaking allies[6] of the enemy, then defeating the enemy in battle[7]. The lowest is to besiege the enemy's city[8]. Siege wars should only be waged if unavoidable. Siege time is very expensive. It takes up to three months to craft and prepare weapons to attack city walls.[9] It takes another three months to build the mounds[10] of construction around the enemy walls. If the general is impatient, he will launch his men to the assault like swarming ants around the citadel so that our troops could lose one third of the casualties while the town still remains untaken. These are dangerous effects of a siege.

Therefore, a skillful leader does not need to use the battlefield to subdue the enemy. He captures the enemy's city without having to attack. He destroys enemy countries without putting his troops in great risk. All is to preserve the force by making use of strategy. Therefore, there is no wear and tear and still there is great benefit. This is the strategy of offensive art.

When deploying the army and we discover that our soldiers are ten times larger than the enemy, then we encircle them. But if we are five times larger, we attack straight up.[11] We divide our troops if we are twice as large.[12] However, if the forces are equal, we make plans to defeat the enemy forces.[13] In situations where the enemy soldiers are more than us, the best thing to do is to avoid direct attacks. If the enemy is too crowded, we retreat completely. So it is better for a small army to persevere rather than be defeated.

The general is the pillar of the nation. If the pillar is solid, the nation is strong. If the pillar is loose, the nation is weak.

We were faced with three challenges. First is that it was unclear if our troops could not advance but we kept them advancing; we were not sure if the troops could back up but we just told them to back up. That's called tying troops. The second challenge is that the position of the internal affairs of the troops was also unclear, but by interfering with the military management, the officers and soldiers would be confused. Thirdly, it was unclear military principle of adaption to circumstances but interfere with the responsibility of commanders, and the generals would be in doubt. If the troops were suspicious and bewildered, the vassal countries would have the opportunity to harass. This is called self-disordered troops and it is to lead others to victory.

In the aspiration of victory, there are five important key elements to observe:

1. Know when to fight and when not if it's going to lead to victory whichever way.
2. Know how to use more troops.
3. Having the same goal and spirit in all ranks will lead to victory.
4. A prepared army will always achieve victory over an unprepared enemy.
5. A talented general who is not restrained by the king will be victorious in battle.

All these five key points, if considered together, are the true path to success.

So we can say that if we know the enemy and know ourselves then we will not be endangered in a hundred battle engagements. If we know ourselves but not the enemy then for every victory gained we will also suffer a defeat. If we know neither the enemy nor ourselves then we will never win.

Chapter 4
Military Disposition 軍形

Good generals in the old days first guaranteed their troops could not be defeated and then waited for the enemy to be self-miserable to win the enemy. We are not defeated because of complete preparation. We can win against the enemy because they are vulnerable. So a good fighter creates conditions that makes him formidable. But there is no sure way to make the enemy vulnerable[1] to defeat them.

While we cannot guarantee victory, then we entrench. When we guarantee victory, then we attack. We will entrench because we know we are in a position where victory is uncertain; and we attack because we have more than enough resources to win. Those who are good at entrencing can hide themselves under nine levels of the earth.[2] Those who are good at attacking can attack enemy from nine levels of heaven.[3] In this way, one can fully protect one's own forces and ensure complete victory.

Just seeing the victory that everyone knows is not really good. A victory welcomed by all people is by no means the greatest of victories. We do not need the strength of a giant to lift a feather. We do not need great eyesight to see the sun. Neither do we need great ears to hear thunder. The great fighters of the past not only won the battles but also won very easily.[4] So the victory of the great fighters is not famed for wisdom, nor is it known for bravery. Being prepared for every winning situation is what guarantees a certain victory. This means we are fighting the defeated enemy.

So a great warrior first places himself in the invisible position and then makes sure he does not miss an important opportunity to defeat the enemy. A successful army first ensures invincibility before not missing the enemy's defeat. A winning army first ensures victorious planning before engaging in battle. A defeated army is first fought before victory is achieved. Those who are good at military use must rectify the righteousness and perfect the rules because this is a clue to make certain the decision to either win or lose.

In the art of war, the following should also be considered:
1. Range
2. Measurement
3. Calculation
4. Weigh
5. Victory

The range is a way of determining the terrains of both sides – wide, narrow, long, short. Then after determining the range, we must measure both sides to know if to use more or less of material resources. The next course of action is the calculation. We have to calculate the number of troops on both sides. Then we must weigh our options by determining military strategy, strength and weakness of both sides. After all these have been put into consideration, then it will be easy to know who will achieve the victory and who would be defeated.

Different terrain is so different resources. Different resources should have different military numbers. Different military forces bring about different results. A victorious army weighs the "dật[5]" with the "thù[6]", while a defeated army will weigh the "thù" against the "dật". A victorious army is akin to releasing a flood of water on a high of ten thousand "knotstick[7]" rushed down. This is referred to as military disposition.

Chapter 5

Military Force 兵勢

The principles for controlling a large force are the same as for a small force. The essential element is organization. Commanding a large army to the battlefield is like controlling a small army. It is a matter of formation and information. To keep the whole army from being broken before the attack of the enemy is by using indirect[1] and direct[2] maneuver. In order to make our attacking power like a stone to smash an egg, we must master the magic of real and unreal.[3]

In combat, directly attack the enemy is very obvious; but what brings about victory is the indirect attack on the side.

A general who understands the use of indirect army has an infinite source of tactics like heaven and earth, like rivers and oceans, which will never run out. He's like the sun which shines in the day, and the moon that illuminates at night, diminishing and replenishing, constantly refreshing the cycle of the four seasons. In music, there are only five basic notes, but their variations are infinite. There are only five primary colors[4] but when mixed, their shades and colors are infinite. There are only five basic flavors[5], but their combination creates many unspeakable flavors. In military strategy, however, there are only direct and indirect, but in which they provide an endless range of tactics. Direct and indirect naturally stick together like a spinning wheel.

The rise of floodwaters slowly sweeping away the rock due to erosion – this is an example of military force. The eagle rushes down and snatches its prey in a flash – this is called the moment. In this case, the military force of the skilled fighter is irresistible and the moment is very accurate. Military force is the tension of the bowstring at full stretch; and the moment is when the arrow is released.

In the chaotic situation of the battle, our army seems to be in chaos, but in reality it cannot be chaotic. In the chaotic and tangled situation, the distribution of our troops seems to be disordered, but in reality is invisible. In this way, chaos clearly masks for real organization, cowardice masks for courage, weak force masks for strong force.

The enemy is chaotic because we are organized. The enemy is cowardly because we are courageous. The enemy is weakened because we are strong. Order or disorder is caused by the level of organization. Cowardice or courage is caused by position. Strength or weakness is caused by formation. The skill fighters keep the initiative, use their troops to entice the enemy to chase. We drop small bait to lure the enemy to take and snare to catch them.

Therefore, a skilled general in combat can create a favorable disposition without blaming his subordinates; he knows how to choose talented subordinates that create advantage position. A skilled general will create a force like a rolling stone wood. The nature of the stone wood is quiet on the plane, moving on slope, stopping on square and rolling on circle. So a skilled combating general like rolling round stone wood from ten thousand knobsticks high mountains down to the foot of the mountain. That is exactly military force.

The military force of the skilled warriors is like a round stone wood rolling down from a thousand meter high mountain.

Chapter 6
Real and Unreal 虛 實

As a general principle, the troops that arrive first at the location of the battle and wait for the enemy will have initiative and will be at ease. The troops that arrive later to the battle position will be passive and exhausted. So the great fighters make the enemy come, he is not lured by the enemy.

Making enemies come themselves by luring them to their advantages. Making enemy not to comes by threating harms to them. Using the same principle, if the enemy is leisurely, we disturb them. If the enemy is well-fed, we make them hungry. If the enemy is stationed, we make them move. Attack at points that the enemies have to scramble to protect themselves, and launch lightning attacks on places they did not expect. Our army can travel thousands of miles without getting tired because of getting in an unobstructed place. If we want a certain win, we only attack where enemy cannot defend. In order to be sure of defending, we have to abide in places where the enemy cannot fight.

Therefore, for those who are good at fighting, the enemy will not know where to defend. Those who are good at defending, the enemy won't know where to fight. Delicate instead! So subtle we can make ourselves invisible. Secret instead! So secretive that we can move without making a sound. That's why we keep the fate of the enemy in our palm. We attack but the enemy could not stop because we fight without people. We retreat and the enemy couldn't follow because we escape quickly. But if we want to fight, even though they have deep moats, high fortresses are inescapable because we fight where they have to rescue. If we do not want to fight, we will strike the ground to defend and prevent the enemy from finding us and fighting because we have been suspected of distracting them.

We make the enemy visible and we hide it so we can keep our forces united while the enemy is forced to scatter defenses everywhere. We gathered our troops into one and the enemy had to disperse into ten so the odds were ten against one. Thus our troop is large, the enemy is small. Using a lot of troops to fight a few troops, the clear victory always leans on us at any time.

Because it was impossible to know where we wanted to attack, the enemy had to send defensive troops everywhere. With thinly scattered enemy forces, wherever we want to attack, the enemy troops there will be few. If the enemy defends on the left, the right wing will have few troops. If the enemy tries to defend everywhere, every position will be weakened.

The weak military force is due to defending everywhere. The strong force is because we have the enemy to defend all over the place. We lack troops because we are distributing troops to guard against the enemy. We have more than enough troops because we make the enemy guard us.

If we know the time and place of the battle in advance, we can easily go thousands of miles to arrive to join force at the battlefield to fight. If we do not know the time and location of the battle, we do not know if we should join forces on the front to save troops on the back, the back cannot save the front, the left cannot save the right, the right cannot not save the left. How much more so if our troops are thousands miles apart? Even if they are several miles away, how can we save each other?

According to my expectation in this condition, surpassing in mililitary number is not necessarily the deciding factor of victory or defeat. So the victory is created by us. Even if the enemy is more numerous, we can prevent them from joining the battle to fight us.

Planning is to discover the enemy's intention and also to calculate the matter of victory or loss. We tease the enemy to know and understand the rules of their operation. We lure them to deploy troops where they we can see their combat skill, including their strength and weakness points. Consider the situation to know if the enemy layout is insufficient or excess troops.

We disguised as cleverly and as invisible for the enemy to not recognize our whereabouts. Being invisible, the enemy spy has deep underground nor detectable. Because they could not investigate our whereabouts, the enemy's general does not know how to deal with us.

Everyone realized that we are in a superior position, but no one realized that we depend on the enemy's situation to transform into victory. People only know how we defeat the enemy, but they don't know how we use that method. That is why we don't use the same strategy twice, we have to adapt flexibly according to the new situation of the enemy.

Military strategy is like flowing water. The characteristic of water is to avoid high places but drain into low places. So victory in the war is due to avoiding strong enemy positions, attacking weak enemy positions. Water depends on the terrain to adapt. Combat depends on the enemy's situation to arrange. So there is nothing certain in war as the water never holds a certain form. Therefore, a general who achieves victory by strategizing his tactics based on the changing situation of the enemy is called miraculous.

Of the five elements[1], no element prospers forever. No season of the four seasons[2] lasts indefinitely. The sun rises and sets. Moon rounds and wanes.

Chapter 7
Maneuvering 軍爭

According to the permission to use soldiers, the general receives orders from the king. It is the job of the general to arrange the available military forces, put soldiers in effective order, build camps and set up battles against enemy. After that, the most difficult task is maneuvering against the enemy. The inherent difficulties in this job are the need to turn curve into straight and turn disadvantages into advantages. So the general can lead the army around using small profits to lure the enemy. Therefore, we arrive at true goal destination before enemy even though we start later. That is the mastery of turning curves into straight.

Bringing troops to maneuvering against the enemy is sometimes beneficial but other times very dangerous. If we wait to gather forces with adequate equipment before attempting to take advantage, we risk coming too late. If we hurry to abandon equipment to take advantage, we risk losing the abandoned equipment. If ordered to force soldiers to march with armor wrapped in military bags, move night and day without rest to double the distance, cross a hundred miles to get to the advantage, the three generals[1] can be arrested. The strong soldiers will come first, the weak ones will come later and only one-tenth of the soldiers will actually arrive to the destination on time. If marched fifty miles, the generals and vanguard forces would be stopped and half the force would come. If marching thirty miles, only two-thirds would come. Therefore, the army that has no equipments must lose, the one with no food must starve, and with no personal supplies must be difficult to live.

Without understanding the vassals' machinations, it was impossible to anticipate the association. The terrain of mountains and forests is not known, so we cannot lead troops there. General must make use of the knowledge of the locals to make the best of the nature's features. So to use the battle army one must rely on improvisation that pretends to act, must rely on the interests that act and depending on the circumstances that improvised. Therefore, the speedy army is as fast as a whirlwind, slowly as dense as the jungle, encroachment is like a burning fire, defense is like a mountain, mystery is like darkness and the attack is like thunder.

Capture the village then distribute that among troops to keep. Expand the territory then divide that benefit to use. Weigh and measure carefully then depending on the situations to take action. Victory belongs to the person who masters the combination of curvature and straightness. That is the way to maneuvering against enemy.

The military book says: in battle, human voices are not strong enough to be heard, which is why we use gongs and trumpets.

Our vision is not accurate enough, which is why we use banners and flags. Set up the gongs and trumplets, banners and flags to let the whole army listen with the ears and see with the same eyes and act unanimously. Unified in understanding, the brave cannot move forward alone and the coward does not withdraw himself. This is the art of military management. So in night fighting, the gongs, trumplets and fire are used as signals and in the day, relying on gongs, trumplets, flags and banners to adapt to the ears and eyes of our army.

For the enemy's three troops[2], we should snatch away their morale. As for the enemy's general, we should cast doubt about their determination. Military morale, when it first arrives, is sharp and strong, after a while it is languid and lazy, and finally wants to return home. Therefore, those who are good at using troops should avoid the morale of the enemy when they first arrive and fight at a time when they want to return home. This is the way that shatters the morale of enemy troops. Take our organized troops, deal with chaotic enemy troops. Take our calmly troops, deal with bewildered enemy troops. This is the way that dissipates the enemy's general determination. Get our near troops to wait for the enemy troops from far away. Get our eased troops to wait for the tired enemy troops. Get our well-fed troops to wait for the hungry enemy troops. This is the way to control military strength. Do not fight with the well organized enemy. Do not fight with the mighty enemy. This is the way to control changes.

Basic principles when using army: do not approach to fight with the enemy troops on a high hill. Do not fight with the enemy troops leaning on a mountain mound. Do not chase with the feint retreated enemy troops. Do not fight with the pungent enemy troops. Do not fight with the lured enemy troops. Do not interfere with the returned home enemy troops. Do not besiege without leaving the exit for enemy troops. Do not press too hard with a desperated enemy troops. This is the art of maneuvering in warfare.

Chapter 8
Nine Changes 九 變

During the war, the general received orders from the king and then arranges the available military forces. The general must know that if the terrain is not favorable, the force must not be stationed. If the roads and communications are good, associate with allies. Do not linger on barren land[1]. If besieged[2], you have to think straight; and situations of life and death[3], risk must be taken. There are roads where we should not step on them.[4] We sometimes do not fight the enemy.[5] We sometimes do not besiege the fortresses.[6] There are places we shouldn't fight.[7] There are even orders from the king that we shouldn't obey.[8]

A general who masters the above nine changes will know how to use his army. A general who does not comprehend these things, even though he knows the terrain, cannot turn them into an advantage terrain for himself. A commander who does not know how to use these nine changes, even if there are five benefits[9], cannot promote the use of military.

The talented one always considers both benefits and harms equally. Considering the disadvantages of a favorable situation, we can certainly achieve our goals. Considering the potential advantages of a dangerous situation, we can find a way to solve our difficulties.

If we want to subdue vassals, then take arms to threaten them. If we want to get vassals to do so, force them into things they cannot help but do. If we want to attract vassals, we must use small profits to buy off.

The principle of using troops is not to rely on the enemy not to fight us but to rely on the available coping tactics. Not relying on the enemy who does not attack us but certainly on the ability to defend our positions.

There are five dangerous drawbacks that often occur to the general: reckless disregard for death will actually lead to death. A living greedy general will be captured. The angry general is easily provoked into enemy superficial action. Self-conceited generals are easy to shame. General who loves the people easily gets troubled. These five are common generals' mistakes and catastrophes to the successful conduct of the war. When the defeated troops and the generals are killed, the reason is not beyond the above five defects. We need to consider them carefully.

Chapter 9
Marching 行軍

In the matter of marching, camping and observing the movements of enemies in different terrains when going through the mountains and valleys, we choose a high position, rely on the stream[1] and face east to camp. Do not climb up[2] to join the battle on the high ground, we should fight down[3], avoid fighting up. That's what we need to know about mountainous terrain and valleys.

Once we cross the river, we move away from it. If the enemy crosses the river to fight us, we do not fight in the middle of the stream. We can gain the advantage by having half of the enemy force overcome and then attack.[4] Do not attack from the other side of the river bank when the enemy approaches the river. Choose an elevated position to the east to wait and do not confront the enemy upstream.[5] This is how to fight on water.

Get past the salt marsh swamp as quickly as possible and don't linger.[6] If you must fight in such marshes, be stationed in a swamp and rely on the trees behind you. This is how to fight in a salt marsh swamp.

On a flat ground, where it is easy to set up a camp, choose a flat place that is easy to move around, has a high ground to the right and behind, leaving danger ahead for the enemy and safety behind. This is how to base your troops on flat ground.

The above four rules are useful for marching and camping operations. Those were the principles that king Huỳnh Đế[7] had used to conveniently defeat four nearby emperors.

When stopping the army camp, avoid the humid place but high places; also, avoid dark places but bright places. If we raise our troops well and have solid refuge, as well as if we take care of the health of the soldiers and camp on the dry ground, the soldiers will avoid all common diseases. This is a guaranteed formula for victory.

When you come to the hillock or dike, take your place in the sun with the high ground to the right and behind you. This will deploy troops to take full advantage of the terrain.

If the river is high and the water is foaming because of the rain on the source and we want to cross, we wait for the water to decrease.[8]

If you encounter a mountain waterfall, dead end, deep bushes, swamps or narrow streams, you must pay attention and stay away. At the same time, try to force the enemy towards such places, then when we go ahead to fight. The enemy will rely on those places and should be in danger.

Close to where our troops are stationed on hilly lands, where there are reeds or dusty ponds, we search carefully because it is the ideal place for the enemy to ambush. If the enemies nearby are quiet and do not attack, they are confident in the strength that would have taken advantage of the terrain. If the enemy is far away but has come to challenge us to fight, then they are luring us to attack. If the enemy camp seems to be open for attack, that's a trap. If trees and bushes seem to be moving, enemies are coming. If the irregular blocks are gathered to prevent our advance between the reeds and the grass, the enemy is setting a trap. If the birds suddenly fly off from trees, there is an ambush below and the terrified animal running away shows that the enemy wants to fight a surprise face down. If the dust is high and pointed, it is the enemy who comes by horseback. If the dust is low and wide, it means the soldiers are approaching by walking. When the dust spreads in different directions, the enemy is collecting firewood. Small dust clouds moving in and out meant that the enemy is setting up camp.

If the enemy envoys speak humble words while increasing their military preparations, it is a sign that the enemy wants to attack. If the envoys speak in violent languages while their force is driving forward as if to the attack, it is a sign that they are preparing to retreat. If light carriages run out and spread out to the two flanks, it is a sign that the enemy was forming a formation to fight.

If the enemy's troops flock and form, a decisive attack is coming. If the enemy troops seem to be half advancing and half retreating, it is a trap. If enemy soldiers are leaning on their spears then they are hungry. If enemy soldiers go to get some water but drink before bringing it back, they are thirsty.[9]

If the enemy could not make use of the obvious opportunities, they would be exhausted. The place where birds gather without disturbance is where there is no enemy barracks. A disturbance in the enemy camp at night means they are scared. The widespread unrest in the enemy troops is caused by a weakness in command. If the flags and banners of the enemy are leaning over, there is disorder among the troops. If the enemy officers are angry and irritable, they are depressed. When enemy troops feed rice to the horses and slaughter animals to eat their meat, and they are not hanging the pots and returning to their tent, they are ready for the final attack. If soldiers are huddled together and whisper among themselves, it is a sign of discontent among the ranks of the soldiers and the commander.

If enemy rewards frequently then they are at the end position of resources. If the enemy punishes frequently, they are in critical condition. If the enemy general is initially fierce towards the soldiers because of fear, it means that the general is ignorant. If the enemy is angry and pulls troops to the battlefield without retreating, we should watch carefully. If we have no advantage in military numbers or a military standoff, then all we need to do is gather our forces in one place, continue to monitor the enemy and increase the troops. A general who is careless by underestimating his enemies will surely be captured.

When the general is trusted by the soldiers even if he punishes them, they will not submit. If, however, the general is admired by his soldiers but he doesn't punish them when appropriate, they will be useless. Therefore, generals must combine soldiers with righteousness and bind them with discipline. This is the path to invincibility.

If the general performs consistency in orders and instructions, the soldiers will be loyal to the general. Without consistency, soldiers won't know where to listen. These are common benefits for both generals and soldiers to maintain consistency.

Chapter 10
Terrain 地形

Terrain can be classified in this manner: accessible ground, entangled ground, dilapidated ground, narrow ground, dangerous ground and far ground.

Accessible ground is the terrain that any party can come and cross. To keep our upper hand in this terrain, be sure to occupy the high, sunny areas[1] and look into our supply roads. Taking over this terrain first and waiting for the enemy to fight will guarantee victory.

The entangled ground is easy to access but difficult to exit.[2] On such terrain, if the enemy is poorly prepared, it will be easy for us to take risks and defeat them. However, if the enemy is well prepared and our attack fails, it will be difficult for us to return because we are in a serious disadvantage.

If both parties could not gain the upper hand by taking initiative, the terrain is called dilapidated ground.[3] When entering this terrain, although the enemy gives an attractive advantage, we control ourselves by leading our troops away to drag the enemy out. After that, when the enemy troops come out halfway, we will return to attack. This way, it will be more beneficial.

For narrow ground[4], we must make sure to occupy and consolidate the position first, then wait for the enemy to enter. If the enemy has been there first and has had the opportunity to strengthen their position, then we should not fight them. However, if the enemy has not strengthened their position, we should come to consolidate and attack.

When we get to dangerous grounds[5] first, we will be able to occupy high, sunny places where it will be easy for us to observe and wait for the enemy. If the enemy goes there first, we should not fight and we should retreat.

Far ground[6] is a far and wide place. If we enter this terrain and the two parties have equal forces, it is difficult to fight and even if possible, we have no advantage.

Above are the six principles of terrain advantage and it is the primary responsibility of any military commander to consider them carefully.

Military matter has six things that fail. None of that comes from the disaster of heaven and earth[7], but all are the faults of the general. These are fleeing troops[8], insubordination troops, ruined troops, collapsed troops, chaotic troops and routed troops[9].

Soldiers flee because the forces are equal but took one-on-ten so they have to run. Insubordination troops are due to the strong of senior officers and the generals' feeble mindedness. Generals are strong but feeble senior officers are called ruined troops. The collapsed troops are caused by the high-ranking officers getting angry and going on their own without waiting for the above order before the prime minister could assess the chance of success. And the general does not not know the competence of high-ranking officers so the troops would collapse. The chaotic troops are caused by a feeble-minded general that lacks dignity, consistency in command, and the soldiers' disgruntled heart. All this leads to chaotic troops. The general does not accurately assess the enemy's strength, take less against much, take weak against strong, combating lack of military elitepioneers. It is the result of a rout troop.

The six paths mentioned above bring failure. Generals who carry the responsibility of their troop must consider these factors and find a way to work around them.

Terrain is a supportive element for maneuver. The ability to accurately assess the enemy's situation in which the army is set to prevail, calculate obstacles, dangerous positions, and distances near or far, this is the path of generals. If we understand all these and apply them in reality, the general will definitely win. If neither understands nor practices, the general will be defeated.

Therefore, after analyzing the rules of the war and seeing all things that only lead to victory, the generals must fight, even if the king does not order. Similarly, generals must know when to refuse a king's order to fight if the signs aren't just for victory. A general who advances without coveting fame and retreats without fear of committing crimes[10] but only thinking of protecting the people and benefiting the king, such generals are truly an invaluable treasure of the nation.

If we treat soldiers like children we can lead them into abyss. By treating soldiers like beloved children, they will stand by us to death. However, if we indulge them but cannot use them, love them but cannot command them, and we refuse to punish them for their crimes, then these soldiers will become useless like spoiled children. The general cannot lead this army to battle.

Knowing that our troops can fight without knowing the conditions that can beat the enemy or not, the victory is only half. Knowing the situation that the enemy can fight without knowing whether our military situation can fight the enemy or not, the victory is only half. Knowing the readiness of both enemies and our troops, but not knowing the nature of the terrain, the victory is still only half. Therefore, those who know how to hold the army do not mislead, the soldiers who fight will not be in danger. Those are the reasons why we say: by knowing the enemy and knowing ourselves, then we will surely win. If we know the atmosphere and the terrain then we will win completely.

Chapter 11

Nine Ground Positions 九 地

In military use, there are nine ground positions: dispersed ground position, shoal groundposition, contested ground position, allocated ground position, linked ground position, important ground position, difficult ground position, besieged ground position, and death ground position.

Fighting on our own land is called dispersed ground position.[1] Taking a short distance into enemy land and fighting is called shoal ground position.[2] The land that is beneficial to any party occupying is the contested ground position.[3] The land that is easily accessible for both parties is called allocated groundposition. The land that connects the border with the three countries, whoever takes it first, is joined by those three countries to be called linked ground position. Deep into the enemy land with many cities occupied behind us is important ground position. Mountains, rugged cliffs, swamps, and wetlands, all hard to cross areas are difficult ground position. The entrance is narrow, there is no way to retreat, so a small force could easily defeat a large force is besieged ground position. If we have to fight to hope for survival and the delay of a certain moment will cause disaster is death ground position.

Therefore, it is not recommended to fight on dispersed ground position[4], do not linger on shoal ground position[5], do not attack on contested ground position[6], arrange the battlefield and maintain contact on allocated ground position, partnership with all vassals on linked ground position, take the opportunity to occupy food on important ground position[7], quickly overcome difficult ground position[8], use cunning tactics when on besieged ground position[9], and on death ground position, fight hard.[10]

So, in the old days, skilled fighters could make the enemy front and rear forces losing contact. Small troops and large troops cannot rely on each other. The general and the troops lose touch. Officers and soldiers cannot help each other. Soldiers are separated, unable to gather. The formation is in disorder. Therefore, if someone who is good at using soldiers sees an opportubity, he will fight; if not, he will halt.

Dare to ask: What if the enemy pulls troops to attack us with a large and well trained army? Answer: Win first the most favorable condition of the enemy, then they will listen to us.[11]

The precious element of military operations is speed. Take advantage when the enemy is not ready, march on unexpected routes and fight the places where they are not taking precautions.

Military plays a guest in the enemy country. If we go deep into enemy territory, the more united our troops will be, making it harder for the host to overcome us. If we find fertile fields, then take them and use them to feed your troops. You have to bolster the morale of your soldiers so as to keep their spirits and preserve their vitality. Do not make them do anything in vain.

When in motion, use strange tricks to keep the enemy from guessing your tactics. Let the troops go into dangerous places, they would risk their life to fight hard because they could not retreat. If the soldiers would risk their lives to fight then nothing will bother them. All ranking soldiers will make every effort and no longer fear in that situation. So your army will show the will to fight a united front when in no other way and fight to the last.

Such an army would not need to emend its team to remain alert, no need to ask if they still fulfill their mission. Even without encouraging them, they will still stick together and support each other, without order they will still obey because they are disciplined. Prohibiting all practices of divination and superstition as well as eliminating suspicions in the army, then such soldiers will die without changing their hearts.

Our soldiers are not abundant, not because of contempt of wealth, nor regret for the life because they hate life. On the day of departure, those who sit are crying with tears soaked in their shirts, those who lie are crying tears on their cheeks. But once at a time of no return, they will show the courage of the Chuyên Chư[12] and the bravery of Tào Quế[13].

The person who knows how to use his troops is like the Suất Thiên[14], the famous snake in Hoành Sơn mountain. If we attack on the head, it attacks back with its tail. If we attack the tail, it attacks back with its head. If we attack the middle part, it attacks back with both its head and tail.

Someone asked: Can soldiers imitate Suất Thiên with their army? Answer: Yes! The people of Wu and Yuet did not like each other, but when they sat in a boat across the river, encountering strong winds and waves, they save each other as their right hand helped the left.

So tying the horse legs, burying the chariot wheels for soldiers determined to fight is not enough to believe. We must urge all the soldiers to apply their military training bravely. Force soft or hard, weak or strong are promoting the forte for taking advantage of terrain. So, skilled generals lead the troops in their hands as if leading a single person that soldiers cannot help but follow.

The strategy of the general must be deep and discreet, he must use tricks and gossip to keep soldiers in the dark to mask his true intentions. A general should change his layout and plans so that soldiers don't know what he's doing. The general should change his location and lead his army around so that soldiers cannot predict his plans.

When the general orders the soldiers into battle, he shouldn't block their way, he should not be the stumbling block on their path to victory, like a person who climbs very high and then kickes the ladder away. The general leads his troops deep into enemy territory, burning boats and smashing pots to promote morale of soldiers like a herder of goats, herding forth then going ahead and herding side then going horizontal. Soldiers don't need to know where to go.

Navigating and leading soldiers into danger is the job of the general. Adaptive improvisation to nine types of ground, assess the dangers of attacking or retreating and understand the mood of soldiers. This is what the general should carefully consider.

The principle of combat in the role of guest in the enemy country is the deeper into the enemy land, the more solid the troops will be. If we are too close to our borders, the soldiers will disperse. When we lead our army across our borders, we enter the secluded land. If the territory is accessible from all four directions, it is allocated ground. If we penetrate deeply into enemy territory, it is important ground. If we only go a short distance into enemy territory, it is called shoal ground. If the enemy is entrenched behind and there are narrow paths ahead of us, that is the besieged ground. When we don't have a way out, it's death ground.

Therefore, in the dispersed ground, we unify the will of the soldiers. At the shoal ground, we communicate closely with the soldiers. At the contested ground, we follow the enemy closely. At allocated ground, we defend. At the linked ground, we strengthen the alliance. In important ground, we protect the food of soldiers. In difficult ground, we try to overcome. At the besieged ground, we block all entrances and exits. In the death ground, we let the soldiers choose the only remaining path between life and death. So we understand the nature of soldiers is to resist being surrounded, forced too much will risk death, and on command when in danger.

Without understanding the strategy of the vassals we cannot take into account the association. The terrain of forests, point of stations, caves, swamps, and canals is not known then do not leading troops there. Without scouting, you cannot gain ground advantage. If the general does not understand even one of the basic above principles of war, he is not a general worthy of his authority.

A worthy general, when attacking a strong country, makes the enemy army unable to mobilize to concentrate forces. We threatened to overwhelm the enemy that other countries could not rescue. Therefore, it is not necessary to fight diplomatic relations with vassals, as well as from the need to strengthen one's power in vassal countries. We only keep our own strength to threaten the enemy. Therefore, we can raze the village and destroy the capital of the enemy.

We give reward without according to the rules, give orders without according to the rules, commanding the entire army as dictating a person. Assigning work to soldiers, not stating the tactics and sending soldiers into dangerous places without showing harm. Launch troops into danger places to turn danger into peace. Launch troops into a dangerous sieged places to turn death into life and win.

So, in carrying out military operations, we pretend to follow the will of the enemy while actually pushing our troops fighting in one direction. This way even thousands of miles will not save their generals from our swords. This is how we use our talents and cunning to achieve our goals.

On the day the war is declared, blockade of the border, cancellation of the covenant, banning of all information and travel of enemy ambassadors. Reviewing the plan discreetly in the temple and carefully arranging the work. If the enemy has a loophole, then we intervene. Take what they value most and limit them with time. Revise the plan according to the enemy's situation until we can bring the enemy to our decisive battle.

So, before the battle, our troops are calm and discreet, shy like a virgin until the enemy showed an opening. At that time, we attack with a speed like an opening cage rabbit so that the enemy has no opportunity to fight back.

Chapter 12
Fire Attack 火 攻

There are five ways to attack enemies with fire. First is to burn enemy troops. Second is to burn enemy food storage. Third is to burn enemy vehicles. Fourth is to burn enemy weapons. Fifth is to burn enemy team.

Fire attacking needs conditions and preparation in advance. To use fire, one must consider the weather of the season and choose the right day. A favoured season is when the weather is dry and the appropriate days are when the moon is in the constellations of the Cơ, Bích, Dực or Chẩn.[1] These are four days with strong winds blowing at night.

When using firepower, we must know flexible improvisation for five cases. If the fire is burning in the enemy camp then we must hurry and respond from the outside.[2] When the fire is burning and the enemy is not chaotic, then do not rush to attack immediately.[3] Wait until the fire has wide spread and see if it can actually strike and act accordingly. Firing from the outside into the enemy barracks does not need to wait for internal effects; we have to rely on the upwind to attack, not attacking at the downwind.[4] The wind blows all day then easily stops at night. The military man should be familiar with the five instances of fire and be prepared accordingly.

By using fire to attack, the effect is clearly visible. Using water to attack makes the army position stronger. Water can be used to block rather than destroy enemy equipments and supplies.

After winning the battle and capturing the enemy stronghold without rewarding the soldiers, it is a disaster. This is called ballast loss. Therefore, the wise lord and the loyal general should know how to take care and arrange these things.

Don't move unless you see a clear advantage. Do not use soldiers unless there is something to gain. Do not fight if we are not in danger. The king cannot mobilize army because of personal anger. The general cannot engage in battle because of personal outrage. Only mobilize army if it is beneficial for the country, otherwise do not move. Anger can turn into satisfaction and outrage can turn into joy, but a country that has been destroyed is hard to recover and cannot give life to those who have died. Therefore a head of state needs to be vigilant and a loyal general should be on guard. This is the way to keep a peaceful country and an intact army.

Chapter 13
Using Spy 用 間

Raising hundred thousand soldiers[1] and marching them thousands of miles away. All costs of hundreds of families and public funds[2] to suffer each day up to thousand taels of gold. There will be widespread disruption at home and abroad, people will be strenuously exhausted on the roadside, neglecting daily work of up to seventy thousand houses.[3]

Spending years to win in a day without daring to spend hundred taels of silver on spies to discover an enemy's situation. This is terribly inhumane. This is not the behavior of a leader for the people, nor is it worthy of being an assisstant for ruler or a master of victory.

For what allows a leader and a general to attack decisively and successfully, where ordinary people fail, is foreknowledge. Foreknowledge cannot be found by consulting with the divine being[4] or by comparing similar situations. Nor could it be found by measuring the movements of heaven and earth but were obtained from people who had accurate knowledge of the enemy's situation.

In this respect, there are five types of spies that we can use: local spy, internal spy, counterspy, suicide spy and reported spy. If we use all five types, no one can understand our scheme. It is a type of sacred organization and the greatest treasure of a wise ruler.

Local spies are recruited from enemy peasants.[5] Internal spies are from enemy court officials.[6] Counter spying means using the enemy's own spies against them.[7] Suicide spies[8] are people who are given false information to take for spies by enemies. Reported spies[9] are the ones who focus on bringing enemy information report to us.

So in the whole army, no one is closer to us than spies. No one is more rewarded than spying. No secret is more closely protected than the spy network. Spies must be used wisely and treated with kindness and virtue. We must use the utmost subtlety to ensure accurate reporting from spies. Subtlety is the key. There are no instances where spy cannot be used.

If a spy reveals information before executing the plan, then both spy and people who known must be put to death. Whether we want to destroy an army, attack a city or assassinate someone, the first important thing is to determine the name of the commander-in-chief, trusted people, assistants, gatekeepers and his bodyguards. We have to order the spy to find out for this information.

When we discover the spy of the enemy who is watching us, we bribe them, take care of them wholeheartedly and release them freely. That way, we can use them as counter spies.

Through these spies, we can recruit local spies and internal spies. Through them our death spies will provide false reports to the enemy. And also through them our reported spies will be able to act as needed.

A wise king must know how to use all five types of spies and this knowledge must necessarily come from a counter spy. So we reward the most to counter agent. In ancient times, when the Ân Dynasty revolted, Y Doãn[10] was on the land of Hạ to investigate and when the Zhou revolt, Khương Tử Nha[11] was on the land of Ân's house to investigate.

A wise king or a sage general should choose only the smartest people to act as his spies, then he will surely achieve great things. This is the necessity of battle action and the army depends on it to act.

The Writing of
Niccolò Machiavelli

THE PRINCE
The Principles Of Victory In Politics

Written by
Niccolò Machiavelli

Translated by
Tham Trong Ma

A Few Words

Niccolò Machiavelli's *The Prince* is one of the most famous books about politics ever written. Perhaps, what sets it apart from the hundreds of books written about the same subject matter is that Machiavelli describes politics as having its own set of rules that should not be influenced by any other source where the goal is not to succeed over others.

In simpler terms, *The Prince* describes politics in such a way that the only rules that apply are the ones that bring the expected results of victory - the end justifies the means.

The book is a thorough analysis of how to obtain and maintain power. It has 26 chapters that can be broadly divided into parts. Chapters 1 - 11 describe the different types of principalities. Chapters 12 - 14 describe the different types of armies, how to manage them, and how a prince must conduct himself as a military leader. Chapters 15 - 23 talk about the conduct of the prince and how one can use them to secure his kingdom for longer. Chapters 24 - 26 describe the dire political situation in Italy. The final chapter is a direct plea to Lorenzo de Medici and the Medici family to save Italy from the humiliation of being enslaved.

To this day, after reading the book, one wonders if the several advices given on how to gain power and maintain it are rooted in evil or simple realism. Most people will argue that some of the things described in the book are jarring. In fact, one of the reasons why the book is so famous is because of the infamy attached to it. The things recommended in the book led to the coining of the adjective "Machiavellian."

When people use the word, Machiavellian, to describe someone they are trying to point out the cunning, devious, scheming, deceitful, and unscrupulous behaviors they find in them.

The essence of Machiavelli's politics, as described in the book, is that you can get away with anything, including murder, if you succeed in your political endeavors. Only those who lost were punished for their actions.

While it might be unproductive to argue against the generally accepted evil significance of his name due to this book, it should be noted that Machiavelli (according to scholars) was not an evil man who taught evil doctrines. Far from it, as his personal life story will show for he was only moderately successful in his political career. In conducting his affairs, Machiavelli was timid and it is only in the literary side of his character that we find a daring boldness to conquer at any means necessary.

Even at that, the harsh implications of the teachings in his book were not known in his time. At the time that he wrote the book, most men lived by the sword and died by it. So, what we would consider "Machiavellian" in this age must have been very normal to them. Machiavelli was clearly a man of great observation, sharp, and brilliant. He noted everything that had happened before him and made his observations based on those events.

Thankfully, a lot of research has gone into helping us understand his mind and interpreting his work more reasonably. These researchers say that Machiavelli much preferred the republics over monarchy and would in no way have supported tyranny and the cruelty involved. Additionally, they argue that his passionate plea for the deliverance of Italy in the last chapter is not in line with the evil tag that has been given to him. These scholars also believe that he was one of the forerunners of modern political science.

All these things, when they come together, show Machiavelli as a republican, patriot, and political scientist. A mild image that heavily contrasts with the reputation that he has. Machiavelli was not Machiavellian after all. Either way, there is one thing that we can gather from all of this, and it is that Machiavelli was an enigma that everyone should have a chance to form their own personal opinions about.

Although over 500 years have passed since his work, *The Prince,* was published, some of the problems that were addressed in the book are still relatable and interesting to debate. That is because, even though we no longer fully practice monarchy (except for some European and Asian countries), at the core of it, the same problems between the rulers and the ruled exist.

As it stands, although most of the code of conduct described in the book was for those that lived in Machiavelli's time, we cannot completely rule them out as being outdated.

Machiavelli draws parallels between historical incidents and people and uses them to illustrate his proposed theories of government and how they should conduct themselves. Some of those parallels still apply to the present-day world.

Leaving out the state of affairs, some of which still plague some European and Asian countries that practice monarchy, there are several proven truths to be gotten from reading the book.

For example, men are still the same victims of their foolishness and greed as you would find in the story of Pope Alexander the Sixth. The decadence and corruption of the Church can also be viewed through Pope Alexander's behavior. Present-day religion still conceals vices, such as those that Machiavelli exposed in the character of Ferdinand of Aragon.

In breaking down the innate character of men, Machiavelli shows that men do not like to see things as they are in reality, but will choose to deceive themselves by seeing them as they wish them to be. The result of this kind of mentality is most often destruction, as can be proven by the historical events in the book.

He also notes that people can be fickle and their affections are easily bought over because they are only invested in their self-interest. As long as there is abundance, you will never run short of people that support you. However, the moment you fall into difficult times, you will be hard pressed to find someone in your corner. People will admire generosity, faithfulness, courage, and honor in others but will rarely display those characteristics themselves.

Of politics, he notes that there is not a perfectly safe course to take. It is your responsibility, however, to chart all the possible risks and choose the one with the least dangers. He also notes that although cruelty and wickedness may win you an empire, the only reward you would get for it is infamy rather than glory.

Of goodwill, he also mentions that for any ruler to remain in power, he has to avoid being hated by his people. No, this does that mean that he has to be completely loved by them, for it is in fact in his best interest that he is revered, rather than loved by his subjects. Goodwill is a ruler's best defense against domestic insurrectionists and foreign attackers. Nobody is more supportive of a government than the people who enjoy benefits from it. On the other hand, when a ruler is completely hated by his people, it brings about his complete downfall.

This part of the book may be contradictory to what he says about using cruelty to govern, but Machiavelli states that a little cruelty is okay, as long as it does not affect the goodwill of the people. He warns rulers against doing things that would lead to hatred.

With these as examples, Machiavelli gives a balanced outlook on the good, the bad, and the ugly of politics as they play out before him. If perhaps, the things written in the book were diabolical and ruthless, then it is a function of the times that the writer found himself in and not a reflection of his personal character.

The book does not contain a moral admonition of what the government should do to hold itself to the highest principles of society because that was a concept foreign to the times that Machiavelli wrote about. Apart from being an artistic piece that retells historical events from a political standpoint, what stands out the most is the unarguable truth of how rulers should relate with their subjects and their neighboring countries.

In translating this book, my aim has been to remain as literal as the original while also using terms that could easily be understood. Most of his words were chosen with care to convey the exact message he wanted. His tone, for the most part of the book, was nobly plain and serious, and it is my hope that I was able to pass that across.

I would like to reiterate that Machiavelli is an enigma that is best discovered on your own terms. So put aside everything that you have read or heard about him and try to read this book with an open mind.

I can only hope that in your eagerness to read this book to get the author's intent, you can overlook some of the roughness in the language that describes it for it comes from merging two different realities into one.

Tham Trong Ma

About Niccolò Machiavelli

Niccolò di Bernardo dei Machiavelli was born on May 3, 1469, in Florence, Italy, and died in the same city on June 21, 1527, at 58. Born to the lawyer, Bernado di Niccolò Machiavelli, and his wife Bartolomea di Stefano Nelli, Niccolò Machiavelli was the third child and first son of the family of six. His other three siblings were named Primavera, Margherita, and Totto.

Niccolò Machiavelli grew up in the district of Santo Spirito, and his family was very popular. Niccolò was a bright young boy. He started studying Latin at the age of seven, and by the time he was twelve, he had successfully translated a couple of native works to Latin. Some Latin authors that Machiavelli read from his early childhood include Platus, Terence, Caesar, Cicero, Sallust, Virgil, Lucretius, Tibullus, Ovid, Seneca, Tacitus, Priscian, Macrobius, and Livy. However, two of his favorite Italian authors were Dante and Petrarch.

When Machiavelli hit twelve years of age, he, along with his brother, went to study with Paolo da Ronciglione, a renowned priest professor who had guided many contemporary humanities. Machiavelli was well on his way to being one of them as well.

By the time he was 29, Machiavelli had got a position at the prime minister's office. In this medieval writing office, he was in charge of the production of official Florentine government documents. Shortly after, he also worked as a secretary for the Dieci di Libertà e Pace. In 1502, Machiavelli met Cesare Borgia for the first time. In that same year, he also married his wife, Marietta Corsini. Together, they had eight children named Bernado, Primerana (dead at a young age), an unnamed daughter (also died young), Baccina, Ludovico, Piero, Guido, and Totto.

While the Medici was out of power, Machiavelli continued to break ground in his career. He was in charge of the Florentine militia from 1503 to 1506. In 1507, Machiavelli was appointed the prime minister to the Nine, a newly formed committee related to the militia. In 1509, Machiavelli commanded the Florentine civilian soldiers to defeat Pisa.

However, in the thick of the Italian wars in 1512, the Medici returned and, aided by Pope Julius II, used the Spanish army to defeat the Florentine troops in Plato. Florence surrendered, and the house of Medici returned to power.

In the aftermath of the Medici's victory, the Florentine government and republic were dissolved. Machiavelli was also stripped of his political position and sentenced to a year's confinement within the Florentine territory.

In 1513, the Medici accused Machiavelli of conspiring against them, and he was forcefully taken into custody. He was tried for conspiracy, imprisoned, and tortured. For three weeks, his jailers hung him with his wrists at his back, forcing his arms to hold his full body weight until he dislocated his shoulder. Even with all the torture and mistreatment, Machiavelli denied his involvement in the conspiracy and was eventually released.

After his release, Machiavelli retired to his estate at Sant'Andrea in Percussina, near San Casciano in Val di Pesa. He devoted his retirement to researching and writing political treaties.

On the 10th of December 1513, Machiavelli wrote to his friend, Francesco Vettori, to tell him about the new book he had worked so hard to write. The book ended up being his most famous philosophical piece, titled The Prince. During this period, he also started writing speeches about Livy. In the years that followed, he, alongside Orti Oricellari, attended literary and philosophical discussions in the Rucellai family's gardens.

In 1518, Machiavelli wrote his most famous play, Mandragola. He spent 1519-1520 writing his book, The Art of War, which was well-received in Florence and Rome upon publication. In 1520, he went on a small diplomatic mission to Lucca, where he wrote about the life of Castruccio Castracani. Eventually, Giuliano de 'Medici awarded him a position at the University of Florence as the city's official historian. Giuliano also commissioned him to write the Florentine history, which he completed in 1525. Machiavelli also directed the production of the first Clizia in January 1525.

After living a remarkable life, Machiavelli died on June 21, 1527, and was buried at the Florentine Church in Santa Croce.

Tham Trong Ma

Chapter 1

Of Different Country Types And How To Acquire Them

All nations around the world practice either of two systems of leadership - republic or monarchy.

Monarchies are either hereditary (in which the title is passed down through a family's bloodline that has been ruling for many years) or completely new. The new monarchies are either entirely new, as Milan to Francesco Sforza[1] was, or they are annexed to the hereditary state of the prince who acquired them, as the king of Spain acquired the kingdom of Naples.[2]

Kingdoms that were acquired or absorbed into a new monarchy could either live in freedom or live under the ruling house. The acquired kingdoms were conquered by either fortune or the talent displayed by the ruler's army or by a foreign army.

Chapter 2

About The Hereditary Monarchy

From now henceforth, I shall leave out everything about republics to focus on only the monarchy. Keeping in line with that order, I will now discuss how to govern and preserve the monarchy.

It is easier to preserve hereditary monarchy, especially when the people are already used to living with their prince's family, than new ones. This is because most people will prefer the stability of customs that they are accustomed to over the new policies of a new ruling family. All that the prince needs to do is preserve his predecessor's customs and carefully resolve conflicts as they arise. Unless affected by extraordinary or excessive things, all he only has to do is maintain himself in this state. This way, if he loses his throne, it is easier for the prince to get it back when his usurper encounters misfortune.

For example, in Italy, we have the Duke of Ferrara[3], who could not have resisted the Venetian attacks in 1484, and Pope Julius[4] in 1510 if his power hadn't been long established. By sticking to old traditions, the successor prince has little reason to offend the people and, perhaps, less need to do so. Unless the prince does something extraordinarily evil to cause him to be hated, the natural inclination of the prince's subject is to treat him well. The longer the duration of his rule, the less the will for change from his subjects, for one change often will usher in another.

Chapter 3

About Mixed Monarchy

Difficulties, on the other hand, will always arise in a new monarchy, especially in a mixed monarchy where a new monarchy is added to an old one. Most of these difficulties stem from the problems that are inherent with all new monarchies.

When people voluntarily change rulers, they do so, hoping that things get better for them. This hope makes them take up arms against the current rulers. However, it is deceptive because they will learn from experience that things usually go from bad to worse under new leadership. It is a natural and necessary result that the new prince's supporters will have to endure other infinite hardships under the new regime.

In addition to the disgruntled supporters who have to endure new hardships under his rule, the prince also has to worry about building resentment from those who were hurt in taking over their territory. The prince cannot keep his supporters that brought him his new status because he failed to meet their expectations and, feeling bound to them because they are his benefactors, the prince cannot use strong measures on them.

Although he may have a heroic army, he would still need his subjects' cooperation if he wants to occupy new territory.

For the above reasons, when Louis the Twelfth,[5] King of France, quickly seized Milan, he quickly lost it. With the first strike, Lodovico Sforza's[6] own forces were enough to drive the French king out of Milan. Those who opened the door to Louis found themselves deceived in their hope of future interests and could not bear this new prince's cruel treatment.

It is true that after the second suppression, they will not lose the territory easily because the prince, with little reluctance, will take advantage of the rebellions to punish rebels, clear suspects, and strengthen his status in the weakest places. All it took for the French to lose Milan the first time was for the Duke of Lodovico to cause mayhem at the border. However, the second time required the cooperation of the whole world to fight them back.

Milan was regained from France after both the first and second attempts at conquering it. The reason behind the failure the first time has been discussed; now, we will discuss the reasons behind the second failure to consider the resources the French king had at his disposal and how he could have safely held on to power in the process.

Old territories acquire new territories, whether they are of the same country and speak the same language or not. When they are the same, it is easier to keep the new territories together, especially when they are new to the autonomous government. The old ruling family must first be destroyed so that both sides can keep the old rules and customs as they live together, maintaining stability and safety.

Examples of this practice can be seen in Brittany, Burgundy, Gascony, and Normandy, bound to France for a very long time. Although there are differences in language, the customs are the same, and the people easily interact with each other.

A prince who wants to keep the throne only needs to note two things. Firstly, he has to destroy the former royal family. Secondly, he does not need to change their laws or taxes, so in a very short time, they will be fully integrated into the old territory.

Managing acquired territories in countries with linguistic, custom, or legal differences is difficult and requires a bit of luck and a lot of effort. One way to work around this is if the prince decides to live in the territory to secure his position. While staying there, he can spot problems immediately and fix them. If he doesn't live in the territory, it might be easy to overlook problems until they become too severe to fix.

Another benefit of having the prince reside in his acquired territory is that it prevents the officials from abusing his new subjects and the easy access keeps the people satisfied. The prince needs to give his subjects many reasons to love him while still maintaining their fear. Any foreign state that wants to attack this territory must also be very afraid. As long as the prince resides there, it will be very difficult for others to take the throne.

Another approach is for the prince to establish colonial settlements in one or two places that tie into his own country. If he doesn't, he would have to keep a portion of the army there. The prince does not need to spend much on such settlements. With little to no cost, he can send in immigrants and keep them there.

This way, only a handful of citizens would be insulted that he took land and houses to provide for the new immigrants. The offended parties, once poor and scattered, cannot do anything to harm him. While the others that aren't affected will keep quiet to ensure they don't also lose their land and homes.

To me, creating these settlements is inexpensive, buys you more loyalty, and causes you less harm. As said, the affected people are poor and scattered and cannot do any harm. However, it is important to note that human beings need to either be treated well or be completely crushed because while they can avenge themselves of smaller slights, they cannot take great revenge. When you want to harm someone, you have to be sure there is no fear of retribution.

If the prince chooses to keep a portion of his army in the territory instead of having immigrants settle, it would cost him more to do so, plunging the entire nation into a loss. The loss could also lead to national alarm because the whole territory feels it. Soldiers often move camp, causing the people to feel hardship, hostile, and even hatred. The people can quickly become enemies, so even though they are defeated on their land, they can still cause damage. When you weigh the pros and cons, it becomes clear that maintaining an army in an acquired territory is in vain, while colony settlements have their perks.

Again, a prince who holds a territory with different languages, customs and laws must become the head and protect the weaker neighbors. He must also weaken the strong territories around him and be careful not to let any foreigner equally as strong get a footing on his land, whether by accident or design. It is clear that the introduction of powerful foreigners into the land can be done by people who have been dissatisfied with the ruler, ambitious, or afraid. For example, the Romans were brought into Greece by the Aetolians[7] and in every other territory where they obtained a footing, they were brought in by the local people.

Usually, when a powerful foreigner enters a territory, all the subjects are drawn to him due to the hatred they harbor towards the current ruler. It is quite easy for an invading foreigner to win this territory because all the subjects will quickly support the country that the foreigner has already acquired.

All he has to do is ensure that the subjects don't hold too much power and authority. With their cooperation and his armed forces, he could easily bring down the most powerful of them to completely master the territory. If he doesn't manage this well, he could quickly lose the acquired territory, but not before facing endless difficulties and troubles.

The Romans used these principles in all the territories they took over. They established settlements and maintained friendly relations with minor powers without increasing their authority. They crushed the more powerful and did not allow any foreign powers to gain authority.

For example, with Greece, the Roman government nurtured the Achaeans and the Aetolians, weakened the Kingdom of Macedonia, and drove out General Antiochus. Although the Achaeans' nation was rewarded, the Romans refused to allow the Achaeans' land to be strengthened.

King Philip was very persuasive and remained cordial with the Jews but within reasonable limits. It didn't matter how strong General Antiochus was; the Romans did not let him keep any private land within the territory. Hence, the Romans acted according to the principles that all careful princes had to follow - to not only be concerned with present problems but also make provisions for future troubles.

When problems are noted before they happen, it is very easy to fix them. If the prince waits until the problem comes before looking for a solution, it might be too late.

Doctors say that severe fever is easy to cure but difficult to detect. If not discovered or treated on time, by the time the fever has been detected, it is difficult to cure. The same thing applies to state affairs. When possible problems are predicted, it becomes easier to avert a crisis. However, if they are overlooked, they snowball into a catastrophe that everyone can see but cannot stop.

Thus, the Romans, predicting troubles, dealt with them immediately. They would not allow those problems to come to a head, even to avoid a war. For they knew that war could not be avoided, only put off when it looked like it would benefit the enemy. For this reason, they suddenly declared war against Philip and Antiochus on Greek soil to avoid having to fight the war over in Italy.

Although at that time, these two wars could have been avoided, the Romans still deliberately started them. This behavior would forever be on the lips of contemporary philosophers who say, "let us enjoy the benefits of time but also the benefits of their courage and wisdom, because time drives everything before it, and brings with it good as well as evil and evil as well as good."

Now let us return to France to see if she followed any of the principles I mentioned an invading prince had to follow. I will begin with Louis the Twelfth, not King Charles IIX,[8] a most obvious choice because he held Italy longer. Louis the Twelfth did the direct opposite of what must be done to maintain a nation composed of different elements. King Louis was brought into Italy by ambitious Venetians under the condition that he gave them half of the territory of Lombardy.

One cannot blame the King for his course of actions because in seeking a foothold in Italy and having no friends and allies there (every door was closed to him due to his father's conduct), he was forced to accept whatever alliance and friendships that he could get. He would have quickly succeeded with his design if he hadn't made mistakes with other matters.

The King, after gaining Lombardy, was able to immediately regain the authority that his father lost. The city of Genoa surrendered, and the Florentines became allies. Marquis Mantua, duke Pharra, the family of Bentivogli, the countess of Forli, the princes of Faenza, Pesaro, Rimini, Camerino, Piombino, the citizens of Lucca, Pisa, and Siena - all appeared to become allies and friends with him. By then, the Venetians had already begun to see the rashness of their decision. In seeking to control half of Lombardy's cities, they helped the King to secure two-thirds of Italy.

Let us now see how the King could have held his position in Italy with little difficulty if he had observed the previously stated rules and kept all of his allies safe and protected. Although the territories were many, they were too weak and scared to do anything untoward. Some feared the church, while others were afraid of the Venetians. This fear and weakness forced them to stand with the King and could have easily given him a safe standing against other powerful forces.

However, as soon as the King first entered the city of Milan, he did the opposite by immediately helping Pope Alexander[9] to occupy the land of Romagna - a move that, unbeknownst to him, would weaken him and cause him to lose his allies. He was unknowingly strengthening the Church by adding more temporal powers to the spiritual and giving the Church more authority.

After the King made his first mistake, he was forced to follow it up, thus, making even more errors. To end Pope Alexander's ambition and keep him from owning Tuscany, he was forced to come to Italy himself. Becoming dissatisfied with how much power he had given the Church and how it had cost him his friends and allies, he went after the Kingdom of Naples and had to divide it with the King of Spain. Where he used to be the sole ruler of Italy, he now had to rule with someone else, a rival that any ambitious person in his kingdom or anyone dissatisfied with Louis' rule could rally behind.

He could have left Naples in the care of a puppet king of his own choosing; instead, he threw him out and replaced him with someone who was capable of driving Louis out from the land.

It is well-known that all humans are capable of displaying greed and ready to conquer if they can. Those who act on this desire and succeed should be praised, not blamed. But if they cannot conquer and they still try to do it anyway, it is foolishness, and they should be blamed. If Louis could have attacked Naples with his own forces, he should have done so. But if he could not, the kingdoms should not have been split with the Spanish. It is understandable and excusable that he had to split Lombardy with the Venetians since it gave him a foothold in Italy. However, the division of Naples with Spain was a foolish mistake that he should be blamed for as there was no need for it.

Louis made five major mistakes. He annihilated the minor powers, increased the power of one of the greater powers in Italy, brought in a foreign power that rivaled him into the country, didn't reside in the territory that he captured, and finally, he didn't send immigrant colonies to settle. However, while still alive, all of these mistakes may not have proved harmful to him if he had not made the sixth mistake of depriving the Venetians of their power.

For if he hadn't increased the authority of the Church or didn't bring Spain into Italy, it would have been necessary and justified to weaken the Venetians. But having made these mistakes, he ought not to have consented to further weakening them. Because if the Venetians had had the same power as before, they wouldn't have let anyone else invade Lombardy; they would never have agreed to anything like that without allowing themselves to retain power. No outside powers would have risked taking Lombardy from France to hand it over to them, nor would they have risked challenging the two powers.

For those who say that King Louis ceded Romagna to Alexander and Naples to Spain to avoid war, I say that, for the given reasons, one ought never to cause a disturbance to avoid war because war cannot be avoided, but only delayed to your disadvantage. And if anyone wants to point out that the French king was keeping his promise to the Pope that he would give him land in exchange for his divorce license and for the appointment of the cardinal of d'Amboise, I will write later on the promises of princes and how they should be kept.

Thus, King Louis lost Lombardy by not following any of the principles observed by those who acquired territory and wished to keep it. There is nothing out of the ordinary about this as it makes sense and is quite natural. As I said, the French do not understand the principles of holding territory. Otherwise, they won't allow the church to achieve such greatness. In fact, we see that the greatness of the church and of Spain in Italy was caused by France. From here, we learn a lesson that never or rarely ever fails, "whoever causes others to become powerful is ruined because that power is due to either cleverness or force, both attributes that are not trusted by those who have been raised to positions of power."

Chapter 4

Why the Kingdom Of Darius[10] Conquered By Alexander The Great[11] Did Not Rebel Against The Successors Of Alexander The Great After His Death

Considering the difficulties that some rulers have had in holding on to newly conquered territories, some might wonder how the territories conquered by Alexander the Great remained loyal, even to his successors. Alexander the Great became the master of Asia for a few years and passed away before completing his mission. Many expected that following his death, the entire empire would be in rebellion. However, the successors all reigned peacefully and had no other difficulties until they became too ambitious.

According to records, here are the reasons why Alexander the Great's legacy remained. The old kingdoms were governed in two different ways - either by a prince with a group of subordinates crafted into ministerial posts by the prince's favor and authority or by a prince and chiefs, who hold the position by virtue of inheritance and not the prince's favor.

These chieftains have their own territory and subordinates who regard them as lords and hold them in high esteem. On the other hand, the kingdoms run by a prince and his subordinates hold their prince in higher esteem because, in the whole country, no one has more power than him. If the people respect another, they do it as to a minister or a prince's official and bears him no special loyalty.

Examples of these two governments in our time are the Turk King and the King of France. The entire Turk kingdom is governed by a king while others are his servants. He divides his kingdom into regions and sends various administrators there, transferring and replacing them at his discretion. However, the King of France is in the midst of a group of long-standing Lords, recognized to have their own power and to receive the hearts of their own subjects. They have their own rights, and the king cannot take them away without risking a rebellion.

Anyone who considers the state of both kingdoms can immediately see that it is very difficult to take the Turk, but once conquered is very easy to keep. The reason behind the difficulty in taking over the Turkish kingdom was that there were no ambitious chiefs to invite the invader in, nor was there any hope of assistance by the rebellion of the king's retainers. The reasons above can explain the reasons why - it is not easy to corrupt the ministers of the prince, for they are all servants, and if by chance the corruption is successful, they cannot carry the people along.

Therefore, anyone willing to attack the Turks must remember that the people are united in favor of the prince, and he would have to rely more on his own strength than on the rebellion of others. However, once the Turks have been conquered and arranged in such a way that the armies cannot be replaced, there's nothing to fear except the prince's family. Once the prince's family has been destroyed, then there is no one left to challenge the invader's claim as none of the powers left have stood with the people. Just as the invader could not count on them before his victory, he does not need to fear them after.

In contrast, it is easy to penetrate kingdoms that are governed like France by gaining the cooperation of a few chiefs because there will always be dissatisfied people who want change. Those people, for whatever reasons given, can pave the way and make victory easy.

However, if you want to keep the territory after acquiring it, you would have to face countless difficulties, both from the people that helped you and those who were crushed by your victory. Destroying the prince's family is not enough to ensure a stable and secure reign, as the chiefs would champion new movements against you, and as you are unable to satisfy or destroy them, anytime the opportunity arises, you will lose the territory.

Now, if we consider the nature of Darius' government, we can see that it is similar to the Turk Kingdom. Therefore, Alexander only had to first conquer him on the battlefield before taking his territory from him. After his victory and the death of Darius, the territory remained secure to Alexander for the reasons explained above. If his successors had been united, they would have safely and comfortably enjoyed the reign as there was no rebellion in the kingdom except for those they created themselves.

It is, however, impossible to have such a secure rule in territories established like France. That explains why there were frequent rebellions against the Romans in Spain, France, and Greece because there were too many lords in these kingdoms and as long as their memories endured, the Romans always held an insecure possession. However, with the power and lasting continuation of the Roman empire, their memories faded, and the Romans could finally enjoy secure possession. Later, when each of the territories fought among themselves, each person held a separate piece of land according to the authority he had there. With the former ruler's family being destroyed, no other ruler, apart from the Romans, was acknowledged.

With these in mind, the question should not be about how Alexander easily kept the Asian empire or the difficulties that others like Pyrrhus and many more faced in securing their acquisitions, as this is not determined by the ability of the conquerors but by the lack of uniformity in the acquired territory.

Chapter 5

About How To Govern Cities Or Countries That Live Under Their Laws Before They Were annexed

In acquired territories where the people are used to living in freedom under their own rules, there are three ways for those who want to secure them to follow. The first is to destroy them, the next is to reside with them in the acquired territory, and finally, the third is to allow the people to live by their own laws while collecting tributes and establishing an oligarchy that will keep the territory friendly to you. Since such a government, formed by the prince, knows that it cannot stand without the prince's authority and interest, they would wholeheartedly support the prince. Therefore, for anyone who wants to keep a territory that is used to living in freedom, the best strategy to secure it is to recruit local citizens into governing positions.

There are two examples of this - the Spartans and the Romans. The Spartans occupied Athens and Thebes, establishing an oligarchy, but they lost them. The Romans, in order to keep Capua, Carthage, and Numantia, destroyed most of them, but they did not lose them. They wanted to keep Greece as the Spartans did, to let the local people live according to their own customs, but they failed. So in order to keep it, they were forced to destroy many cities in the country as there was no other way to secure them apart from ruining them.

Any new prince who occupies a territory used to living in freedom without destroying it should expect to be destroyed by it. That is because rebellion will always be the outcome of having tasted freedom and its privileges. Time or benefits will never make the people forget what they enjoyed when they were free. No matter what you do or protect against, they will never forget what it was like to have their old rights or freedom unless they are dispersed.

However, if a territory is accustomed to living under a prince and the ruling family is destroyed, they, being accustomed to obeying orders and not having a prince, would be unable to raise one from among themselves or rule themselves. For this reason, they would be slow to rebel against the new prince, and he would be accepted as their leader, making it easier to secure them.

However, in republics, there is more vitality, greater hatred, and more desire for revenge, which will never allow them to forget their old freedoms. Therefore, the safest way is to destroy them or to settle in their own land in person.

Chapter 6

About New Countries Acquired With Your Own Abilities

It should come as no surprise to anyone that, in speaking about entirely new monarchies, I always mention the highest examples of princes and territories. This is because people who follow the path that others have and imitate their behaviors do not entirely keep to the ways others or attain the power of those they imitate.

A wise man ought to follow the paths that great men have taken and to imitate those who have been successful so that if his abilities fail to equal theirs, he can at least enjoy some traces of it. We should act like clever archers who, when aiming for a mark that is far from range, and knowing the limits of their bows' strength, aim much higher than the target. This maneuver is not to push the bow's limit or to cause the arrow to fly higher, but because the arrow has to go up in a detour before it can hit its target.

In completely new territories where there is a new prince, the difficulty in keeping them depends on the abilities of the ruler.

Now it is clear that for an ordinary person to rise to the position of a prince either by his ability or luck, one of these will help to mitigate difficulties to an extent. However, those who depend on luck the least will come out stronger. Furthermore, it is extremely beneficial when the prince, having no other territory, is compelled to live there personally.

When it comes to people who rose to become princes through their personal abilities and not luck, I say that Moses, Cyrus, Romulus, Theseus, and the likes are great examples. Although we cannot discuss Moses because he was executing God's command and not his personal interests, we can admire him, if not for anything else but the favor that made him worthy to speak with God. However, when it comes to Cyrus and others who have established or acquired territories, all will be found admirable. If you consider their works and conducts, you will find that they are no less than Moses, even though Moses had great guidance from God.

When considering their actions and lives, we can see that they do not owe anything they achieved to luck beyond the opportunity that gave them the material to mold into any shape that best suits them. Without that opportunity, their abilities would have been wasted, and without those abilities, the opportunity would have been in vain.

It was necessary for Moses to find the people of Israel enslaved and oppressed in Egypt in order for them to be disposed to following him to freedom from bondage. It was necessary for Romulus not to remain in Alba and that he should be abandoned at birth for him to become the king of Rome and the founder of that kingdom. It was necessary that Cyrus found Persians who were dissatisfied with the government of Medes and that the Medes be weak and soft from enjoying long-lasting peace. Theseus could not have proven his ability if he hadn't found the Athenians dispersed.

All of these opportunities made these men fortunate, but it was their great abilities that helped them realize the opportunity to make their country stronger and famous.

Those who, like these men, become princes from brave deeds acquire territories with difficulty, but they keep it with ease. The difficulties they face in acquiring it arises partly from the new rules and methods they are forced to enforce to establish their government and secure it. It is important to remember that there is nothing more difficult to solve and more dangerous than the adventure of creating a new regime. This is because the founder will meet enemies who have enjoyed many privileges under the old regime, and lukewarm supporters, in those who enjoy the new laws, will not actively protect the new collaborators.

This resistance arises partly due to the fear of the opponents who have the laws on their side and in part from the doubt of men who do not readily believe in the new regime until they are sure that it will last a long time. So that whenever there is a chance for the enemies to riot, they attack ferociously while the others defend only superficially, endangering the prince along with them.

It is, therefore, necessary, if we wish to thoroughly discuss this issue, to ask whether these founders can rely on themselves or have to depend on others. That is to say, in the bid to achieve their goals, do they have to use prayer, or do they have to use force?

In the first instance, they always succeed badly and never achieve anything, but when they can rely on themselves and use force, they are rarely endangered. Hence, it is that all armed religious leaders conquered while those who were not armed were destroyed. Besides the above-mentioned reasons, human nature is very fickle - it may be easy to persuade them but harder to hold them to it. Therefore, it is important to take measures that, when they no longer believe in you, make them believe by force.

If Moses, Cyrus, Theseus, and Romulus had been unarmed, they would not be able to enforce their constitution for a long time, as happened in our day with Fra Girolamo Savonarola.[12] He was destroyed shortly after the new regime was established because the people lost faith in him, and he had no way to keep that faith or to make the unbelievers follow.

All those armed religious leaders had a lot of difficulty in achieving their goals because all the dangers are in achievement, but with the ability, they overcame them. Having overcome these dangers and eliminating those who envied their successes, they began to be respected, and afterward, continued to feel powerful, secure, honored, and happy.

To these great examples, I want to add a smaller one with similarities, making it a good example - the Hiero[13] of Syracuse. This man went from being a commoner to the prince of the

Syracusans with no form of luck outside of opportunity. The Syracusans were under threat, so he was chosen to be their commander and then rewarded by being made their prince. He had so many outstanding abilities that it was written that the only thing stopping him from being a prince except having a kingdom. He disbanded the old army and created a new one; he discarded old alliances and made new ones. By creating his own soldiers and allies, he built himself a solid foundation to build anything on. So that even though he had difficulties acquiring it, it was easier to secure and keep it.

Chapter 7

About Newly Acquired Territorial Lands Either By Arms Of Others Or By Luck

Those who become princes from commoners through good fortune have little difficulty rising to the top but find it hard to remain on the throne. They experience no hardships on the way up because they fly but once they get to the top, they have many. Such goes for people who acquire a state by buying it or by the favor of one who bestows it. Examples of this can be found in Egypt, the cities of Ionian and Hellespont, where princes were ordained by Darius to keep the cities both for his security and glory. The same thing also applies to rulers who, by the corruption of soldiers, came into power.

One thing that all of these people have in common is that they were elevated on the goodwill and fortune of others - two of the most volatile and fragile things. These men are not qualified to hold this position. Because unless they have great talents and abilities, there is no reason to expect them to know how to command, having always lived as commoners. Besides, they do not have any loyal forces to help them hold their positions.

Territories that rise too quickly, like all things in nature that are born and grow rapidly, cannot lay the proper foundations and groundwork fixed in such a way that the first storm does not destroy them. Unless, as noted, that those who suddenly become princes have great abilities that they know they have to be ready at once to hold on to what luck has given them. They must understand that they need to lay a solid foundation for their status, like others that had come before did.

In relation to the two methods of becoming a prince, either by ability or fortune, I would like to allude to two examples of our time - Francesco Sforza and Cesare Borgia.[14]

Francesco Sforza, by the right means and with outstanding talent, went from being an ordinary citizen to the Duke of Milan. He acquired power with a hundred thousand difficulties but kept it very easy. On the other hand, Cesare Borgia acquired many territories while his father, the sixth Pope, Alexander, was in power. After his father's death, he lost all the acquired land as well. This notwithstanding that he had done everything a wise and able man could do to fix his roots in the territories that the army and fortunes of other people had given him.

As stated above, any prince that does not lay his foundation may be able to do so after with outstanding talent, but with so much trouble and danger to the building. If we consider all the steps taken by Cesare, we will see that he laid a solid foundation for his future power, which should be considered because I do not know of any other advice to give a new prince but the example of his actions. If his plan failed, it was by no means his fault but simply the irony of life.

Alexander, the sixth Pope, in wishing to elevate the status of Cesare, his son, met many difficulties before and after. First, he could not give his son territory except those belonging to the Church. If he was willing to use the Church's territory, he knew that the Duke of Milan and the Venetians would disagree. Besides, he saw that the Italian army, especially those who could have helped him, was under the control of those who did not want to see the Church gain any more power.

Therefore, it became necessary to disturb this state and create confusion among the powers to make him more stable on the territory. This he did easily because he found the Venetians, motivated by other reasons, were inclined to bring the French into Italy. He decided not to object to this but made it easy by helping the righteous King Louis to end his previous marriage.

So the French king came to Italy with the help of the Venetians and with the consent of the Holy Father Alexander. No sooner had the King settled did the Pope approach him about Romagna. King Louis himself had to take his soldiers, who came simply out of fear of the king, to help the Pope. Thus, Cesare, after taking Romagna and defeating Colonnesi's army, in wanting to keep it and go further, was thwarted by two things. First, his forces did not appear to be loyal to him. Second, they had the goodwill of the French.

He was afraid that the forces of Orsini[15], which he was using, were not loyal to him. He feared that not only would they prevent him from winning but also seize what he had won for themselves and that the French king would do the same.

His fear of the Orsini forces began when he saw them take Faenza, and when he attacked Bologna, he found them unwilling to attack. Of the King, he learned his intentions when, after taking the Duchy of Urbino, he tried to attack Tuscany but was stopped by the king. From then on, Cesare decided not to depend on the military forces and fortunes brought by others.

First, he weakened the power of Orsini and Colonnesi in Rome by manipulating all nobles and honorable subjects with good pay and honored them with office and command according to their ranks. Within a few months, all the loyalty of the old factions had been destroyed and was completely under Cesare's control. After he had scattered the supporters of Colonnesi, he then waited for the opportunity to destroy Orsini.

This opportunity came soon, and he used it well. For the Orsini, having realized that once Cesare and the Church became more powerful, they would be in danger, called a meeting in the province of Magione in Perugia. From this meeting sprung several rebellions in Urbino and Romagna with endless dangers for Cesare.

However, he overcame these dangers with the help of the French. After his power was restored, Cesare was determined not to risk relying on France or other outside forces. So he decided to be more strategic and hide his intentions. Through the mediation of the priest Pagolo, whom Cesare poured out all of his attention, money, clothes, and horses, the Orsini reconciled themselves with him.

Their simplicity made them fall into his trap and brought Cesare more power. He exterminated their leaders and turned their supporters into friends. Thus, holding the entire territory of Romagna and the Duchy of Urbino, he gained all the power for himself. It also helped that the people began to enjoy better, improved living conditions, so they were happy to support him.

As this part is worthy of note and of use to imitate, I won't leave it out. When Cesare acquired Romagna, he found it ruled by a bunch of weak masters dedicated to plundering rather than ruling. Thus, giving the people more reasons to rebel than unite so that the country was full of robbery, quarrel, and violence.

Cesare thought it necessary to establish a good governor to help restore peace and order to the country. So he appointed Ramiro d'Orco, a cruel and effective man, as governor and gave full authority to act. Within a short time, the whole country was at peace and unified.

However, Cesare felt it was not advisable to confer such excessive power on just one person, for he had no doubt that it would corrupt. So he set up a domestic tribunal and appointed one outstanding judge in every city.

Because he knew that his harsh treatment in the past must have caused the people to hate him, so to clear himself in the minds of the people and buy their loyalty, he wanted to prove that if any cruelty had been done, it originated from Ramiro and not himself. With this claim, he took Ramiro and one morning and executed him, leaving him in the Cesena construction site with the chopping block and a bloody knife beside the body. The barbarity of this symbolic statement caused people to both be satisfied and worried.

Now, let's get back to where we started. Cesare, now finding himself powerful enough and somewhat protected from direct dangers by arming himself in his own way and having crushed those neighboring forces that could have him if he went on with his quest, turned to his next target - the French. He knew that the King, now belatedly aware of his mistake, would not support him.

So from here, he began to look for new alliances and was slow to help the French king with his royal campaign to the kingdom of Naples against the Spanish who were attacking Gaeta. It was his intention to secure himself against them, and he would have quickly been successful if his father, Pope Alexander, had been alive.

This was his policy in present state matters. But as to the future, he first had to fear that the new pope would not be as friendly to him and might seek to take away what his father, Pope Alexander, had freely given him.

Therefore, Cesare decided to act in four ways. First, he could kill all the families of the Lords he defeated, so the new pope could not use that as an excuse to attack him. Second, he could gain the loyalty of all the nobles of Rome so that they could not support the new pope. Third, he could gain the support of the College of Cardinals.[16] Fourth, he could gain a lot of power before the death of Pope Alexander so that by his own means, he could resist the first shock.

By the time Alexander died, he had fulfilled three of those four acts. He had killed as many of the dispossessed lords he could lay his hands on, except the few that escaped. He won over the Roman nobles and gained control of the majority of the College of Cardinals. As for gaining more power, he intended to become the Lord of Tuscany, for he already possessed Perugia and Piombino, while Pisa was protected by him.

He no longer had to worry about the French because the Spanish had expelled them from the kingdom of Naples, and in this way, both were forced to seek his support. He capitalized on this to take Pisa. After that, Lucca and Siena gave in at the same time, partly out of hatred and partly out of fear of Florentine.

The Florentines would have had no remedy if he had continued to succeed, for he was prospering in the year that Alexander died. Cesare had managed to gather enough power and fame to stand on his own and no longer had to depend on the forces and luck of others but on his own strength and abilities.

However, Pope Alexander died five years after he drew his first sword. Alexander left Cesare with only the state of Romagna in peace, but the remaining territories were in a state of unrest, between two powerful enemies and in poor health.

There was no shortage of courage and talent in Cesare, and he knew so well how to gain power. In such a short time, he had laid firm foundations that if the two armies had been slow to attack or if he had been in good health, he would have overcome those difficulties.

Apparently, his foundations were good because Romagna waited for him for more than a month. Even though he was only half alive, he remained secure in Rome, and while

Baglioni, Vitelli, and Orsini could go to Rome, they couldn't do anything against him.

If he could not have chosen the pope he wanted, at least the person he didn't want could not have been elected. If he had been in good health when Alexander died, everything would have been different for him. On the day that Julius the Second was elected to be Alexander's successor, he told me that he had thought of everything that could happen at his father's death and had provided a remedy for them all. Except that he never anticipated that when the death occurred, he himself would be at the point of death.

When we consider all the actions that Cesare took, I cannot criticize him. Rather, as I have said, I must keep it as a model for all, whom by the good fortune or force of others, are raised to a position of power. Because Cesare, having a noble spirit and far-reaching goals, could not have adjusted his behavior otherwise. Only Alexander's short life and his own illness ruined his plans.

Therefore, whoever considers to secure himself in a new territory, to win friends, to overcome either by force or deception, to make the people love and fear him, to be obeyed and respected by soldiers, to destroy those who have the power and cause to harm him, to change the old order of things to new, to be severe and gracious, to be generous and liberal, to destroy a disloyal army and establish a new one, to maintain a friendship with kings and princes in such a way they must help him with eagerness and offend with caution, we cannot find a more lively example than the actions of this man.

He can only be criticized for the election of Pope Julius the Second, in which he made a bad choice because, as has been said, if it was impossible to elect the Pope according to his own choice, he could hinder any other person from being elected pope. He should never have agreed to the election of any cardinal that he had harmed or who had reason to fear if they became pope. This is because humans tend to cause injury to others either out of fear or hatred.

Cesare had injured many cardinals. The rest, on becoming Pope, would fear him. Cesare should have created a Spanish pope, and if he could not, he would have chosen a pope who depended on him and had a good relationship with him. Anyone who believes that new interests will make people forget old injuries has been deceived. Therefore Cesare made a mistake in his choice, and that was the cause of his final destruction.

Chapter 8

Of Countries Captured By Wickedness

There are two ways for one to progress from an ordinary citizen to a prince, neither of which can be entirely attributed to luck or talent. These methods are when, either by wicked or nefarious means, one acquires a kingdom or when by the favor of his compatriots, a common citizen rises to become the prince of the state.

The first method - wickedness - will be illustrated with two examples, one ancient and the other modern, and without getting too much into it, I think these two examples will be enough for anyone who wishes to imitate.

Agathocles[17], a Sicilian, became King of Syracuse not only from an ordinary citizen but from a low and humble position. This person, a potter's son, through all the changes in his luck, led a life of crime. Nevertheless, he accompanied his wickedness with great strength and ability that, having dedicated his life to the military, he rose through the ranks to become the leader of the army in Syracuse.

Once in this position, and having determined to make himself a prince and to take by violence without considering others and the power they gave him, for this purpose, he joined forces with Amilcar and his army, the Carthaginian, who was fighting in Italy.

One morning, he gathered all the people and the Senate of Syracuse as if to discuss state affairs, and at a certain signal, the soldiers killed all the senators and the richest people. He seized and held the princedom of the city without any civil rebellion.

Although he was defeated twice by the Carthaginian and was eventually besieged, he was able to not only defend the city but, leaving part of his soldiers to secure the city; he attacked the Carthaginians with the rest in Africa. Within a short time, the Carthaginians were forced to give up the siege of Syracuse. Out of necessity, the Carthaginian was forced to compromise peace with Agathocles, ceding Sicily to him to occupy Africa.

Anyone who the actions and genius of this man will see that nothing, or little, can be attributed to good fortune. He achieved all of his success, as seen above, not by anyone's favor but by advancing through the military ranks. He acquired the state by thousands of troubles and dangers and, afterward, he held on to his state despite many more dangers.

However, we cannot call this talent because he had to kill his fellow citizens, deceive friends, to be without mercy and religion. Such methods may get you an empire, but not glory. Although, if we consider his courage in entering and exiting dangerous places, together with his will to overcome difficulties, it might be seen that he was admirable as a talented leader. However, his inhumanity and immense cruelty did not allow him to be ranked among the most perfect. Therefore, one cannot attribute what he achieved to luck or talent.

In our day, during the rule of Alexander the Sixth, Oliverotto da Ferno[18], having been left an orphan, was raised by his uncle, Giovanni Foglani. In the early days of his youth, he was sent to fight under Pagolo Vitelli so that, being trained under his discipline, he could be assigned to a high rank in the military.

After Pagolo died, he fought under his brother Vitelleschi. In a very short time, due to his intelligence and skill, he became the first leader in the army. However, he did not like serving under others. He decided, with the help of the Fermo people and the support of the captain Vitelleschi, to take the city of Fermo. So he wrote to his uncle, Giovanni Foglani, that, since he had been away from home for many years, he wanted to visit him in the same city. He also claimed that he wanted to see what his parents had left for him.

He wrote that, although he had not worked to acquire anything besides honor so that the people of Fermo could see that he hadn't spent his time in vain, he wanted to return home honorably, accompanied by a hundred soldiers, a group of friends, and staff.

He asked Giovanni to arrange for him to be honored by the Fermo, all of which would be not only a recognition of his own achievement but also a reflection of Giovanni himself, who raised him.

Giovanni, therefore, could not afford not to give his nephew his best, causing him to be honorably received by the people of Fermo. Oliverotto stayed in his uncle's house, and after a few days of perfecting what was necessary for his wicked plans, he held a solemn banquet which he invited his uncle and the leaders of Fermo to.

When food and all other sorts of casual entertainment ended, Oliverotto artfully steered the conversation to more serious matters, talking about the greatness of Pope Alexander and his son, Cesare. Giovanni and the rest responded to his speech, but Oliverotto suggested that such grave matters were better discussed in a more private setting.

He took himself into another room, and Giovanni and the leaders of Fermo all went in with him. However, before they could sit down, troops swooped in from secret places in the room and slaughtered them all.

After this massacre, Oliverotto went up and down town on horseback and surrounded the board. The people were compelled to obey him out of fear, and Oliverotto created a government where he was the prince. He killed all those who could harm him and strengthened himself with new civil and military laws, in such a way that in the year that he held the kingdom, not only was he secures in the city of Fermo, but he became formidable to all the neighboring kingdoms. To destroy Oliverotto, like Agathocles, would have been very difficult if he had not been deceived by Cesare Borgia. Thus, a year after killing his uncle, Oliverotto was killed.

Some may wonder how it was possible for Agathocles and his likes, after their immense cruelties and treachery, could live for a long time in his country, defend himself against foreign enemies, and never have a rebellion among his people. This is understandable because many others were not able to hold their cities, after obtaining them through cruelty, in peaceful times, let alone in the middle of a war.

I believe that this happens after brutal measures have been badly or properly used. They may be called 'properly used' if they are applied in one blow and are necessary for the security of the government, and it is not allowed to persist unless they are used to take advantage of the subjects. Brutal measures are 'badly used' if, although they start easy and are few in the beginning, they gradually increase with time.

Those who practice the first method can, with the help of God or men, to some extent to soften their rulership as Agathocles did. However, it is impossible for those who use the second brutal tactic to contain themselves.

It is, therefore, noted that in conquering a territory, an invader carefully considers all the necessary injuries he has to inflict and does them all at once so as not to repeat them daily. Because he is not constantly unsettling his people, it is easier to make them feel more secure and win them over with benefits.

Anyone who does otherwise would be compelled to always keep his knife in his hand. He cannot rely on his courtiers, and they cannot attach themselves to him either, owing to their constant and repetitive mistakes. Cruelty should be done all at once so that in less tasting, the people are less offended. The benefits should also be given little by little so that their flavor lasts longer.

Above all else, a prince must live among his men in such a way that no unexpected event, good or bad, will cause him to change. For if the need for change arises in troubled times, he would be too late for serious measures. Mild ones would not help him either because they would be seen as forced from him, and no one would be obligated to him for them.

Chapter 9

About Civil Monarchy

Coming into another point, when an ordinary citizen becomes a prince, not by cruelty or violence, but by the favor of his people, this is called a civil monarchy. One does not need genius or good fortune to attain it, but rather fortunate intelligence. Such a country is obtained either by the favor of the people or the favor of the nobles. Since both distinct groups are present in all cities, it goes that the people do not wish to be ruled or oppressed, but the nobles want to rule and oppress the people. From these two conflicting desires, there can be three outcomes - monarchy, self-government, or anarchy.

A monarchy can be created by the people or by the nobles, depending on who has the opportunity. The nobles, seeing they cannot resist the people, begin to push one of their own to the front to make him a prince so that under his shadow, they can fulfill their own ambitions. As for the people, they know that they cannot oppose the nobles, so they chose one of their own to be a prince so that he may protect them and their interests.

Anyone who obtains power with the help of the nobles finds it hard to secure his position than one who comes to it with the help of the people. That is because he finds himself surrounded by nobles who think they are equals. Therefore, he cannot rule or manage them to his liking. However, if he obtains power from the favor of the people, then no one, or only a few people, will disobey him.

Besides this, he cannot by fair dealing, and without causing harm to others, satisfy the nobles. However, he can satisfy the people because their intentions are usually more reasonable than the nobles who only seek to oppress.

A prince can never defend himself against hostile people because they are too many. On the other hand, he can protect himself from the nobles because they are few in number. The worst that a prince has to fear from hostile people is being abandoned. However, from the hostile nobles, he not only has to fear abandonment but also that they may rise in opposition against him. For they, in these matters, are more insightful and astute, always respond promptly to keep themselves safe, and have the support of the person they expect to prevail.

Additionally, while the prince will always have to live with the same people, he does not need the nobles to rule well. Each day, he can change them by giving or taking away authority from them as he so wishes.

To make this point clearer, I say that the nobles should be viewed primarily in two ways - they either shape their interests to match the prince's, or they don't. Those who fit their interests to the prince's and are not greedy must be honored and loved, while those who do not fit into the prince's interest can be handled in two ways. They may act this way due to cowardice and lack of natural courage. In this case, the prince ought to make use of them, especially those who give good advice. So, in good times, you honor them, and in bad times, you do not have to fear them.

However, if they refuse to align with the prince's interests due to their self-interest, it is a sign that they are thinking more about themselves than the prince. He should defend himself against such people and fear them as if they were his open enemies because, in difficult times, they will turn against him and help to ruin him.

Therefore, for this reason, one who wishes to become a prince through the favor of the people should remain friendly with them. This should be easy to do, seeing as all they want is not to be oppressed by him. However, one who, without the support of the people, becomes a prince through the favor of the nobles ought to seek to win the people over to his side.

He could easily do this by taking them under his protection because human beings when they receive good from one who they were expecting evil, are more attached to this benefactor. Therefore, the people become more devoted to him than if he had been raised to power by their favors.

The prince can win their support in many ways, but as these things change depending on the circumstances, one cannot set fixed rules, and so I must omit them. However, I repeat, it is necessary for a prince to remain friendly with the people, or he will have no security in difficult times.

Nabis[19], the prince of Sparta, defended his country and government against all of the Greek attacks and Roman invasions. To overcome this danger, it was only necessary for him to make himself secure against a few. This wouldn't have been enough if the people had hated him. And do not let anyone attack this with the old saying that, "He builds on people, builds on mud." This statement is true when an ordinary citizen lays his foundation there and foolishly convinces himself that the people will liberate him when he is oppressed by the enemy. In such a case, that man will find himself deceived, as it happened with Gracchi[20] in Rome and Florentine with Messer Giorgio Scali.[21]

But if the man is a prince who has established himself as a man of command and a brave man, equally capable, and a person who by his spirit and abilities, keeps everyone inspired - such a person will never find himself abandoned by the people and will be proven that he has built a strong foundation.

These civilian states become dangerous when they are transferred from civil power to a dictatorial government because such princes either rule by themselves or through councils. In the latter case, their governments are weaker and less secure because they rely on the goodwill of the citizens placed on the council, and they, especially in difficult times, can easily disrupt to annihilate the government by deception or rebellion.

The prince will have no chance in the middle of an uprising to exercise absolute power because the citizens and subjects, being accustomed to receiving instructions from the council, will not be willing to obey his orders. In unstable situations, he will always have a shortage of people that he can trust.

Therefore, a prince cannot rely on what he observes in peaceful times when the people need the state because then, everyone agrees with him. They all promise, when death is yet far away, to die for him. But in troubled times, when the state needs the people, the prince will only find a few. Indeed, this experiment of moving from civil ruling to a totalitarian government is dangerous because it can only be tried once.

Therefore, a wise prince must always seek to adopt a course that will cause his citizens, in any sort of circumstance, to have need of the state and need of him so that they will remain loyal to him.

Chapter 10

About The Way Of Measuring The Strength of Nations

In order to examine the characteristics of nations, one more point must be considered, which is whether a prince has the power, that in times of need, can support himself with his own resources or that he has to rely on others for assistance.

To make this quite clear, I consider those who can support themselves with their own resources as those who can, by the abundance of men or money, build a sufficient army to join the battle against anyone that attacks them. I also consider those who always rely on others for assistance as those who cannot stand against their enemies in battle but are forced to defend themselves by cowering behind a wall.

The first case has been discussed, but I will mention it again if the need appears. In the second case, one cannot say anything but to encourage the princes to take care of the provision and fortification of their towns and not on any account to defend the town. Anyone who fortifies his town well, and manages other concerns as outlined above, will never be attacked without caution. Humans are always averse to obviously difficult circumstances, and it will be seen as not easy to attack one who governs a town that is well fortified and a people that don't hate him.

German cities[22] are completely free; they own very little of the surrounding countryside and only obey the king's orders when it suits them. They are not afraid of this or any possible power around them because they are fortified in such a way that everyone thinks that taking it by the direct attack would be tedious and difficult.

This is because they have strong fortifications, with sufficient artillery and enough supplies in public warehouses to eat, drink, and fight for a year. In addition to this, in order to keep the people alive without wasting money, they always create jobs for the community with city-building works, and from this, the people are well-fed and supported. They value military training, and more than that, they enact many laws to support it.

Therefore, a prince who keeps a strong city and does not make himself hated will not be attacked. If anyone dared to attack, he would only be pushed back in defeat.

Because the situation of the world is always changing, it is almost impossible for anyone to keep an army idle in a siege for a year. One might object by saying, "If people have property outside the city, caught on fire, they will no longer be patient because the siege is too long and the destroyed property will make them forget their prince." To that I answer that a powerful and courageous prince will overcome such difficulties by giving his subjects, one hand, hope that the evil will not last for long, and on the other hand, fear of the enemy's cruelty to deal with those subjects that have a propensity for being too bold.

Furthermore, the enemy would naturally instantly burn and destroy the countryside upon arrival at the time the people's spirits are boiling and ready for defense. For these reasons, the prince has nothing to worry about. Because after, when their spirits have cooled down, the damage has been done, and there are no longer any remedies.

The people will, therefore, be more willing to unite with the prince, seeing that he is indebted to them after their houses have been burned and their possessions ruined in his defense. This is because people, by nature, are bound by the benefits they give as much as the benefits they receive. Hence, if these things are carefully considered, it will not be difficult for a wise prince to keep the minds of his citizens strong and loyal from start to finish as he continues to support and protect them.

Chapter 11

About The Church Nations

Now, all this left to discuss is church nations, touching all difficulties that occurred prior to their possession because they are acquired either by fortune or ability and can be secured without either, for they are upheld by ancient religious laws. These laws are very powerful and of such character that these states may be secured regardless of how the princes behave and live.

These princes alone have nations that do not need them to defend and subjects that do not need a ruling. The nations, although unguarded, are not taken from them. The subjects, although not ruled, do not care, and they do not have the desire or ability to rebel.

Therefore, only these types of nations are secure and happy. Being kept by powers that the human mind cannot reach, I will not talk more about that. Since it was created and maintained by God, it would be a presumptuous and foolish act to discuss it.

Nevertheless, if anyone asks me how the Church can achieve such great achievements in earthly power, seeing that up until the time of Alexander, the Italian leaders did not place much value on the Church's earthly power. Yet now, a French king is trembling before the Church, and the Church has been able to drive the French king and to ruin the Venetians - although this may be very obvious, it is worth describing once more.

Before Charles, King of France, came to Italy, this country was under the control of the Pope, the Venetians, the King of Naples, the Duke of Milan, and the Duke of Florentines. There were two major concerns among these leaders - the first was that no foreign troops should enter Italy, and the second was that none of them should take other people's lands. Those whom they worried the most about were the Pope and the Venetians.

To limit the Venetians, a union of all the others was necessary, as it was for the protection of Ferrara. To restrict the authority of the Pope, they used the barons in Rome, made up of two groups - the Orsini and the Colonnese. These two groups always had reasons for quarrel and often showed their mighty forces against the pope to keep him weak and helpless. Although there was sometimes a brave pope, yet neither luck nor wisdom could help him eliminate these problems. Additionally, the short life of a pope was also a cause of weakness, for each pope had an average of ten years in office, and it was very hard to reduce the power of one of the groups. If for instance, one pope almost eliminates the Colonnesi group and then another pope hostile to the Orsini takes the position, the Colonnesi would rise again, and he wouldn't have enough time to destroy the Orsini. This was the reason why the powers of the Church were not highly respected in Italy.

However, this was not the case during the time of Pope Alexander the Sixth. Of all the popes that have ever been, he showed how successful a pope with both money and power could be. With the help of his son, Cesare Borgia, and the French invasion of Italy as an opportunity, he did all the things I discussed above in the act of Cesare.

Although his intentions were not to the benefits of the church but to Cesare, his actions contributed to the Church's greatness, which after his death and Cesare's end, became the heir to all his labors.

Pope Julius succeeded right after Pope Alexander and found that the Church was strong, possessing the entire land of Romagna, the barons of Rome reduced to nothing, and through the efforts of Alexander, the Colonnesi and Orsini were completely weakened. He saw an opening to accumulate money in such a way that had never been done before Alexander's time.

Such things were not only followed by Julius but also improved. He intended to gain Bologna, wreak havoc on the Venetians, and to drive the French out of Italy. He not only achieved these goals but had others to his credit. He did all he could to strengthen the Church and not any individual entity.

He also kept the Orsini and Colonnesi factions within the boundaries he found them. Although some of them tried to cause trouble, he nevertheless kept two things firmly - the greatness of the Church with which he terrified them, and he didn't allow them to have their own cardinals, as they could stir quarrels. Whenever these groups had cardinals, they didn't remain silent for long. The cardinals fostered the groups like the Orsini in Rome, and the barons were compelled to support them. Thus, from the ambitions of the cardinals arose turmoil and rebellion among the barons.

For this reason, Pope Leo is the most powerful, and one may hope that if the other popes made it great with arms, he would make the Church even greater and more respected with his goodness and boundless virtues.

Chapter 12

About Soldiery Types And The Mercenaries

As I have described the features of each of the monarchies as I had proposed to discuss in the beginning, and having considered to some extent the causes of them being good and bad, and having shown the methods by which you can acquire and secure territories, it now remains to discuss the general rules of attack and defense for each case.

We have seen from above the need for a prince to lay a solid foundation. Otherwise, it follows that he would be destroyed. The main foundation of all nations, new or old or mixed, is the good rule of law and strong military force. As there cannot be good laws without a strong military force, it follows that a nation with a strong military force has good laws. I will leave out the part of the laws in this discussion and focus on only military forces.

The armies that a prince uses to protect his nation are either his own or mercenaries or auxiliary or mixed. The mercenaries and auxiliary forces are useless and dangerous. If a prince holds a nation that relies on these armies, then it is unstable and insecure because they are disunited, ambitious, indisciplined, unfaithful, courageous in the presence of friends, and cowardly in the presence of enemies. They are not afraid of God and are dishonest to people.

Destruction is postponed only as long as an attack is postponed, for in peace, they will plunder you, and in war, your enemy will. In fact, they have no other interest or reason for fighting other than a small stipend, which is not enough money to make them die for your cause. They are willing enough to be your soldiers while you are at peace, but if war comes, they either disappear or run from the enemy.

I shouldn't have little difficulty proving this, for the destruction of Italy was caused but nothing else but relying on mercenaries for help for many years. Although they used to make some feats in the past and appeared brave among themselves, yet when enemy nations came, they showed us the truth about them.

Therefore, it was that Charles, the French King, was allowed to take over Italy without any resistance. Anyone who says that our weakness caused it speaks the truth. However, they are not the weaknesses he imagined but those that I have described. As they are the weaknesses of the prince, it is also the princes themselves who have suffered the consequence.

I want to further demonstrate the dangers of these soldiers. The mercenary captains are either capable men or not. If they are, one cannot trust them because they always aspire to their personal greatness, either by oppressing you, who is their master, or others against your will. But if the captain is incompetent, then you are destroyed in the usual way.

Suppose it is argued that any soldier would act in the same manner, whether mercenaries or not, I would reply that when soldiers are used, either by a prince or a republic, the prince must go in-person to perform the duty of a captain while the republic must appoint a citizen to hold the position. When one who is sent fails to fulfill his duties, a replacement should be made available. When you have a worthy captain, you must hold him to the laws so that he doesn't step out of bounds.

Experience has shown that both princes and republics do better single-handed, while mercenaries do nothing but cause damage. It is harder to bring a republic with its own army under the hands of a citizen than it is to bring one armed with a mercenary army. Rome and Sparta stood for a long time with their own armies and kept their freedom. The Swiss people had their own powerful army, and they were very free.

An example of ancient mercenaries is the Carthaginians[24], who were oppressed by their mercenaries after the first war with the Romans, even though the Carthaginians had their citizens as captains. After the death of Epaminondas,[25] Philip of Macedon came to command of their soldiers by the Thebans, and after his victory, he deprived them of their freedom.

Duke Filippo[26] being dead, the Milanese hired Francesco Sforza to fight the Venetians, and he, after overcoming the enemy at Caravaggio, joined the Venetians to crush the Milanese, his master. His father, Sforza, was hired by Queen Giovanna[27] of Naples, but he did not protect her, instead of forcing her to throw herself into the arms of the king of Aragon to preserve her kingdom.

On the other hand, the Venetians and the Florentines expanded their territory by using mercenaries, yet the captains did not take the crown but protected them. However, I think that the Florentines, in this case, were fortunate because out of the able captains they could have been afraid of, some could not win, some had opposition, and others had turned their ambitions elsewhere.

One of those who lost was Giovani Acuto, and since he did not win the battle, his loyalty couldn't be proven. However, everyone acknowledges that had he won the battle, the Florentines would have been at his mercy.

Sforza was always opposed by Bracceschi, so they kept an eye on each other. Francesco shifted his ambitions to Lombardy, and Braccio turned against the Church and the kingdom of Naples.

Now, let us go back to what happened recently. The Florentines appointed Paolo Vitelli[28] their captain, a very careful man who had risen from an ordinary citizen to become very famous. If he had taken Pisa, no one could deny that it would have been proper for the Florentines to be on good terms with him. That's because if he had stood with the enemy, then they would have had no means of resistance and if they had been cordial with him, they would have had no choice but to obey him.

TIMELESS CREEDS FOR WINNING

The Venetians, if their achievements are considered, will be seen to have acted safely and gloriously, and providing they brought their own troops to war, performed valiantly with the nobles and subjects armed. This was before they turned their attention to land. When they started fighting on land, they renounced this virtue to follow the custom of Italy.

At the beginning of their land expansion, because they did not have a lot of lands to control and their great reputation, they were not afraid of their captains. However, as they expanded, they began to taste the failure of hiring mercenaries. Having found a brave figure in Carmagnola, seeing as they defeated the Duke of Milan under his leadership, and on the one hand, knowing how lukewarm he had gotten to war, feared that he wouldn't bring them any more victory. On the other hand, they were not willing or able to let him go because they didn't want to lose what they had acquired.

They were forced to kill him to protect themselves. They afterward had new leadership in the military made up of the captains Bartolomeo da Bergamo, Roberto da San Severino, count Pitigliano and many similar people. Under these captains, they had to fear loss and not gain, as happened at Vailà[29], where in just one battle, the Venetians lost everything they had acquired within eight hundred years.

In using these mercenaries, the rewards come slowly and inconsiderably. However, the losses are sudden and damaging. Through the above examples, we can see that Italy has been ruled for a long time by mercenaries. I would like to discuss them more thoroughly so that having seen their rise and progress, one may be better equipped to counteract them.

One must understand that the empire was recently destroyed in Italy. The Pope gained more temporal power, and Italy was divided into several states, being that many of the great cities wielded weapons to revolt against the nobility who, in the past, relied on the ruler's power to oppress the people. While this was happening, the Church was favoring them so as to gain more power.

In many other cities, their citizens became princes. Thus, Italy partly fell partly into the hands of the Church and republics. The Church, being made up of priests, and the republics, being of non-military citizens, had to hire foreigners as mercenaries.

The first to become a famous mercenary was Alberigo da Comio[30] from Romagna. Later there was Braccio and Sforza, who were the masters of Italy during that time. Since then, many other captains have continued to command these armies.

The outcome of all their valor has been that Italy was invaded by Charles, robbed by Louis, exploited by Ferdinand, and insulted by Switzers. The rule that has been guiding them has been to first lower the reputation of the infantry so that they would increase theirs. They did this because living on their salary and without land, they were unable to support many soldiers.

Furthermore, they had no authority over the infantry and were forced to use the cavalry. This way, with a moderate amount of force, they could maintain their reputation. However, this meant that out of an army of twenty thousand soldiers, there was a maximum of two thousand infantry.

They had, besides this, used all kinds of tricks to reduce the fatigue and the danger for themselves and their soldiers. These procedures included not killing people in battle but taking prisoners and releasing them without asking for money. They did not attack towns at night, nor did the soldiers of the towns attack their camps at night. They didn't surround the camps either with stockades and trenches, nor did they fight in the winter.

All of these things were permitted by their military rules, put together by them, as I said, to avoid fatigue and danger. As a result, they ruined Italy's reputation and put it into slavery.

Chapter 13

About The Auxiliary Army, The Mixed Army, And The Private Army

Auxiliary armies are another kind of useless soldiers recruited when a prince needs to take up arms, as was done in recent times by Pope Julius. The Pope, in the attack against Ferrara, after having poor results from the mercenaries, turned to the auxiliary soldiers. He negotiated with the King of Spain, Ferdinand, to borrow troops to help. These soldiers can be helpful and good to their master, but it is a disadvantage to the one who asks for it. Because if they lose, the prince is ruined, and if they win, the prince becomes under their control.

Although ancient history may be full of examples, I do not want to ignore the recent one of Pope Julius the Second - a danger that cannot be ignored. Pope Julius, in wanting to acquire the land of Ferrara, put himself entirely in the hands of foreigners. However, his good fortune brought about the third event so that he was unaffected by this bad decision.

His auxiliary soldiers were thoroughly defeated in Ravenna, and the Swiss suddenly came and drove the conquerors away. Therefore, he didn't become prisoners to his enemies since they were chased away and did not fall under the control of his auxiliary because they were destroyed by his enemies.

The Florentines, being completely without troops, sent ten thousand French soldiers to take the land of Pisa, after which they incurred more danger than in any other of their troubles.

The Emperor of Constantinople[31] sent ten thousand Turkish soldiers to occupy Greece to fight against the state. When the war ended, the Turks did not leave Greece, thus, beginning Greek's slavery with the foreign states.

Therefore, let those who have no ambitions to conquer use auxiliary troops, for they are much more dangerous than mercenaries. For them, your ruin is predetermined because they are all united and obey their commanders. But with the mercenaries, when they have won the battle, need more time and better opportunities to hurt you. They are unified, having been found and paid by you. Their commander is a third party installed by you, therefore, making it impossible for him to immediately have the authority to hurt you.

In summary, with mercenaries, cowardice is the biggest danger, but with auxiliary soldiers, courage is. A wise prince will, therefore, always avoid these types of soldiers and use his own army. It is better for one to lose with his own army than to win the battle with auxiliary soldiers, as you cannot consider any victory won with them as being real.

I will not hesitate to cite Cesare Borgia and his actions. Cesare attacked Romagna with auxiliary soldiers, taking only the French soldiers, and with them captured the land of Imola and Forli. But then he found it impossible to trust the auxiliary soldiers and turned to the mercenaries, discerning that they were less dangerous. He enlisted the help of Orsini and Vitelli, and finding them unreliable, unfaithful, and dangerous, he destroyed them and formed his own army.

The difference between these types of an army can immediately be seen when one considers the difference in Cesare's reputation when he had the French soldiers, when he had Orsini and Vitelli, and when he had his own soldiers. When he relied on his own soldiers, his reputation increased. More people held him in high esteem when they saw that he was the absolute master of his own army.

I had no intention of going beyond the Italian and recent examples, but I do not want to leave out Hiero, the Syracusan, who was one of those mentioned earlier. This man, as I said, was made the captain for the Syracusan army and soon discovered that an army of mercenaries couldn't be used. When he realized that he couldn't keep them or fire them, he tore them apart and destroyed them. After that, he used his own soldiers to fight and not foreigners.

I wish to also mention an example from the Bible that applies to this topic. David[32] dedicated himself to King Saul to fight Goliath. To give David courage, King Saul equipped him with his own weapons, which David refused immediately after wearing them. He said he couldn't use them and instead wished to confront the enemy with his own simple weapons. In conclusion, someone else's weapons will either fall from your back, weigh you down, or tie you down.

Charles the Seventh, the father of King Louis the Eleventh, who by good fortune and heroic valour, freed France from England, acknowledged the need to be armed with his own forces. In his kingdom, he established laws concerning soldiers. Afterward, his son, King Louis, abolished the infantry and began to hire the Swiss. This mistake, followed by the latter ones, is now seen as a danger to that kingdom. This is because he completely devalued his personal army to increase the reputation of the Swiss. Because he had no infantry, his other soldiers were led by the Swiss and, having being used to fighting side by side with them, could no longer fight alone.

So it appeared that the French could not fight against the Swiss and, without the Swiss, could not fight others. The French army, thus, became mixed - part mercenaries and part soldiers of the nation. The reputation of this type of army is higher than a mercenary or auxiliary army but inferior to that of one's own army. This example proves it - the kingdom of France would have been stronger had the laws of King Charles being strengthened and maintained.

However, the naivety of most people, when starting a new job that looks good at first, will not let them see the poison that is hidden in it, as I have said before of severe fevers. Therefore, if a prince cannot recognize the danger until it is already happening, he is not really wise; this insight is only assigned to a few.

If the first fall of the Roman Empire is examined, we will see that it started with the recruitment of the Goths.[33] From that time, the power of the Roman Empire began to decline, and all her prestige was passed on to the Goths.

Hence, I conclude that no kingdom is safe without its own army. On the contrary, it is completely up to good fortune as there is not enough courage during difficulty to self-defend. It has always been the opinion and judgment of wise people that nothing is so uncertain or unstable as a reputation or power that is not founded on one's own strength.

One's own army is one that consists of either subject, citizens, or dependents of the country. Any other form would be mercenaries or auxiliaries. The way to create and make ready a national army would be easily found if the rules I suggested earlier are carefully considered. Also, if one would consider how Philip, the father of Alexander the Great, and many other republics and princes, have armed and organized themselves.

Chapter 14

Of The Prince On The Art Of War

A prince should not have any other goal or thought, nor choose anything else for his research, anything else but war and its rules and discipline. This is the only art that belongs to the ruler, and it enables those who weren't born princes to not only defend their status but also helps ordinary citizens rise to the princedom.

It is common to see that when princes who think more of peace than of war lose their state. The reason why they lose their states is that they neglected this art. Along the same vein, the reason they expand their territory is from the mastery of this art. Francesco Sforza, having mastered the art of war, changed from being a regular citizen to becoming the Duke of Milan. On the other hand, his children, avoiding the difficulties and troubles of war, turned from dukes to commoners.

Among the many evils which not having a military will bring you is that it causes you to be despised. This is one of the dangers that a prince must guard himself against. There is a big difference between the armed and unarmed. It would be unreasonable to expect one who is armed to willingly yield to one who is unarmed or that the unarmed man feels secure in the midst of armed servants. This is because while one person holds disdain towards the other, the other would be suspicious of them. Therefore, making it hard for them to work together.

Hence, a prince who does not understand the art of war, among other mentioned disadvantages, cannot be respected by his soldiers, nor can he rely on them. Therefore, a prince must never let the art of war leave his mind and, even in peace, ought to practice more than during the war. He can do this in two ways, by action or research.

With action, the prince must, above all things, keep his soldiers well trained and organized. In addition, it is advisable to practice as if in battle so that the body can endure and learn the nature of the natural terrain. The prince must understand the terrain of the mountains, valleys, plains and understand the nature of the rivers and marshes. He must learn about all of these terrains for careful analysis and planning.

This knowledge may be useful in two ways. First, the prince learns to know his country and is able to defend it better. Then, with the knowledge and observations of the terrain in his country, the prince can easily understand any aspect that needs to be studied more. This is because the hills, valleys, plains, rivers, for instance, in Tuscany, have a certain resemblance to those of other countries. So, with this knowledge about one aspect of one's country, one can easily gain knowledge about others.

Any prince who lacks this skill lacks the essentials that every military leader should have. It taught him how to surprise enemies, choose a campsite, dispatch and organize troops during combat, and lay siege to the towns in the best way.

Philopoemen,[34] the prince of Achaeans, among the other praises that writers have written about him, is commended because, in the time of peace, he never had any other thought on his mind beyond the rules of war. While wandering around the fields with his friends, he would often stop to reason with them, "If the enemy is on that hill and we are here with our army, who will have the advantage? How can we advance to meet the enemy without losing ranks? What if we wish to retreat? If the enemy runs, how do we go after them?"

He would put forward suggestions on all the possible scenarios of war that could befall an army and would listen to their opinions, expressing his with valid reasons as well. Because of these constant discussions, there could never be any unexpected circumstances that arose during a war that he was not prepared to deal with.

But to exercise his brain, the prince should read the history and study the actions of famous people, see how they behaved in war, find out the causes of their victory or defeat in order to avoid the latter and achieve the former. Above all, the prince ought to follow what these famous men, who found someone who had been famous and praised before them to imitate, have done in the past and keep their achievements and actions in mind.

It has been said that Alexander the Great imitated Achilles, Cesare imitated Alexander, and Scipio imitated Cyrus.

Anyone who reads the life of Cyrus, written by Xenophon, will then recognize afterward in the life of Scipio how much that imitation of Cyrus brought him glory and how much in friendliness, kindness, and generosity Scipio conformed to those things that had been written of Cyrus by Xenophon.

A wise prince should observe some of such rules. He must never remain idle during peaceful times but increase his knowledge in such a way that he is always ready to respond in the face of adversity so that when his fortune changes and bad luck comes, he is always prepared to resist them.

Chapter 15

Involving Men Things, Especially Prince About Praising Or Blaming

Now we consider what should be the rules of conduct for a prince towards his subjects and friends. I know that many articles have been written on this subject, and people may think me presumptuous to bring it up again, especially as I will not be following other people's methods. However, my intention is to write what the reader might find useful by telling the real truth of the matter rather than the imagination of it.

Many have imagined republics and kingdoms in ways that, in fact, have never been known or seen. That's because the way a person lives now is far different from the way one ought to live. Anyone who ignores the apparent reality for the imagination of what ought to be will sooner cause his own destruction rather than protection. A person who chooses to act completely moral will soon be destroyed among so many in the world who are not good.

Hence, a prince who wants to survive must know how to do evil or not according to his need. So let's put aside the fantasies regarding the prince and discuss the realities. I say that all human beings, when mentioned, especially princes due to their high status, are notable for their particular values that either bring them blame or praise. This is why people are known for being generous or miserly, generous or greedy, cruel or compassionate, unfaithful or loyal, soft and cowardly or daring and brave, friendly or proud, lascivious or chaste, sincere or cunning, easy or serious, religious or disbelieving, and so on.

I know that some people will confess that it is praiseworthy for a prince to have all the above good qualities in him, but our human nature does not allow us to have all of those perfect qualities. Therefore, the prince needs to be careful enough to avoid the reproach of those vices that would make him lose his state. Additionally, the prince should try, if possible, to also keep himself from those bad habits that will not lose him his state. But if he cannot avoid it, he should not hesitate to do those things. Moreover, he does not need to concern himself about being criticized for evil behaviors, especially in states that need them to be preserved. Sometimes, if considered, morality may cause the prince to be destroyed, while something that looks evil may yet bring him security and prosperity.

Chapter 16

Of Generosity And Miserliness

Of the two qualities above, being generous is better. However, being generous done in a way that doesn't bring fame harms us. If a person is genuinely generous and not popular, then the opposite criticism cannot be avoided as miserliness.

Therefore, anyone who wishes to maintain a reputation of generosity must be outlandish in his display of generosity. A prince who does this will use up his fortune on such acts and, in the end, would be compelled to unduly burden his people by taxing them and doing everything possible to make more money.

This will soon make the people hate him, and when he becomes poor, he will be worthless to everyone. With his generosity having offended many but rewarding little, he will be affected by every trouble and run into risk at every sign of danger. Once he recognizes this and wanting to avoid this problem, he will be criticized for being miserly.

If he is wise, then he should not be afraid of being labeled as miserly. With time, the prince will be appreciated than if generous because it would become clear that the economy is in abundance, that he can defend himself from all attacks, and that he can carry out his projects without burdening his subjects. Therefore, it happens that the prince exercises generosity towards the many who are his subjects and miserliness to the few who he does not give.

We have not seen extraordinary things being done in our time except by those who have been considered miserly; the rest have all failed. Pope Julius the Second was notorious for being generous before becoming pope. However, later, he did not try to keep up that character when he declared war on the French king. He waged many wars without imposing any extraordinary taxes on his subjects because he administered his extra expenses during the war from his long thriftiness.

The present king of Spain would not have undertaken or conquered on so many difficult adventures if he had been generous. Therefore, a prince, who does not want to exploit his people but wants to be able to defend himself, not become poor, hated, or greedy, does not need to worry about having the reputation of a miser, for it is one of those vices that would allow him to rule.

And if anyone tries to say, "Cesare acquired an empire due to generosity and many others achieved the highest positions by being generous or just by being considered to be generous," I answer, "it is either you are already a prince or on the way to becoming one."

In the first instance, generosity is dangerous, while it is very necessary to be known as being generous in the second. Cesare was one of those who wanted to attain the highest power in Rome. However, if he had remained generous after he had gained that position and didn't curb his expenses, he would have destroyed his government.

Also, if anyone should reply, "Many people have become princes and have done great things with the military and remained very generous," I would say, "Either the prince uses his own money or that of his subjects, or that of others."

In the first instance, one should be very careful, and in the second, any opportunity for generosity should not be overlooked. If a prince who has an army conquers and acquires the properties of his enemy or anything that belongs to others, then generosity is necessary. Otherwise, the soldiers will disobey. Following the examples of Syrus, Cesare, and Alexander, when a prince obtains wealth from others, it would cost him nothing to be generous with it. It will not make him lose his reputation but improve it because he only squanders what belongs to others. It only becomes dangerous when you squander your own belongings.

Nothing disappears as quickly as generosity because even while you are exercising it, you are quickly losing your power to do so. The prince, while wasting his resources, becomes poor or despised and, in avoiding poverty, becomes greedy and hated for exploiting the people. Above all things, the prince should protect himself from being despised and resented. Generosity leads to both. Therefore, it is wiser to have the reputation of being miserly without being hated than to be compelled, by seeking a reputation of being generous, to incur greed that will cause everyone's hatred later.

Chapter 17

Of Ruthlessness and Mercy, And Whether Love Is Better Than Fear

Coming down to the other qualities mentioned above, I say that every prince should expect himself to be seen as benevolent and not ruthless. However, the prince must be careful not to allow his mindedness to be abused.

Cesare Borgia was considered ruthless, but in spite of it, managed to reconcile Romagna and unify it, bringing peace to the land and the people's loyalty. If we consider this carefully, he will be seen to be more merciful than the Florentines, who, to avoid a reputation for being cruel, allowed the whole province of Pistoia to be destroyed.

Therefore, the prince, as long as he keeps his people united and loyal, should not be bothered about the reputation of cruelty. With only a few examples, the prince will show himself to be more benevolent than those who, through too much mercy, allow riots that lead to killing and looting to arise. Such incidents are capable of hurting a large population, while the executions that could have quelled them would only affect a few individuals.

Out of all princes, it is impossible for a newly crowned prince to avoid the reputation of cruelty. This is because new territories are full of dangers that need to be checked. Nonetheless, the prince must be slow to believe or act and should not show fear. He must act calmly with concern and empathy for his people, such that overconfidence does not cause him to be careless, and too much caution does not cause him to be suspicious and intolerable.

In relation to this, a question arises, "Is being loved better than being feared or feared better than being loved?" I will tell you immediately that a prince ought to strive for both, but because it is difficult to combine them both in one person, if he had to choose one, it is safer to choose being feared over being loved.

The reason for this is that people are generally ungrateful, fickle, false, cowardly, and greedy. As long as you remain successful, they will remain with you, willingly offering their blood, properties, lives, and children when the need is far away. However, as soon as the need arises, they will turn their backs against you.

Any prince that completely believes their promises and neglects to place other precautions would be completely destroyed. This love is caused by the things they stand to gain and not by sincere or noble feelings. It may be earned but is often insecure and cannot be relied upon in times of need. People are less afraid to offend the one who is beloved than one who is feared. This love is held by a chain of obligation that, due to the fickle nature of man, would break at any opportunity for their advantage. The fear of severe punishment, on the other hand, never fails.

However, the prince should inspire fear in people in such a way that, even if he doesn't win affection, he cannot be hated. His reign would endure being feared without being hated, which will continue as long as he does not steal his subjects' properties or their women. When it becomes necessary to take someone's life, he must do it on proper justification and an obvious reason for it. Above all else, he must keep his hands off the possessions of others because, while people can quickly forget the death of their father, it is harder to forget losing possessions.

Besides, there are several pretexts by which one can take properties away. Anyone who has once robbed others of their possession would always find more pretexts to take what belongs to others away. On the contrary, the reasons for taking a life are harder to find and exhaustive. When a prince has his personal army, with hundreds of soldiers under his command, then it is very necessary for him not to worry about having a reputation for cruelty because, without it, he will not be able to keep the army united or control them to do their duties.

Among all of Hannibal's[35] great deeds, he is depicted as leading a huge army, comprised of many different races, to fight in foreign countries, with no disagreement between them or against the prince, whether in his favor or against it. This came from nothing but his inhumane cruelty, which, together with his boundless courage, made him respected and feared in the eyes of his soldiers. Without that cruelty, none of his other virtues could have achieved that effect. Many myopic writers admire his achievements on the one hand, and on the other, they condemn the actions that led to those achievements.

It is true that none of his other virtues could have been sufficient, as can be seen in the case of Scipio, the greatest man, not only in his times but also in all of human history. Nonetheless, this did not stop his army from rebelling against him in Spain.

This rebellion arose from nothing but his excessive kindness, which gave his soldiers more leeway than was customary with military rule. For this, he was criticized in the Senate by Fabius Maximus and called a bad leader. Someone in the Senate, wanting to let him off the hook, said that there were more people who knew much better how not to make mistakes than to correct other of their mistakes. His agreeable nature, if he had continued in command, would have, in time, completely destroyed the fame and glory of Scipio. Fortunately, he was under the control of the Senate, so this dangerous behavior was not only concealed but contributed to his glory.

Returning to the question of being feared or loved, I have come to a conclusion that, because people love according to their will and fear according to the will of the prince, a wise prince would do well to establish himself on that which is under his control and not in the control of others. However, as noted, he must endeavor not to attract hatred.

Chapter 18

About How Prince Keeps His Promise

Every one admits how exemplary it is for a prince to be a faithful man and live a life of integrity, not deceitful. However, our experience shows that princes who have done great things are those who do not bother about keeping promises and have been known to get around people's intelligence by deception.

There are two ways to win - by the rule of law or by force. The first method is appropriate for humans, while the second is suitable for animals. However, because the first method is hardly ever effective, the second must also be used. It is, therefore, necessary for a prince to know how to use both the beast and the human ways.

This has been taught to princes by ancient writers, who described how Achilles and many other ancient princes were given to Chiron,[36] the centaur, to raise, discipline, and teach. This means that they had for a teacher, a half-animal and half-human. Therefore, it is essential for a prince to know how to use both natures, for one without the other is hardly ever enough.

If a prince is compelled to behave like a beast, he ought to choose the fox and the lion. As the lion cannot protect itself from traps, and the fox cannot defend itself against wolves. Therefore it is necessary to become a fox to sniff out the traps and a lion to fight off the wolves. Those who simply rely on the lion do not understand what they are doing.

Hence, a wise prince should not keep the faith when such a promise can be turned against him or when the reasons behind such promise cease to exist. If humans were entirely good, then there would be no need for this rule, but since they are evil and will not keep their promises to you, you are also not bound to keep your promises to them. A prince will never lack good legitimate reasons to justify not keeping his promise. Innumerable modern examples can be given, showing how many treaties have been broken by princes and how they know the best ways to deploy the fox to become successful.

However, a prince ought to know the cleverness to disguise this behavior and be a good actor. Humans are so simple and, therefore, only concerned with present necessities, such that anyone who seeks to deceive will always find one person who will allow himself to be deceived.

A recent example I cannot ignore in silence is Pope Alexander the Sixth, who did not do anything else but deceive people, nor did he think of doing anything else. He always found victims to deceive, for there was no one with more convincing and promising words who, yet, would honor it less. His lies always succeeded according to his wishes because he understood this aspect of people well.

It is, therefore, necessary for the prince to have all the good qualities that I have described, but it is also necessary for him to pretend to have them. I dare say this too, to have these qualities and to always exhibit them is dangerous. However, it is helpful for a prince to appear to have them - to appear to be benevolent, loyal, generous, religious, straightforward but flexible enough to take display the opposite of these qualities when needed.

We have to understand that a prince, especially newly crowned, cannot do these things that everyone is praised for because, in being forced to secure the nation, he has to act contrary to honesty, generosity, loyalty, kindness, and religion. Hence, the prince needs to have a flexible mind that is ready to turn in any direction the wind of fortunes and variation of things come. Although, as I have said above, he should not give up the good if he can avoid doing so, if he finds it necessary, then he should know how to go about it.

For this reason, a prince should take care not to let anything slip out of his mouth that is not fully in line with the five qualities listed above. He must appear to everyone who sees and hears him to be full of kindness, loyalty, generosity, honesty, and religion. There is nothing more important to appear to have than the last one because people generally judge more with their eyes than by their hands. Most people can see your appearance, but very few will get close enough to be in touch with you. And those few that do, dare not object to the opinion of the majority because they have the support of the government. In human actions, especially princes, it is not wise to challenge because everyone judges according to the results.

For that reason, let the prince be given credit for acquiring and securing the nation, and the means he used will be considered honest, and he will be praised by everyone. This is because the majority is always taken by the appearance and outcome of a thing. In this world, when the majority unanimously support a thing, no one cares to pay attention to the minority that opposes it.

A prince in our present time, whom I will not foolishly name, never preaches anything else but peace and faith but is hostile to both of them in reality. If he did what he preached, he would have lost his reputation and kingdom so many times.

Chapter 19

Of Avoiding Being Scorned And Hated

Now, because I have talked about the important characteristics that a prince must display, I would like to briefly discuss under the general topic the things that a prince should think about to avoid those things that would make him hated or despised. If he can play his part to the best of his ability, then he needs not to fear any dangers of other criticisms.

As I have said, what makes people the most resentful is the exploitation of the properties and women of his subjects. The prince must abstain from doing both of these things. When neither property nor honor is threatened, the majority of them will live happily. Then, the prince only has to contend with the ambitions of a few that he can easily control in many ways.

A prince is scorned if he is considered to be fickle, weak, indecisive, wicked, or lowly. All of these attributes should be avoided by the prince. In his actions, the prince should strive to show greatness, courage, bravery, and somberness. In his private dealings with his subjects, let him show that his orders are absolute. He must maintain his reputation in such a way that no one can hope to deceive or manipulate him.

A prince who demonstrates these good qualities would be respected and will not easily be conspired against. For this reason, a prince only has two things to fear - an attack from within from his subjects and one from without from foreign forces.

Against the latter, the prince is defended by being well-armed and having food allies, and if he has good arms, he will always have good allies. Things within will remain quiet if the things outside remain quiet, as long as it isn't disturbed by rebellion. Even if he is disturbed on the outside, if the prince has learned to prepare and act, as I said earlier, as long as he does not despair will be able to resist any attack. As in the case of Nabis of Spartan, I discussed above.

However, regarding his subjects, if there is an external disturbance, the prince also has to worry that his subjects are secretly plotting a rebellion. The prince can easily protect himself from this by avoiding hatred and contempt and by maintaining good relations with his subjects. This is important for him to achieve, as I have discussed above.

One of the most effective measures that a prince can take to prevent a rebellion is ensuring that he is not hated or despised by his people. That is because he who starts a rebellion against the prince expects to please the people by his removal. But when he sees that, instead of pleasing the people, he would be offending them, the traitor will not be able to summon the courage to carry out his plan. As we know from experience, the difficulties involved in staging an uprising are limitless, and so, many rebellions have started, but so few have been successful.

A traitor cannot plan an uprising alone, but he cannot find fellow conspirators except for those he believes to be equally dissatisfied. As soon as he exposes himself to one who is considered dissatisfied, he gives him material to find satisfaction because he will look for every advantage. So, on the one hand, the dissatisfied person sees the benefits, and on the other hand, he sees the dubious risks and reckless dangers involved. He must either be a very good friend of the traitor or an enemy of the prince if he decides to keep it a secret and go on with the plan.

In summary, I say that on the traitor's side, there is nothing but distrust, jealousy, and fear of punishment to contend with. While on the prince's side, there is the law, the majesty of his throne, the protection of friends, and the government to defend him. If the general goodwill of the people is added, then it would be very difficult for anyone to successfully start a rebellion. For whereas, under normal circumstances, the traitor should only be afraid before the execution of his plot, but now he also has to be afraid of the aftermath of committing the crime. This is because the people now see him as an enemy, and thus, has all hope for escape cut off.

Multiple examples can be given on this subject matter, but I will focus on just one that happened in the days of our fathers. Messer Annibale, Lord of Bologna and the grandfather of

Annibale, having been murdered by the Canneschi, who had plotted against him, didn't have any surviving family except the newborn baby named Messer Giovanni. Immediately after the murder, the people rose up and killed all of the Canneschi rebels. This was the result of the general goodwill of the people towards the Bentivogli clan those days in Bologna. It was so great that after the death of Annibale left no one else to rule the state. Having heard that there was a descendant of Bentivogli in Florence who was a blacksmith, they sent for him and made him the temporary ruler until Messer Giovanni was old enough to rule.

For this reason, a prince should not be afraid of a rebellious plot, as long as he knows how to make the people show him goodwill. However, when they hate and scorn him, he has reason to fear everyone and everything. Well-ordered states and wise princes have taken care not to drive the nobles to despair and to keep the people satisfied, for this is an important issue that a prince must consider.

Among the best ordered and governed kingdoms of our time is France, where we find innumerable good institutions that depend on the king's freedom and security. Among these, the first is the parliament and its administration. Those who founded the kingdom, knowing the ambition and arrogance of the nobility, found it necessary to tighten and restrain them.

On the other hand, knowing that the hatred of the people was founded on the fear of the nobles, they wished to protect them, but they did not want it to be the specific responsibility of the king. So, to take away the criticism that the king could have gotten from the nobility for supporting the people and from the people for supporting the nobles, they formed a parliament of people who would be responsible for beating down the nobility and supporting the people without reproach to the king.

You could not have a better, more efficient, or more secure arrangement for both the king and the kingdom. From this, one might draw another important conclusion that the prince ought to leave the matter of reproach for others to manage and keep only the matters of grace in his hands. However, I think that the prince should care for the nobles but not in such a way that would make the people hate him.

It may appear, perhaps to those who have studied the life and death of the Roman Empires that many of them would be an example contrary to my opinion. Seeing that many of these emperors lived nobly and displayed many great qualities, yet, they lost their empires or were killed by subjects who plotted against them. In response to these objections, I will, therefore, describe the characters of several emperors and show that the causes of their destruction were not that different from the causes I have described. At the same time, I will only consider the things that are relevant to those who studied events of those times.

It will be sufficient for me to bring all of the emperors who succeeded the empire from the philosopher Marcus down to Maximinus. They were Marcus and his son Commodus, Pertinax, Julian, Severus, and his son Antoninus Caracalla, Macrinus, Heliogabalus, Alexander, and Maximinus.

It should be noted that while in other countries, the princes only had to contend with the ambitions of the nobles and the insolence of the people, the Roman emperors had a third difficulty to consider - the cruelty and greed of the soldiers. This is such a difficult issue that brought the ruin of many, for it is hard to satisfy both the soldiers and people. The people love peace and will respect a peaceful emperor, while the soldiers love war-like emperors who must be bold, cruel, and greedy. The soldiers will want the emperor to carry out these acts on the people so that they could reap the double benefits of both their greed and cruelty.

As it so often happens, these things always cause the emperors to lose power if, by virtue of their birth or training, they do not have enough authority to hold both in check. Most of them, especially those who are new to power, recognizing the difficulty of managing these two opposing forces, tend to give in to the demands of the soldiers rather than care for the vulnerability of the people. Unfortunately, this is a necessary course of action to take because if the prince cannot avoid being hated by someone, they ought to avoid being hated by everyone, and when they cannot do this, the best thing is to avoid the hatred of the more powerful group.

As a result, those emperors who, through inexperience, needed favors to support the soldiers against the people. Whether or not this line of action is effective depends on the prince knows how to wield his authority over them.

For all of these reasons, it became that Marcus, Pernitax, and Alexander, being all men who lived modest lives, lovers of justice, enemies of cruelty, kindness, and pride, all came to a sad ending, except Marcus. Marcus was allowed to live and die honorably because he came into power by hereditary and owed nothing to his soldiers or people. Having so many qualities that made him respected while he lived, kept both forces in their places, and was neither hated nor despised.

However, Pertinax was made prince against the wishes of the soldiers. They were used to living freely under the laws of Commodus and could not bear the decent life that Pertinax wanted to force on them. Therefore, having reasons to hate him, to which scorn was added to the hatred because he was old, he was overthrown at the very beginning of his reign.

We should note here that one can be hated for doing both good deeds as well as bad deeds. So, as I have said before, any prince who wants to hold on to this throne is often forced to do evil. When the body that you need to maintain power is corrupt, be it the people, soldiers, or nobility, you must submit to their whims to satisfy them, and then, good deeds will not harm you.

Let us return to the story of Alexander. He was of such greatness that one of the praises attributed to him was this, "during the fourteen years of his reign, no one was put to death without trial." However, since he was seen to be effeminate and a man who allowed himself to be governed by his mother, he was despised, and the army conspired against him and killed him.

Reviewing these behaviors now with the contrasting ones of Commodus, Severus, Antoninus Caracalla, and Maximus, you will find that all of them were cruel and greedy. These people, in order to satisfy their soldiers, did not hesitate to inflict any kind of injury on the people. Yet, all of them, except for Severus, had a bad ending.

There was so much courage in Severus that, even by supporting the soldiers and oppressing the people, he was always able to rule peacefully because his virtue made him admirable to both the soldiers and people. The people were kept in awe and astonishment of him, while the soldiers were respectful and satisfied.

Because the actions of this man, as a new prince, were great and notable, I would like to point out briefly how well he knew how to use the power of the fox and lion, whose natures, as I have said above, are important for a prince to emulate.

Since Severus knew about the laziness of Emperor Julian, he persuaded the army of Sclavonia, of which he was captain, to go to Rome to avenge the death of Pertinax, who had been killed by the Praetorian army. Under this pretext, without showing that he aspired to collect the seat of power, he moved his army against Rome.

He was already in Italy before the news of his departure spread. After he arrived in Rome, the parliament, out of fear, elected him as emperor and killed Julian. After this beginning, if Severus had wanted to be the ruler of the entire empire, he only had two challenges - one in Asia, where Niger, the master of the Asian army, had declared himself emperor and the other in the West, where Albinus also aspired to be emperor.

He saw the danger in declaring war with both of them, and he decided to attack only Niger and deceive Albinus. He wrote to Albinus, saying that since he had been elected by the parliament to be emperor, he wanted to share the honor with him. He sent him the title of Cesare and, by the decision of the parliament, accepted him as a co-emperor. Albinus believed all of this to be real. But Severus, after defeating Niger, killing him, and securing the East, came back to Rome and complained to the parliament that Albinus, hardly grateful for all the benefits he had received from him, had tried to kill him treacherously. Thus, it was necessary for Severus to find Albinus and punish him for his ingratitude. Then he went to find Albinus in France and took away his kingdom and life.

Anyone who closely examines the actions of this man would find him a very brave lion and a cunning fox. He will find him feared and respected by everyone and not hated by the army. It need not be surprising that Severus, as a new prince, was able to hold the empire so well because his courageous reputation protected him from the hatred that the people could have harbored against him for his atrocities.

His son, Antoninus, was a man of great power and quality. This made him admirable to the people and accepted by the soldiers. He was a military man, very capable of enduring every hardship and disdainful of all delicate food and other luxuries, earning him love from the army. However, his ferocity and ruthlessness were so great and unbelievable - after endless single murders, he killed a large number of the people of Rome and Alexandria. He became hated by the whole world and feared by those he had around him, so much so that he was murdered by a soldier in his army.

It should be noted here that such murders, which are deliberately done with resolve and desperate courage, are inevitable for the prince because they are done by those who do not fear death. However, a prince does not need to be so afraid of them because they are so rare. All the prince has to do is to be careful not to seriously offend the retainers serving under his rule. Antoninus was not careful about this. He had killed that soldier's brother and threatened him every day, yet he retained him as a bodyguard. As it turns out, this was a foolish thing to do and proved to be the end of the emperor.

Now let us come to Commodus, who held on to the empire with great ease because he won it by hereditary right as the son of Marcus. It was enough for him to follow in his father's footsteps and he would have satisfied both the people and the soldiers. But he was born with a cruel and stubborn temper. So as to practice his cruelty, he gave his soldiers too much freedom to treat people badly. In addition, he did not maintain the proper respect for his position, frequently descended into the halls to compete with soldiers and did evil deeds unworthy of being emperor. So he was despised by the soldiers, hated by this group, and despised by the other. He was conspired against and killed.

Now, it remains to discuss the character of Maximus. He was a very warlike man, and since the army was disgusted with Alexander's weakness, of which I spoke of above, they killed Alexander and elected Maximus as emperor. However, Maximus did not hold the thrones for too long because of two things that had him hated and scorned.

The first was that he came from the lower class, formerly a shepherd. Everyone knew this, and it brought him great disdain, for they considered it an unsuitable background for an emperor. The second was that when he officially became emperor, he deferred going to Rome to take possession of the imperial seat. He established a reputation for himself as being cruel since he had committed many cruelties through his representatives in Rome and everywhere in the empire.

Therefore, the whole world resented him for having a low status and feared his cruelty. Africa rebelled first, then the parliament, along with everyone in Rome, and all the people in Italy conspired against him. They were later joined by his own army, which after besieging the citadel of Aquileia and having difficulty in capturing it, were disgusted by his cruelty. Seeing as how many people were already against him, the army was not afraid of him any longer and killed him.

I do not want to discuss Heliogabalus, Macrinus, or Julian, who, because they were despised, were quickly assassinated. However, I will conclude this discussion by saying that princes in our time have less trouble with this difficulty of giving their soldiers too much satisfaction. Notwithstanding, one has to give them some form of indulgence. Yet, this is quickly settled because none of the princes has an army with the same experience in government and administration of parts of the empire as the army of the Roman empire. Then, if it was necessary to satisfy the soldiers rather than the people, it was because the soldiers could do more than the people. But now, it is more necessary for the princes, except the rulers of the Turk and Egypt, to please the people and not the soldiers because they are strongest.

As mentioned above, I excluded the ruler of the Turks because he always keeps around him twelve thousand infantry soldiers and fifteen thousand cavalry soldiers to defend and secure the kingdom. It is necessary for that ruler to put aside all consideration for the people and remain affable with the soldiers. The kingdom of Egypt is similar. Being completely in the hands of the soldiers, the ruler, without worrying about the people, must keep the soldiers as his friends.

One must note that the kingdom of Egypt is unlike any other kingdom because it is similar to being ruled by the Pope and cannot be called a hereditary or new monarchy. The sons of the old prince do not become the heir but remain noblemen. Anyone who becomes king is elected to that position by those who have the authority for it. Therefore, this being an old custom, cannot be called a new monarchy because some of the difficulties of the new monarchy cannot be met here. Even if the prince is new, the customs of the nation are old and framed to receive him as if he were its hereditary ruler.

However, let us return to the main issue. I say that anyone who carefully considers the discourse above will deduce that resentment and contempt have led to the ruin of the emperors mentioned above. Additionally, we also see why, although some princes ruled in one way and others in the other, they all had tragic endings except one.

It was useless and dangerous for Pertinax and Alexander, being new princes, to imitate Marcus as he was the hereditary prince. Likewise, it was disastrous for Caracalla, Commodus, and Maximinus to imitate Severus, as they did not have as much courage to allow them to follow in his steps.

Therefore, a new prince in a new kingdom cannot imitate the actions of Marcus or follow those of Severus. But he should take the necessary parts from Severus to establish his kingdom and from Marcus, those which are useful and glorious to keep his already established kingdom safe and secure.

Chapter 20

Whether Citadels And Many Other Things The Prince Used Are Useful Or Useless

Some princes, to keep the kingdom safe, have disarmed their subjects; some have kept their population divided into faction towns; some have fostered opposition against themselves; others have tried to win over those who were originally against their government; some have built citadels; others have knocked down and destroyed citadels. No one can make a final judgment on all this unless one knows the details of the state for which one has to make such a decision. However, I will speak as comprehensively as possible about these matters.

There has never been a new prince who has disarmed his subjects. On the contrary, whenever he has found them unarmed, he has always armed them. For when they are armed, those arms become yours; those who used to be mistrustful become loyal, and those who were loyal remain the same; from your subjects, they become your loyalists. Although not everyone can be armed, when those who you do arm benefit, the others can be dealt with more freely.

Although the treatments are different, they fully understand. Those who are armed become your supporters, and those who aren't armed, accepting that those who have more dangerous responsibilities should have the highest reward would excuse you.

On the contrary, when disarmed, the prince insults them by showing that he does not trust them, either out of cowardice or for want of loyalty. Both of these prejudices create hatred against the prince, and because he cannot be unarmed, he has to turn to the worthless mercenaries, as I have discussed. Even if the mercenaries are good, they wouldn't be good enough to protect the prince from powerful enemies and untrustworthy citizens. Therefore, as I have said, a new prince in a new kingdom must always create arms there. History is full of such examples.

But when a prince occupies a new kingdom and adds it to his old one, it is necessary for him to disarm the newly conquered people, except those who helped the prince occupy the territory. These people, also, with time and opportunity, should be rendered weak and cowardly. Matters need to be managed in such a way that those who are armed in the state are only the prince's soldiers, who were raised in the old kingdom.

Our ancestors, and those who were considered wise, were accustomed to saying that it was necessary to keep Pistoia by creating opposing factions and Pisa by citadels. With this idea in kind, they encouraged quarrels in some of the acquired towns to keep them divided and easier to secure. This may have been a good idea to do during those times when Italy was balanced, but I do not believe that it should be recommended as a present-day rule. I do not believe that opposing factions could be of any use. On the contrary, in the event of an enemy attack, the divided cities are immediately lost because the weakest group will always support the external force, and the other will not be able to resist.

The Venetians, affected, as I believe, by the above reasons, encouraged the Guelph[37] and the Ghibelline factions in their acquired cities. Although they never allowed the people to kill each other, the Venetians nurtured these quarrels among the people so that the subjects, caught up in their differences, could not unite against them. This, as we have seen, did not work out according to their plan later, for when the Venetians were defeated at Vaila, one of the factions immediately became daring and took over the whole nation.

Such methods showed the prince's weakness because these opposing factions would never be allowed in a strong kingdom as they are only useful to the prince when there is peace. But when war comes, such a policy will only be a mistake.

Certainly, princes become great when they overcome the difficulties they face, and therefore fortune, seeing that a new prince more than a hereditary prince needs to prove himself great, creates enemies and plots against him, so that he has an opportunity to overcome them and rise higher than the difficulty caused by his enemy. For this reason, many believe that a wise prince, when he has the opportunity, should encourage some enmity against himself so that when he crushes them, it increases his prestige.

Princes, especially new princes, have found more loyalty and assistance in the men who were initially distrustful of him at the beginning of his rule than those who trusted him at first.

Pandolfo Petrucci, Prince of Siena, ruled his country by people who were initially distrustful of him than others. However, on this subject, one cannot generally speak because it varies a lot according to the person. I will only say that the prince would always be able to win over those who were initially hostile to his government if they have qualities that require them to depend on others for support. They will be bound to serve the prince more faithfully because they know that it is essential for them through their actions to change the bad opinion that the prince must have of them. Therefore, by employing these people, the prince would have more usefulness from them than if he would have from those who, while serving him enjoy a secure position, would neglect their work.

Since the matter calls for it, I will not forget to warn the prince, who by means of secret favors acquired new territory, to carefully consider the reasons why they moved to support him. If it was not a natural feeling of affection to him but a result of the dissatisfaction with their old government, then it will be hard for him to remain in their good graces because he wouldn't be able to satisfy them. Carefully considering the reasons for this, with examples taken from ancient and present affairs, we will find that it is easier for the prince to remain in the good graces of those who were satisfied with the old government and therefore his enemies than those who, because they were dissatisfied with the old government, supported and helped him to seize their state.

It is a custom of princes, who wish to keep their kingdoms more secure, to build citadels as a warning to those who might plan to attack them and as a place of refuge from sudden attack. I commend this system because it has been used in the past.

Nonetheless, in our time, Nicolò Vitelli[38] has destroyed two citadels in Citta di Castillo to acquire that territory. Guido Ubaldo, the duke of Urbino, when he returned to his kingdom after being chased away by Cesare Borgia, destroyed all the citadels there down to the foundations and assumed that without them, it would be very difficult to lose his territory again. Bentivogli, returning to Bologna, made a similar decision.

Whether the citadel is, therefore, useful or not depends on the circumstances, for if it's good for one thing, it may bad for another. With this issue, one may further reason that any prince who is more afraid of his subjects than of foreign invades ought to build a citadel, but one who is more afraid of foreigners than his people has no need to build one.

The Milan citadel built by Duke Francesco Sforza has caused more trouble for him and his family than any other rebellion in the state. For this reason, the best stronghold is not to be hated by the people. Although the prince can keep the fortresses, they will not do much to protect the prince if the hearts of the people resent him. This is because there will always be foreign invaders to support the people when they rebel against the prince.

In our times, we do not see the citadel having any effect on the prince except in the case of Countess Forli[39] when the duke Girolamo, her husband, was killed. With the stronghold, she was able to resist the famous attack while waiting for help from Milan, and, thanks to that, she kept the country. The situation at that time was that the foreign countries could not support the people. However, the strongholds were of no value to her later when Cesare Borgia attacked her and when her hostile subjects were supported by foreigners. So, both before and after, she would be having been safer not being hated by the people than to have citadels.

So having considered all of this, I will praise those who build citadels as well as those who do not. But I would blame anyone who, trusting them, has little regard for the resentment of the people.

Chapter 21

How The Prince Must Behave To Be Famous

Nothing makes the prince more famous than his great achievements and exemplary gestures. In our day, there is Ferdinand of Aragon, the present King of Spain. He could almost be called a new prince because he successfully and glorified himself from an insignificant king to become one of our most famous monarchs in the world. If we look closely at his actions, we will find all of them are wonderful, and some are extraordinary.

As soon as he ascended the throne, he attacked Granada, and this was the foundation of his success. Initially, he quietly did this and did not have any fears of others being against him because he kept the mind of the Castile preoccupied, and while thinking of the war, they didn't innovate.

Therefore, they were not aware that with these actions, he was exerting power and authority over them. He used the money of the church and the people to sustain his army, and because of the long war, he laid the foundation for military skills, which has since made him stand out.

In addition, he always used religion as a justification for larger schemes. He applied cruel policies to push people out of the Moors[40] kingdom. We cannot find a more admirable or rare example than that. Using the same excuse, he invaded Africa, waged war in Italy, and eventually attacked France.

Therefore, his achievements and plans have always been great and kept the mind of his subjects in admiration and occupied with the outcome. He continued from war to war, leaving his subjects not enough time to think about opposing him.

It is very helpful in the rule of the kingdom if a prince acts extraordinary, similar to what was told about Bernabo da Milano.[41] When he had the opportunity as a civilian to do something extraordinary, either for good or bad, he always had a unique way of rewarding or punishment that got people talking. A prince should, above all else, strive in every action to be famous for being great and remarkable.

A prince is also respected when he is a true friend or an absolute enemy; this is when without hesitation, he declares himself for one side against the other. This is always more advantageous than being neutral. If the two neighboring powers fight and one of them becomes victorious, the prince must either fear them or not.

In either case, it would always be beneficial for the prince to assist one of them to actively wage war. If the prince does not declare himself, he will fall prey to the conqueror. Then, the loser will be pleased and happy. As for the prince, there is no reason to ask for help, nor anything to protect or shelter him. For whoever wins will not want people he doubts would help in difficult times, and the loser will not be willing to protect him because the prince was not willing to bring his troops to share his fate.

Antiochus went into Greece and was sent by the Aetolians to drive away the Romans from Greece. He sent messengers to the Achaeans, who were friends of the Romans, urging them to remain neutral. On the other hand, the Romans urged them to take up arms. This matter was discussed in the Aetolians assembly, where the Antiochus representatives called them to be neutral. To this, the Roman representative replied, "As for that which has been said, that it is better and more favorable for your country not to interfere in our war, nothing could be more wrong. Without interference, your country will be abandoned and will become the conqueror's prize."

So it always happens that the people who are not your friend will ask for your neutrality, while your friends will beg you to hold your weapon by their side. The weak princes, in order to avoid the present danger, often go neutral and are often defeated. But when the prince bravely declares in favor of one side and if his side wins, even though the conqueror may be strong and have the prince at his mercy, he would still be indebted to the prince, and a friendship is established.

Men can never be so lowly that they become a symbol of ungratefulness by oppressing the prince. Victories, after all, are never so clear that the winner must not show some regard, especially justice. But if one who the prince supports is defeated, the prince will be protected by them, and when it is possible, he may assist the prince and they both become companions on a fortune that may come again.

In the second case, when the two neighboring powers go to war but the prince does not feel threatened by whoever wins, it is even of more importance for the prince to support one side. By so doing, the prince helps to sabotage one side by helping the other. With the prince's necessary help and interference, the winner will always be indebted to him.

However, it must be noted here that the prince should never ally himself with someone stronger than him to fight someone else unless absolutely necessary. As said before, if he wins, he becomes his prisoner. A prince must avoid, as much as he can, being in a position of indebtedness to anyone.

The Venetians joined the French against the Duke of Milan, against all better judgment, and it caused their destruction. However, when it is unavoidable, as it happened to the Florentines when the Pope and Spain sent troops to attack Lombardi, then in this case, for the above reasons, the prince must assist one of the parties.

No government should imagine that it can choose a completely safe course; rather, let it expect to always have doubtful ones. For in the natural order of things, one should always foresee that in seeking to avoid one obstacle, we always run into another. The best course of action is to know how to characterize problems and choosing the less evil option.

A prince should also show himself to be a lover of talent, giving recognition to talented men and honoring those who are skilled in the arts. At the same time, he should encourage his citizens to do their jobs peacefully, both in commerce and in agriculture and in every other sector. That way, the people do not need to worry about increasing wealth for fear that their possessions are taken away or worry about opening a trade for fear of taxes. The prince should reward anyone who wants to do these things that would bring honor to his city or country.

In addition, the prince must also organize festivals and ceremonies for the people's entertainment at appropriate times of the year. Every city is divided into commercial or social unions. The prince oughts to respect such groups and sometimes even associate with them to show himself as a prime example of good and generous behavior. However, he should take care to always maintain his rank.

Chapter 22
Of The Prince's Personal Staff

The choice of personal staff is very important to the prince. Whether they are good or not depends on the prince's discrimination. The first impression that one gets of a prince is by observing those around him. If they are capable and loyal, the prince can be considered wise because he already knows how to recognize their abilities and keep them loyal. But when they were the opposite, people would unfavorably criticize the prince for the grave error that he made in choosing the wrong person.

Everyone who knew Antonio da Venafro[42] as the minister of Pandolfo Petrucci, the prince of Siena, considered Pandolfo to be a very smart person to have Venafro in his staff. The human mind has three types. The first one understands things by itself, the second has to listen to explanations to understand, and the third doesn't self-understand nor understand when it is explained. The first is the best, the second is good, and the third is useless.

It follows, therefore, that Pandolfo, if not necessarily the first, is definitely second. He had the judgment to know the good and the bad when it was said and done, and although he may not have the initiative himself, he could recognize the good and the bad in his employees. He praised the good and corrected the bad. Therefore, they could not hope to deceive him but were kept honest.

But how does a prince know the qualifications of his employees? There is an experiment that never fails. When a prince sees an employee thinking more about his own interests than prince interests and searching for his own profits in everything, such a person never makes a good servant. The prince could never trust him either, because he who has the responsibility of another in his hands should never think of himself but always of the prince and never pay attention to matters that the prince does not care about.

On the other hand, to keep his servants honest, a prince must reward, honor, enrich, be kind, share his glory, and care for them. At the same time, he must show them that they cannot stand alone. So that receiving a lot of honors will not make them want more, much wealth does not make them desire more, and many burdens make them afraid of changes. Once the relationship between the prince and the servants is kept at that level, they can trust each other. Otherwise, the end is always destructive, either for one or the other.

Chapter 23

How To Avoid Flatterers

I don't want to leave out an important matter because it is a difficult danger for the princes to watch out unless they are very careful and discerning. These are the flatterers that every court is filled. Because people are so wrapped up in their own affairs or deceived within them, it is difficult to protect themselves from this danger. If they want to protect themselves, they risk being despised. The only way to protect oneself from flattery is for people to understand that letting the prince know the truth is not offensive. However, when everyone feels free to speak the truth, the prince's respect fades away.

Therefore, a wise prince should hold a third method by choosing wise people in the country and giving only them the freedom to speak the truth. Even then, they can only speak the truth of the things the prince asks and not say anything else. But the prince should ask them about everything and listen to their presentation, and afterward, he can conclude himself. With these councilors, both individually and collectively, the prince must behave in such a way that each of them should know that the more freely they speak, the more they will be preferred. Outside of this group, the prince doesn't need to listen to anyone but pursue what has been settled and stick to his decision. Any prince who does otherwise will be buried in his career by flattery or often changes his mind because of different opinions and be laughed at.

I want to give a modern example of this. Fra Luca, the servant of Maximilian[43], the current emperor, said of the emperor, "The emperor did not listen to anyone's opinion, nor did he do his own." This happened because he followed a method that was the opposite of the way above. The emperor is a secret man - he does not communicate his plans to anyone, nor does he accept anyone's opinion. However, in putting them to practice, the plan is revealed and known. They are debated by those around the emperor; when they protest, he is immediately dissuaded from doing them. Therefore, the things he does today would be undone the next day without anyone understanding what he wanted to do and no one can rely on his decisions.

So the prince must always listen to advise, but only when he wants, not when others want it. He must make it clear that he does not want advice unless asked. However, he must constantly ask questions and then be a patient listener about what he asks. Also, knowing that anyone, on any matter, has not told the prince the truth, he should let his anger be felt.

There may be some who think that a prince can be wise not because of his own abilities but because he has good advisers around him. Such a belief is clearly false, for an unwise prince would never take good advice unless, by chance, he completely entrusted full control over to a brilliant and intelligent courtier.

Indeed, in this case, the prince may be well governed, but it wouldn't be long, as such an eminent person would depose him within a short time.

If an unwise prince takes advice from many people, he always takes different advice, and he won't know how to handle it. Each advisor will think about his own interests and the prince will not know how to control or observe them. This is obvious since people always want to deceive the prince unless they are bound by a necessity to be honest. Hence, good counsel, from wherever it comes, is the result of the prince's wisdom. Not that the prince's wisdom comes from good advice.

Chapter 24

Why The Italian Princes Lost The States

The recommendations in the above chapters, if they are carefully observed, will allow a new prince to be well established in his kingdom and strengthen his status in his kingdom, than if he had ruled for a long time. This is important because the actions of a new prince are observed more often than those of a hereditary prince.

When the new prince is considered capable, he attracts more people, and they are more loyal than the ancient princes. This is because people are more attracted to the present than the past and when they find good in the present, they enjoy it and don't seek more. They will also strongly defend the prince if he does not harm them in other matters. So it will be a great glory for the prince to have formed a new kingdom and made the country rich with good laws, good troops, good allies and good leadership. Likewise, it will be a great contempt for those born as princes to lose their country for their lack of wisdom.

If we look at the princes who lost their kingdoms in Italy during this era, such as the King of Naples, the Duke of Milan, and others, we will find in them, first and foremost, a common problem involving poor troops from the causes discussed at length above. Second, we will see that some of them were hated by the people, or if being loved by the people did not know how to leverage it against the nobles. For in the absence of these problems, the kingdoms with enough strength to keep an army in the field cannot be lost.

Philip[44] of Macedon did not have a great kingdom compared to the greatness of the Romans and the Greeks who attacked him. However, because he knew how to lead armies, attracted the hearts of the people, and protected himself against the nobles, he maintained the war against his enemies for many years. In the end, he lost some of his cities, but he kept his kingdom.

Hence, our princes should not blame fate for losing their power after years of possession but rather their own laziness. In peaceful times, they never thought that times could change (it's a common human weakness that in peace, no one thinks to prepare for a storm). When chaos came, they only thought of running away instead of protecting themselves. They hoped that the subjects, who were disgusted with the attitudes of the conquerors, would call them back. This, when other things fail, might be good, but it's a bad thing to ignore all the other factors to choose this course. For one should never let go in the belief that someone else would pick everything back up. Whether it happens or not, it is not good for the prince's security because being saved is of no use except by your own effort. The only reliable, sure, and sustainable way is to depend on yourself and your courage.

Chapter 25

Effects Of Human Fate And How To Fight It

It is not unknown to me how many have had, and still have, the idea that the affairs of the world are governed by destiny and God. That humans, with their wisdom, cannot direct themselves, and no one can even help them. Because of this, they don't think they need to do much work but let fate rule them. This opinion gets more credit in our time because major changes have been seen and can still be seen, each of these, beyond all human predictions. Sometimes thinking about this, I am somewhat inclined to their opinion. However, in order not to destroy our free will, I believe destiny determines half of our actions. But destiny will leave us half or perhaps a little less to control.

I compare destiny to one of the violent rivers, which, when in floods, cover the plains, wipe out trees and homes, and carry soil from one place to another. Everything flies in front of it, all destroyed by its violence, without any way of resisting. Yet, though it is its nature, it does not follow that men, after the weather became quiet, shall not make provisions to build canals and defenses so that in the future, when the water level rises, we could direct them away and its destructive power is no longer raging and dangerous. Destiny is also like that; it exposes its power to people where there is no preparation to resist. It exerted strength where it knew that the walls had not been raised to limit it.

Now, if we look closely at Italy, the center of change that has given it some strength, we will see it as an open field without barriers and defenses. If Italy had been protected with the same courage as Germany, Spain and France, then this invasion would not have made such great changes or it would not have happened. This I have covered enough to talk about the resistance of fortune in general.

Now, getting to the point, a prince can see the glory of today and be destroyed tomorrow without having him change his nature or character. This, I believe, arises primarily from the causes that have been discussed at length, namely, that the prince who firmly believes in fate will lose his throne when the situation changes. I also believe that the prince will be successful if he directs his actions to the spirit of the times, and if his actions are not in accordance with the spirit of the times, he will not succeed.

People gain fame and wealth by various methods - either with caution or with haste, either with force or with talent, either by patience or its opposite - and each person succeeds in achieving their goal in a different way. One can also see that out of two people who are cautious, one may achieve his results, and the other fails. Likewise, two people may equally be successful, one by being cautious, the other by taking risks.

All these differences arise from nothing else except whether or not they follow their methods in the spirit of the times. This is true of what I said that two people working differently deliver the same effect and two people doing the same thing, one will achieve the goal and the other will not.

Changes in state affairs also come from this. If the prince behaves cautiously and patiently, the time and circumstances come together properly to make sure he succeeds, and his destiny is achieved. But if times and circumstances change, he will be destroyed if he does not change his way of acting. But often, people are not smart enough to know how to adapt themselves to change. This is because the prince cannot deviate from what nature wants him to do and also because, having always prospered by acting in one way, he cannot be convinced that it is better to change. So a cautious prince, when it's time to become daring but not knowing how to, is destroyed. If he knows how to go with the times, his fate will not change.

Pope Julius the Second worked boldly and enthusiastically in all of his works. Times and circumstances matched those actions very well, so he was always successful. Consider the first campaign he took against Bologna when Messer Giovanni Bentivogli was still alive. The Venetians did not agree with him, neither did the king of Spain, and he still had the campaign to discuss with the French king. However, he single-handedly put it in motion with his boldness and fervor - a move that left Spain and the Venetians indecisive and passive. The Venetians due to fear and the Spaniards from a desire to recover the kingdom of Naples.

On the other hand, he pulled the French king to join because the king, having observed the movement, and wanting to turn the Pope into his friend and humiliate the Venetians, found that he could not deny him. Consequently, Julius, with his daring act, achieved what no pope other than simple human intelligence could do. If he had waited in Rome until he could go with his plans arranged and everything fixed, as any other pope would have done, he would never have been successful. Because the French king would have invoked thousands of reasons, and others would have raised thousands of fears.

I will put aside his other actions since all were the same and all were successes; for the shortness of his life, he did not let him experience the opposite. However, if circumstances had arisen that would have made it necessary for him to behave cautiously, then his ruin would come, for he would never deviate from his innate qualities.

I conclude, therefore, that fate can change, and people act fixed on their instincts, as long as both are in agreement, then men will be successful but would fail without agreement. In my opinion, I think the risk is better than caution because fate is like a woman; if you want her to be submissive, you must firmly resist and treat her poorly. She allows herself to be mastered by risky actions rather than those who treat her coolly. Fate, therefore, always like women, is a lover of young men because they are more reckless, violent, and always daring to command boldly.

Chapter 26

An Exhortation To Free Italy From The Barbarians

After thinking about what I discussed above, I wondered if the present moment in Italy is right for a new prince and if there are any factors that give a wise and virtuous person a chance to introduce a new order to bring honor to him and goodness to the people of this country. I think a lot of things have come together to support a new prince that I don't know what will ever have a more convenient opportunity than now.

As I said, if it was necessary for the Jews to be in chains so that Moses' mission would be clear; that the Persians had to be oppressed by the Medes to discover Cyrus' heroic temperament; and the Athenians had to scatter in order to illustrate the talent of Theseus, then, at the present time, in order to discover the virtue of an Italian spirit, it was necessary for our country to be in the trouble she is in right now. That Italy should be more enslaved than the Jews, oppressed than Persians, more dispersed than the Athenians - with no leadership, without order, bullied, exploited, torn, invaded - and to have endured severe griefs of bad times.

Although there have also been some characters lately of hope, leading us to think that they were chosen by God to save us, however, as seen, they were later rejected by fate. Thus, Italy exists as a soulless nation, waiting for some hero to heal her wounds, to end the destruction and exploitation in Lombardi from deception, fraud, and taxation of the kingdom of Tuscany, and to clean the country's festering wound. The entire people seem to be pleading with God to send a world-saving hero to destroy all the barbarians. The people are willing and eager to follow the waving flag if anyone would raise it.

Currently, in Italy, there is no one else who people can hope more than in your[45] aristocratic house, with its courage and fortune, favored by God and the Church, of which it now rules, surely it can head this national restoration. It wouldn't be difficult if you can remember the actions and lives of the people I have outlined in this book. Even though they were great men, they were just human beings and each of them did not have as many opportunities as the present. For their campaigns were neither more just nor more permissive than this, nor was God more their friend than He is yours.

There is great justice on our side because war is just to whom it is necessary and the weapons are blessed when there is no hope other than them. Here there is the greatest willingness, and where there is willingness, the difficulties are easy to overcome if you just follow the example of those that I bear witness to. In addition to this, the miraculous signs of God are evident in the divided sea, a leading cloud, water pouring out of rocks, and rain of food from heaven. Everything has contributed to your greatness; you must do the rest. God is not willing to do anything to take away our free will and share in the glory of what is ours.

Unsurprisingly, none of the aforementioned Italians has been able to achieve all that is awaiting from your glorious lineage. During many revolutions in Italy and many wars, the spirit of the martial arts was almost always suppressed. This happened because the old regimes were rotten, and none of us knew how to find a new one. There is nothing more glorious for you than setting new rules when you first ascend the throne. Such things, when they are established and appropriate, will make you loved and admired, and in Italy, there are plenty of opportunities to do so.

Although we lack leadership, our limbs are strong. Take a closer look at individual duels and hand-to-hand combats to see the Italian excellence in strength, speed, and skill. But when it comes to the army, they are hopeless. This is purely the result of poor leadership since those who are capable do not obey. Everyone thinks they were capable since no one stood out from the rest, both by talent or fortune. Thus over a long period of time and in the course of fighting for the past twenty years, whenever there was an army, Italy was completely defeated. The first example of this is Taro II and is followed by Alexandria, Capua, Genoa, Vaila, Bologna, and Mestri.

So if you want to imitate the heroes who saved their country, what is needed first is the real foundation for every campaign, providing your own forces; for then will you have a loyal, true, and perfect army. Although each of them is good individually, together, they are better, directed, cherished and nurtured by their own prince. Hence, it is necessary to form an army so that you could defend against foreign aggression with the courage of the Italians.

Although the Swiss and Spanish troops can be considered very strong, there is a weakness in both, by which a third force would not only be able to oppose them but might be relied upon to overthrow them. For the Spaniards, it is impossible to fight cavalry soldiers and the Swiss were afraid of infantry soldiers in close combat whenever they clash. Due to this, as was and can be seen again, the Spaniards cannot resist the French calvary and the Swiss are defeated by the Spanish infantry. Although complete evidence of the latter cannot be shown, there is, however, some evidence of it in the battle of Ravenna, when the Spanish infantry faced German soldiers, who fought in the same way as the Swiss. The Spaniards, through their skill, speed and with the help of their wooden shields, stormed under the spear of the Germans without any danger, able to attack while the Germans were forced to stand still. If the cavalry hadn't struck quickly, it would have been over for the Germans. Maybe, therefore, knowing the weaknesses of both types of soldiers, we will invent a new army that can withstand the cavalry's attack and not be afraid of the infantry. This does not need to create a new army but a change in the old ranks. These are the types of improvements that bring fame and power to a new prince.

Hence, this opportunity for letting Italy see their liberator appear should not be overlooked. Nor can one fully express the love he would receive in all the regions of Italy that has endured so much from foreign invaders, with a longing for revenge, with strong conviction, with conscientiousness, and with tears. What door is not open to welcome you? Who would refuse to obey you? Who dares to be jealous to stop you? What Italian dares to refuse to honor you? The domination of barbarians has disgusted all of our people.

I sincerely implore your illustrious family to accept this mission with enthusiasm and hope to wage the fight to protect justice, to once again under your banner, bring our homeland glory, and under your leadership, what Petrarch wrote may come true:

> Take virtue against cruelty,
> The war will soon take off:
> For the old Roman courage did not die,
> Still warming in the hearts of Italians.

The Writing of

Lao Tzu
老 子

THE BOOK OF ETHICS
道德经

Blessing Peace

Written by
Lao Tzu
老子

Translated by
Tham Trong Ma

A Few Words

If a man writes a book, let him set down only what he knows. I have guesses enough of my own.

Johann Wolfgang von Goethe – *German poet, novelist, playwright, and philosopher*

This book should not be considered a book of ideas or one giving the difference between the forces of good or evil or the distinction between right and wrong. However, while it may touch on these subjects, those are not the foundation upon which this book is written. This should be considered a book of timeless principles that have been practiced for thousands of years. A personal study has been done on the principles inherent in this book, and the result has been outstanding. But it should also be known that as much as this book is generally available for everyone who wants to read it, it is not meant for everyone. Some may find problems understanding the concepts explained within the pages or the nuggets of wisdom that may be hidden to a layman due to writing style. To enjoy this book and the treasure within, one must bare their minds and give a critical view to the words, for the words are not just made up. Every line has a purpose.

This book is divided into two parts: The *Way* and the *Virtue*. While these two elements may seem mutually exclusive, to some extent, they are also similar. And this book is here to offer insights into them.

Some scholars have considered *Tao Te Ching (The Book of Ethics)* to be a compilation of various sayings; even the text authorship, date of compilation, and date of composition have been greatly debated. These subjects are still being debated even today. Researchers are working tirelessly to gather the facts, but this mystery might continue for many generations to come. However, there is no doubt that the book – or a major part of it, as the case may be – is hugely credited to Lao Tzu. And until a different fact emerges about the true authorship of *The Book of Ethics*, Tzu will continue to be known as the original author, which is most probably the truth anyway.

The oldest version of the book was dated as far back as the 4th century BC, when it was reported to have been excavated. However, some other dates emerged concerning the historical appearance of the book. Some have claimed that some parts of the text have been compiled later than the earliest portion of the *Zhuangzi*. A controversial manuscript about the *Tao Te Ching* inked on silk, which was reported to have been written in the 2nd century BC, has also been unearthed from Mawangdui.

The Book of Ethics is regarded as a fundamental text for philosophical and religious Taoism; indeed, it has strongly influenced other Chinese philosophy and religion schools. It also has a great influence on Legalism, Buddhism, and Confucianism. The text was largely translated and interpreted through the use of the Taoist concept when it was first introduced to China. Such professionals like artists, painters, poets, calligraphers, and gardeners have used *The Book of Ethics* as their source of inspiration.

Over the years, the book's influence has spread widely beyond the shores of East Asia; and it has held the title as one of the most translated works in world literature. It is no surprise that it has been translated into many widely spoke languages all over the world.

In the title, Tao Te Ching, *Tao* means 'way' in English or any of its close synonyms. However, the term was later extended to mean 'the Way". This term, *Tao*, and its meaning were later adopted by other Chinese philosophers such as Hanfeizi, Mozi, Mencius, and Confucius. The word, and its meaning, has its concept in Taoism, where it implied the essential process of the universe.

However, the *Te* in *Tao Te Ching* means 'virtue' which, of course, has further meanings with 'inners strength,' 'personal character,' or 'integrity'. Modern terms have also chosen it to mean 'goodness' or 'moral excellence'.

Now from the two words, the term *tao-te* means 'ethical principles', 'morality', 'morals', or 'ethics'. Then *ching* also has its own meaning, which, in this context, is 'great book', 'classic', or 'canon'; hence the general title *The Book of Ethics* – or, if to be named more appropriately, should be titled *The Great Book of Ethics*, but we feel *The Book of Ethics* is appropriate; there should be no reason for verbosity since everyone who has read it has agreed that it is indeed a great book.

Tao Te Ching can also be given other synonymous titles, such as *The Classic of the Way's Virtues, The Book of the Way and of Virtue,* or *The Book of the Tao and Its Virtue.* Some translations have been titled *The Tao and its Characteristics; The Classic Book of Integrity and the Way; The Canon of Reason and Virtue;* and *A Treatise on the Principle and Its Action.*

As everyone familiar with it knows, *The Book of Ethics* has a long and complex textual history. It has been claimed to have dated back to two millennia, including silk, paper, and bamboo manuscripts discovered in the twentieth century.

The original *Tao Te Ching* is a short text that contains not more than five thousand Chinese characters in 81 brief chapters; the structure has been carefully followed in this translation. However, there is some evidence that the chapter divisions later had some additions simply for the sake of commentary or as an aid for easier memorization. Besides all the adulterations, revisions, translations, and abridgments, the original text was still more fluidly organized. There was the *Tao Ching* that begins from chapter 1 to chapter 37, and followed by *Te Ching,* which continues from chapters 38 to 81.

As you will soon notice, even in this translation, the writing style is somehow concise and mysterious. All in all, the style is poetic. So while reading, you may feel that you are reading poetry. It is easy to get lost in the stanzas and lines, but the message will be fully received if you pay careful attention to the text. The writing style combines two major strategies – the first strategy creates memorable phrases, and the second forces the reader to reconcile supposed contradictions in the general work.

The original version, written in Chinese characters, contained three writing styles: the first style is in the *zhuànshū* (seal script) form; then another version was written in *lìshū* (clerical script) and then finally *kăishū* (regular script). These three styles have been maintained over millennia.

There have been many transmitted editions of *Tao Te Ching*, but there are three primary editions named after early commentaries. The first is the 'Yan Zun Version', which is just the extant of *Te Ching*, derives from a commentary attributed to Han dynasty scholars that went by the name Yan Zun. Then the second version is the 'Heshang Gong Version', which is named after the legendary Heshang Gong who lived during the reign of Emperor Wen of Han. The third version is the 'Wang Bi Version', which has a more verified origin than either the Yan Zun or the Heshang Gong. The man Wang Bi was a famous Three Kingdoms period philosopher on the *Tao Te Ching* and the *I Ching*.

In 1973, archeologists discovered copies of early Chinese books, known as Mawangdui Silk Texts, in a tomb dating from 168 BC. The texts have been associated with *Tao Te Ching*. Also, in 1993, the oldest known version of *Tao Te Ching*, written on bamboo tablets, was found in another tomb near the town of Guodian in Jingmen Hubei, and the text was dated before 300 BC. The Guodian Chu Slips has about 800 slips of bamboo with a total of 13,000 characters; 2,000 of those characters correspond with the *Tao Te Ching*.

The text in *The Book of Ethics* has thematic concerns with the Dao, otherwise known as 'Way', and how it is expressed by virtue. The book talks specifically about the virtues of naturalness and inaction, or non-action, as specifically referred to in the text.

Tao Te Ching has been translated over 250 times into Western languages, most of which are English, French, and German. According to Holmes Welch, "It is a famous puzzle which everyone would like to feel he had solved." It is hard to determine when *Tao Te Ching* was first translated to English, but the first English translation was publicly produced by John Chalmers, a Scottish Protestant missionary. He titled the book *The Speculation on Metaphysics, Polity, and Morality of the "Old Philosopher" Lau-size.*

However, translating *Tao Te Ching* didn't come easily to people; there were challenges. Since the text was written in ancient Chinese characters, some people had difficulty identifying some words' meanings. They only had to rely on the thematic approach of the general lines in the chapters before they could use suitable words to replace the ones they couldn't understand. Also, because there are no punctuation marks in Classical Chinese, it was difficult to determine where one sentence ended and where another began. So generally, it can be impossible to understand some chapters without moving sequences of characters from one place to another.

This particular translation has been made in the most straightforward and understandable way possible. I hope that you find this translation highly satisfying and refreshing.

Tham Trong Ma

About Lao Tzu

According to *History*, a book written by Tư Mã Thiên, Lao Tzu was from Khúc Nhân village, Khổ district, country of Sở. His family name was Lý, and his name is Nhĩ. He decided to rename himself Bá Dương and his nickname was Đàm. In his early days, he worked as a library keeper for the Zhou kingdom. It is predicted that he was born in 601 BC and resided in seclusion in 531 BC; he was 70 years old at that time.

According to legend, Lao Tzu was tired of the contemporary government, so he resigned from the library and rode the buffalo to hide. When he was passing through the gate, he met Doãn Hỷ, who was the gatekeeper at Hàm Cốc. Doãn Hỷ pulled him back and said: If you decide to stay in hiding, please write something for our descendants so that they may know what is happening in our world this time. Lao Tzu decided to put the gatekeeper's request into consideration. He stayed at the gate of Hàm Cốc and wrote the book called *The Book of Ethics* (Tao Te Ching). When he finished writing, he handed the book over to Doãn Hỷ and went into hiding. Since then, no one knows how and where he lived or died.

The only book Lao Tzu ever wrote was *The Book of Ethics*. This book was later divided into two parts consisting of 81 chapters. Part one has 37 chapters, talking about the Way and the second part has 44 chapters, talking about the Virtue. With a total of 5250 words in 1745 sentences, Lao Tzu denied and deconstructed the whole scale and organized the face of contemporary feudal society to construct a "non-existent" doctrine. *The Book of Ethics* advises people to live in harmony with nature, harmony with the universe, transform themselves and give up desire. He explained that if people and nature were in harmony, they would all be inanimate and desireless, so there was no need to fight and conquer. Therefore, humans will have peace, well-being, and happiness.

According to scholars today, *The Book of Ethics* is a spiritual book for those who follow the mystical and transcendent path. But objectively, one must recognize that the book is, first of all, a book written to urge the rulers and politicians to use the Way to rule the country. Lao Tzu was a sage who tried to bring ethics into politics, using his spiritual experiences to form a philosophical system.

Lao Tzu in *The Book of Ethics* also did not forget to advise politicians that if they know the Way, they do not need to take humanity, righteousness, courtesy, and wit to teach the people, just making them keep their simplicity with nature. The ideal society for Lao Tzu was a small country with few people. There was no need for deception, no need for civilization, no need for soldiers, no need for traffic, no need for luxury items. As long as one can eat fully, dress warmly, live peacefully, keep the custom of being gentle and courteous. So in chapter 80, he advised:

> *Food is simple but delicious.*
> *Cloth is rudimentary but beautiful*
> *The house is primitive but peaceful*
> *Tradition is pure but fun*

Lao Tzu is considered a semi-legendary figure in the entire Asian community. He was often portrayed as the contemporary of the powerful Confucius. However, some modern historians believed that Lao Tzu lived during the Warring States period of the 4th century BC; one could argue that it was the politics of war that inspired him to write the single book he wrote. The book, however, has been considered one filled with a lot of symbolism and deep meaning. Even Lao himself mentioned in his book that many people do not understand him and do not understand his teaching, so they do not know him. Even in his lifetime, before he left to live a life of isolation, Lao was often considered a strange person because of how he talked. He rarely spoke directly; most of his words were laced with deep meanings that required even deeper thoughts to understand, which is reflected in his writing. He was regarded as a sage (a very wise man).

It is hard to mention central figures of the Chines culture and not mention Laozi. He was claimed by both the emperors of the Tang dynasty and the modern people who have the Li as their original surname; these *Li* people often considered Lao Tzu as the founder of their lineage. The accuracy of this claim, however, is only speculative.

Even after thousands of years since it was written, Laozi's work is still being embraced by Chinese legalism and various anti-authoritarian movements.

A consensus emerged around the mid-twentieth century when some scholars claimed that Lao Tzu's history is doubtful and that *Tao Te Ching* does not refer to a single individual. Some claimed it to be a Taoist compilation of sayings written by many hands. The oldest text of the *Tao Te Ching* that has so far been recovered as part of the Guodian Chu Slips. The text was written on the slips of bamboo around the late 4th century BC.

The *Tao Te Ching*, according to some other scholars, was an otherwise name for Laozi. It has been considered the source and ideal of all existence. The theme of the writing is to lead students to return to their natural state in harmony with Tao.

A lot of people have been influenced by Laozi and his work. They have advocated a restrained approach to statecraft and humility in leadership, either for tactical ends or for ethical and pacifist reasons. On another hand, however, various anti-authoritarian movements have accepted the teachings of Laozi on its emphasis on the power of the weak.

In an article for the *Encyclopædia Britannica* of 1910, Peter Kropotkin considered Laozi as among the earliest proponents of anarchist concepts. In the same vein, David Boaz of the Cato Institute took a passage from *Ta-Te Ching* and included it into his 1997 book titled *The Libertarian Reader*. But a philosopher such as Roderick Long believed that libertarian themes in Taoist perspectives are originally from earlier Confucian writers.

Tham Trong Ma

Part I
The Way
道

1

The Way[1] that can be spoken of is not the way of truth
A name[2] that can be called is not an eternal one

Anonymous is before heaven and earth
Having a name is the mother of all species

Nonbeing, we infer mystery
Being, we recognize the quintessence[3]
The two elements mentioned above have the same origin
But contain different names

Both are deep
Deep in the deepest level
That is the door to the occult

2

Under the dome:
Knowing the beautiful because there is the ugly
Knowing the good because there is the evil

Being and non-being that are born together
Are sometimes difficult and easy to complement each other
Long and short compare together
High and low lean together
Sound and voice mingle together
Before and after chase each other[4]

So sages:
Act without moving
Teach without using words
Everything is spontaneously and can self-destruct

Create, but do not take over
Do, but don't count on
Succeed, then withdraw
Therefore, do not lose

3

Do not respect the meek,
Do not make people scramble.
Do not make the rare precious,
Do not make people steal.
Do not provoke desire,
Do not make people confused.[5]

Rule of the saint:
Makes people's mind empty, fill their stomachs
Weaken the heart and soul but make the bone strong
This often makes people mindless
Without desire
So intellecturists do not dare to bother
There is nothing that cannot be corrected by
following the Way.

4

The Way is empty but not used up
The deep Way is like the root of all species

The Way blunts the sharp
The Way unties the trouble
The Way softens the glare
The Way harmonizes with dust
The Way is dark but it seems to exist

I do not know who are the Way's children
But the Way appeared out
Before heaven and earth.[6]

5

Heaven and earth do not have kindness
Consider all species like stray dogs
Heartless saints
Treat everyone like a stray dog

Between heaven and earth
Like a fire pipe
Empty but endless
The more blow, the more dynamic

Many words, little value
Better keep this in mind.[7]

6

The Way is the eternal breath
The Way is a woman
Mother of beginning stage
The mother's gateway is the root of heaven and earth
Like a veil very hard to see
Using the Way will never dry out.[8]

7

Heaven is undying
Why is it undying?
Because Heaven does not live for itself
So Heaven is undying

Saint stands behind
So people push to the front
Saint stands outside
Therefore, get along with everyone
Act carefree
Then results come.[9]

8

The perfect one is like water
Water provides life for all things
Without competing with anything
Water lives where people hate
Therefore, suitable with the Way

Accommodation is humble
Thinking is deep
Treatment is forgiven
Talking is genuine
Assertiveness is fair
Working is competent
Action is timely

No contest, therefore no mistakes.

9

Better to lack a little than be too full
When the sharpening knife is too sharp, it will quickly become blunt
Houses are full of gold, and pearls are hard to keep
By pretending to be rich, one would harm himself

When done, retreat[10]
That is the Way of heaven

10

Keep body and soul together
Is it possible to keep them apart?
Pay attention to breathe to be soft
Can one become an infant?
Spiritual cleansing
Can the stain be gone?
Love people and rule country
Maybe not talented?

The heavengate opens and closes
Can be a female?
Through everything
Can't do anything?

Born and raised
Instructions without possession
Made without merit
Instruction without ruling
That is the root of the Way

11

Thirty wood sticks make up a cart axle
Emptiness then self-contained
Create soil into pot
The empty space of the pot is where it is used
Cut the doors and windows to make the house
The empty space in the house is used for living

The existence of things is wealth
The non-existence of things is what to use

12

Five colors make people's eyes blind
Five sounds make people's ears buzz
Five flavors make people's tongue lose taste
Chasing hunting horses makes people go crazy
Rare and precious possessions make one to degrade
Sage prays for full stomach
Not spectacular
Therefore, leave this, get that

13

Be open to humiliation
Accept bad luck like it's human destiny

What does "be open to humiliation" mean?
Reception is not important
But don't worry about loss or gain
It is called "be open to humiliation"

What does "accept bad luck like it is human destiny" mean?
Bad luck comes from one body
If not, where does that bad fortune come from?

Be precious to one's body like people
As people believe one's body in everything
Love this world like one's body
Then one can fulfill everything.[11]

14

Look but not seeing because of formlessness
Listen but not hearing because of soundlessness
Get it but can't keep it because of being inanimate
Those three things cannot be traced
Because they are one

Above, do not illuminate
Underneath, do not overshadow
Far away from being great
Can not describe

Then back to nothing
The form of the formless
The shadow of the shadowless
That is called indescribable, non-visualizable

Standing in front, one can't see the head
Following, one can't see the tail
Keeping the Way of the past in harmony with present
Knowing primitives is the precepts of the Way

15

In ancient times, one skillfully practiced the Way
Then delicate, mysterious, profound and enthusiastic

We are deeply unpredictable
Because people can't guess
So people are forced to describe his looks
Cautious like one crossing the river in winter
Calm like one in times of danger
As polite as when welcoming guest
Soft as when ice melts into water
Rustic like untouched wood
Deep hollowlike cave
Nebulous like muddy water

Who can wait for the nebulous water to settle?
Who can remain still until the moment of action?

The Way users don't want to be filled
Don't want to be full so one can change without being sacked

16

Make it all empty
Keep your mind calm

All species born and pass away
Then go back to the original source[12]
Returning to the origin is stillness
It is according to the law of nature
The natural law is immutable

Knowing the circulation of heaven and earth is lucid
Do not know the circulation of heaven and earth is dark

Knowing the circulation is lucid
Lucid, then the soul is exuberant
Exuberant, then behave fairly
Fairness is everywhere
Everywhere is suitable with nature
Suitable with nature is suitable with the Way

Being one with the Way is the true Way
Even when the body dies, the Way remains

17

If the king is superior, the people only know the people
Lower, the people love and praise
Lower than that, the people are afraid
Lowest, the people are contempt

The sage says little
Quiet, why value words?

Work is accomplished
Things are done
People said: "They do it themselves"

18

When great Way is forgotten, benevolence appears
When wisdom and talent are born, lies appear
When the family is in conflict, good man appears
When the country is in turmoil, loyal ministers appeared[13]

19

Eliminate intellectual, discard knowledge
People benefit a hundred fold
Eliminate humanity, discard justice
People are blessed
Eliminate artistry, discard profit
Thieves and robbers dissipated

These three things are external manifestations
They are not sufficient enough by themselves
Should be more important:
The outside keeps rustic
Keep pure in mind
Less esoteric
Reduce longing

20

Eliminate learning, less worry
What is the difference between good and evil?
Why are we scare of what others are afraid of!
So immense, it is impossible to know

Everyone is as cheerful as enjoying buffalo feast
Like spring on the hill
I alone am silent
Like infant who cannot yet laugh
Hang down walking like a homeless

People have redundant
I alone am destitude
My mind is like a fool
How dumb!
People are all bright and sharp
My own as dark and dull

People like ocean wave
Personally, I do not know which way the wind is blowing

People are busy
My own boorish
I am different from people
I'm unlike from people
I treasure mother's milk to feed all species

21

Great Virtue practice is with the Way
The Way cannot be touched or captured
Cannot be touched or captured
But there's an image inside
Cannot be touched or captured
But there is category inside[14]

The Way is dim
But inside has a substance
This substance is very real
Which contains belief

From primitive to present
The Way is eternal
The Way is creation

How do we know that Way is the root of all creatures?
Because!

22

Concede is sure to win
Curvy is sure to straight
Low is sure to full
Worn is sure to new
Less is sure to more
More is sure to chaos

Sage embraces one to be an example for the world
Not showing off, should shine like the sun and moon

Not explain away, should stand out
Regardless merit, should be merited
Not brag, should not embarrassed
Not contest so no one contested

Because the ancients said that concede is sure to win
Must not be an empty statement?
To be completely honest, everything will follow

23

Nature is quiet

Strong wind does not blow the whole morning
Heavy rain does not fall all day
Why? Heaven and earth!
If heaven and earth can't do it
How can human do it?

One with the Way
Then becomes one with the Way
One with Vitue
Then become one with Virtue
One who lose the Way and the Virtue
Then become one with loss

When one is one with the Way
The Way welcomes one
When one is together with the Virtue
The Virtue is always there
When one is together with loss
Loss also follow one

One is disbelieved
Should not be believed

24

Tiptoe cannot stand firm
Long steps do not go far
Ostentatious is not illuminant

Self-important is not respected
Pompous does not achieve anything
Haughty cannot exist

The follower of the Way must stay away
from the above habits
Like leftover food
As unnecessary things

25

There is a mystery taking shape
Born before heaven and earth
Quiet and empty
Stand alone without changing
Mobile forever without getting tired
Probably the mother of all species
I don't know what to call it
So temporarily called the Way
Because the lack of nouns
So be called big

Because big, so be moving
Moving far away
Going far away, so come back

Therefore, "The Way is big
Heaven is big
Earth is big
Human is also big"

Those are the four big things in universe where human is one

Human follows the earth
The earth follows heaven
Heaven follows the Way
The Way follows nature

26

Heavy is the root of light
Static is the owner of the disturbance

The sage walks all day
Eyes do not leave the luggage
Though there is beauty to comtemplate
But still self-controlled and calm

Why does the king hold ten of thousand soldiers
and consider the court very light?
Because light is to lose oneself
And acting heavy is to lose control.[15]

27

Skilled walker leaves no footprints
Skilled talker does not miss words
Skilled mathematician does not need comparison

Skillfully close needs not locking
But no one can open it
Skillfully knot needs not tie
But no one can remove it

Sage takes care of everyone
Not missing one
Sage takes care of everything
Nothing missing anything
That is called: Bright hearted!

What is a good person?
The teacher of the bad person
What is the bad person?
It's for good person

If the teacher is not respected
And student does not loved
Though the talent is also confused
That is the pivotal point of the mystery

28

Know the male, keep the female,
Making streams for people.
Making streams for people,

Vitue does not leave
Return to the childhood

Know the light, keep the dark,
Be an example for the world.
Be an example for the world,
Vitue does not leave
Return to infinite

Know the honor, keep the humiliation,
Make a cave for the world.
Make a cave for the world,
Virtue is full
Return to the rustic

Rustic is not divided
Sage use to provoke hundreds of officials

So the great spell is not undercut

29

You want to bring people to reform?
I don't believe that is possible
People are holy
You cannot reform
Change is awry
Keep is lost

Sometimes things are in front, sometimes in rear
Sometimes the wind is hot, sometimes cold

Sometimes strong, sometimes weak
people sometimes is above, sometimes below

The sage avoids excess, luxury and complacency

30

Those who use the Way to help king
Do not rely on soldiers but submit to the world
Where the soldiers stomped, the thorns grew there
After winning big battle, there must be a crop failure

Skillful rescue only!
Do not rely on soldiers to be strong

Achieve results, not complacent
Not self boast, not elate
Because that is natural
When there is no violence

Losing power, so use violence
That is not the path of the Way
Acting opposite with the Way will soon be destroyed

31

Good weapons are ominous tools[16]
All species hate them
The gentleman respects the left side
The war user respects the right side

Weapon is an ominous tool
Gentlemen don't use it

Only used for reluctance
Peace is a precious thing
Victory is not rejoicing
Victory is rejoicing, is a ferocious man who likes to kill
Enjoy killing, one cannot satisfy people

Good works value to the left
Evil works value to the right
Vice general stands to the left
The general stands to the right
That is to take the funeral to judge

One should be grieving and sad because many people die
That is why when victorious
One performs the funeral

32

The Way is forever indefinable
Small and formless
Not to hold on
If King keeps it
All species obey
Heaven and earth bind
Drizzle rain falls
People do not need anyone to prevail but submit themselves

Once the Way is divided, the name creates
When name has enough
One would know how to stop
Know how to stop to avoid danger
The Way in the world like river water back to the sea

33

Knowing people is clever
Knowing oneself is lucid
Winning people is strength
Winning oneself is potent

Knowing enough is wealth
Working hard is an ambition
Keeping yourself will last long
Death without loss is called longevity

34

Great Way spreads everywhere
Move to the left, move to the right
Depended on by everything
Create without holding back
Work is accomplished, yet taking credit

The Way fosters all species without mastering
No desire so called small
All species come back without mastering
So called great

In the end, the Way doesn't receive as great itself
That is why it accomplished great thing

35

Keeping the great Way, the people will follow
Because the Way is a comfort and peaceful place

Passersby stops for music and food
But talking about Dao is dull and tasteless
Look but seeing
Listen but hearing
But using it does not end

36

Wanted contract, first stretch
Wanted weak, first strong
Wanted dump, first mania
Wanted receive, first give
It is: "The hidden object in the daytime"

Soft wins hard[17]
Big fish cannot leave the abyss
National vested interests cannot be displayed

37

The Way does not act
But nothing is not done
If king noticed this
Then everything will change itself
If one wants to do
Be simple and rustic

Invisible without desire
No desire, therefore undisturbed
This is the path to self-healing[18]

Part II

The Virtue
德

38

The highly virtuous people do not pray for virtue, they
already have virtue
The lowly virtuous people want virtue, so
they don't have virtue

The highly virtuous people do nothing
Yet nothing is undone
The lowly virtuous people always do
Yet many more things need to be done

The humane person works, not to let the job go unfinished
The righteous person works, the undone jobs are many
The polite person works, but no one responds

When the Way dies, the Virtue is born
When the Vitue dies, humanity is born
When humanity dies, the righteous is born
When the righteous dies, the polite is born

Politeness is a shell of disloyalty
The clue of chaos
Using mind to foresee is flashy of the Way
The clue of foolishness

High virtuous people live faithfully
Not respectful of politeness
On the fruit, not in the flower
One chooses this, but leaves that[1]

39

The old things are from One
Heaven is One, therefore clear
Land is One, therefore firm
Soul is One, therefore holy
Cave is One, therefore full
Everything is One, therefore alive
King is One, therefore the world is righteous
This is called Virtue of One[2]

Clear heaven prevents breaking
Firm land prevents cracking
Holy soul prevents dissipating
Full cave prevents dried up
Alive specie prevents destruction
Righteous king prevents collapse

Wealthy takes petty as the base
High takes low as foundation
King sees himself as orphan, widow, and useless
So is it petty as the base?
Isn't that so?
Therefore, being praised loses honor

Nonvociferant as jade
It is better to be disdainful like pebbles

40

Coming back is acting of the Way
Birth is the effect of the Way
The Way produces all things
Being is born out of being

41

Bright people who listen to the Way try hard to execute
Ordinary people who listen to the Way are in doubt
Dark people who listen to the Way laugh
There is no Way without laughter

So the old saying goes
The bright Way seems to be dim
Forward seems to be backward
Seeing easy seems difficult

The highest Virtue seems empty
Clear seems to be cloudy
Broad Virtue seemed helpless
Strong Virtue seems weak
Real Virtue seems virtual
The real square has no corners
Doing great things takes long
High pitch is hard to hear
Large shape seems without form

The Way is hidden without name
Only the Way has skillful birth and creation of all things

42

The Way gives birth to one
One gives birth to two
Two gives birth to three
Three gives birth to the universe[3]
Everything that carries negative holds positive
Combined, they are in harmony

The human hates orphan, widow, and useless ones
But the king sees himself like that
Therefore, his thoughts increase but also decrease
And thoughts decrease but also increase

The words that others promote and I also promote is
"Violent man has brutal death!"
That is the main point I recommend

43

The softest thing in the universe
Win the hardest in the universe
Empty can get into empty space because there is gap
So one knows the value of nothingness

Teaching without words is the benefit of inaction
Few people in this word can understand

44

Fame or fate: Which is more important?
Fate or asset: Which is more valuable?
Gain or loss: Which one hurts more?
Ambition is a loss
Containing many, loses much
Knowing enough is not disappointed
Knowing when to stop ikeeps one from danger
So one is forever sustainable

45

Perfectly good seems lacking
Its use is unending
Fully full seems empty
Its use is inexhausting

Straight seems crooked
Wise seems stupid
Good reasoning seems awkward

Action restrains cold
Inaction restrains hot
Inaction is the natural state of the universe

46

When people have the Way
Horses are used for farm work
When people do not have the Way
War horses are fighting outside the city

Catastrophy is nothing more than do not know enough
Harm is nothing more than endless greed
Because who knows enough is always enough!

47

Do not go out but know the world
Do not look out the window but see the Way
The more one goes, the less one knows

So a sage does not go out but knows
Do not only look but see
Do not only do but accomplish

48

Learn knowledge, then its increase
Learn the Way, then its decrease

Less, then more less
To reach the point of not doing
Because one does not do, so nothing is not done

People follow the natural law
But can not be annoying
If annoyed
The work will not be completed

49

A sage does not have a heart of his own
Get the heart of the world as his heart

One is good to good people
One is also good to those who are not good
Because Virtue is good
One believes those who believe
One also believes those who do not believe
Because Virtue is believing

Sage in the world is carefree
Harmony with everyone
So people look and listen
But sage sees them as children

50

Being born is called living
Coming back is called dead

Three-tenths live long
Three-tenths die prematurely
Three-tenths may live long but die early
Why?
Because they consider life is too heavy

People who knows how to nourish life are not afraid of rhinos or tigers
They fight without armor
Because rhino has no place to pierce horns
Tiger has no room to use its claws
The weapon has no room to penetrate
Why?
Because they don't fall into hazardous location[4]

51

The Way births
The Virtue nourishes
Thing shapes
Circumstances complete

Everything respect the Way, precious Virtue
No one says to respect the Way, precious Virtue
But that is the nature of all species

Therefore the Way births
Virtue keeps, nurtures, matures, ripes, protects, and buries

Born without receiving
Accomplish without holding
Raised without mastering
That is the miracle of Virtue[5]

52

Everything has origin
At the beginning of everything is the mother of all
Keeping the mother, one knows the child
Know the child, so one keeps the mother
Therefore, one should not in danger for lifetime

Close-lipped, hold breath
Life is full
Open-lipped, always busy[6]
Life is futile

Seeing hidden is bright
Hold strength is strong
Use Virtue to return to the Way
Do not let body be in trouble
Thus, the Way is eternal

53

If we have a little knowledge
One will walk on the main road and only fear losing the path
Keeping the main road is easy
But people love the short cut

When the court displayed its splendor
The farm fields are full of weeds
The food warehouse is empty
Courtiers are displayed in luxurious dresses
Wearing a sharp sword
Excess eating
Excess wealth
They are bandits
That is certainly not the road of the Way

54

Skilled plant, difficult to eradicate
Skilled grasp, difficult to slip
Virtue will be honored from generation to generation

Fix Virtue in oneself, Virtue will be real
Fix Virtue in the house, Virtue will have redundancy

Fix Virtue in the village, Virtue will grow
Fix Virtue in the country, Virtue will be in abundance
Fix Virtue in the world, Virtue will be everywhere

So, by oneself that considers other
By one's house that considers other houses
By one's village that consider other villages
By one's nation that conders other nations
By one's people that considers other people

How do we know what people are? Thanks for that!

55

People with deep Virtue like babies
Bees and snakes cannot spit poisonous nibs
Wild beasts cannot grab
Birds can't peck
Soft bones, weak tendons
But hold firm
Don't know how to have sexual intercourse between men and women but perfect
Vitality living in abundance
Screaming all day but not hoarse
That is called harmony

Knowing the harmony is invariant
Knowing invariants is bright

Greed is catastrophe

Keeping greedy is not harmony
Non harmony is opposite of the Way
Opposite of the Way is soon destroyed[7]

56

Those who know don't say
Those who say don't know

Fill the hole
Close the door
Break the sharp
Unravel tangle
Shield bright
Mix with dust
That is called sociable

Who understands this state
Then there is no longer a distinction between friends or foes
Beneficial or harmful, noble or despicable
This is the most precious person in the world[8]

57

Use the truth Way to rule the country
Use surprise to attack in battle
Do not fight but subdue the people

How do we know that?
Because of this:
The more laws forbid, the poor people become

The sharper the weapon,
The more turmoil the country becomes
The more talented people, the more mischief happens
The more laws, the more robbers

So sage:
One does nothing but people transform themselves
One is at ease, but the world is pure
One gives the laws, but people become rich
One does not pray lust, but people return to rustic[9]

58

Politics blurred, the people merely
Politics clearly, the people are cunning

Disaster is the fulcrum of blessing
Blessing hides under the shadow of disaster
Who can understand how disaster and blessing are?
They are not in a certain direction
Honesty becomes lying
Goodness becomes suspicious
Humans have been in a sodden for a long time!

So sage:
Sharp without hurting
Just without harm
Straight without offending
Bright without blinding

59

In caring for others and worshiping god
Nothing like restraint
Restraint begins with giving up one's will
This belongs to Virtue gained from experience
If you store a lot of Virtue, nothing can be undone
If there is nothing one can't undo, then there's no restraint
If there is no restraint, then one can cure the country
Knowing the root of country treatment is long-lasting
That is called deep roots, durable descent
That is the Wayto live long and see throughout

60

Treating a big country likes cooking a baby fish

If a sage uses the Way
Then the devil will not be efficacious
And deity can't harm people either
Not only can deity not harm people
Nor do sage harms people
The two sides do not harm each other
So Virtue kept coming back[10]

61

Big country seems to locate in low land
That is the gathering place of all species
Mother of all things

Females prevail over males due to their stillness
Take stillness as low place

Therefore, if a big country is humble with small country
Then it will conquer small countries
If small country is humble with big country
Then it will be protected by big country
So staying below to get it
Or staying below to be protected

Big country wants to accommodate many people
Small country needs many people to accommodate
Each side gets what they want
So the big country should learn to be humble

62

The Way is the root of all species
A treasure of good people
A place of refuge for bad people

Sweet words can buy fame
Doing good deeds can add respect
But if it's a bad person, why quit?

So on the day the king is crowned
To appointing three ministers
Two hands offered jade in front of the four-horse carriage
Better by kneeling in the mud to pray for the Way

Why do people in ancient times like the Way?

It's not what one is looking for?
And if guilty, one will be forgiven?
So the Way is the most precious to people

63

Action without moving
Do without getting your hands embedded
Taste the tasteless
Increase the small
Extra the few

Plan the hard work while still easy
Plan the big work while small or not yet present
Hard work in the world
Surely starts from easy
Big work in the world
Surely starts from small

Sages are not doing the big
So accomplishes the big

Empty promises, so believe few
Despise things, so face difficulty
Sage considers everything difficult
Therefore, no trouble[11]

64

Stillness is easy to grasp
Not yet form is easy to plan
Crisp is easy to break
Small pieces are easy to disperse
Prevent at yet present
Treat at yet chaos starts

Big tree as one hug
Born from a small seed
Nine-storey high floor
Erect from a crate of soil
Walking thousands of miles away
Starting with the first step

One who acts, fails
One who holds, loses
Therefore:
Sage doesn't act
Thereupon he doesn't fail
Doesn't keep
Thereupon he doesn't lose

Things often fail when they are about to be accomplished
Because not as cautious as at first
If the following caution is used as before, the job will not fail
So the sage avoids ambition
No precious desire
Just want to teach the uneducated
Bring people back to the Way

Helping things grow naturally
Therefore, one should not interfere with anything

65

The sage of the past, did not use the Way to enlighten the people
Only use the Way to make people honestly emanate

People of plots are difficult to rule
If one uses wit to govern the people, one will harm the country
If one does not use wit to govern the people, one will bless the people

Understanding these two things is understanding the law of heaven
Through these two spells, it is called legend Virtue
Legend Virtue is deep
Then everything is back to the original
Then it's compliance with nature[12]

66

River and sea are the king of hundreds of streams
Because you should be smart staying in the lower place
If one wants to be in the higher places in the world
One has to say humble words
If one wants to stand before the world
One has to step back

Therefore, sage:
Above, but people do not feel heavy
In front, but people do not feel obscured
So people worship without knowing boredom

Because no contest
So no one contested[13]

67

People say my Way is very big
There is nothing like the Way
If so, the Way is already small

There are three treasures that I always carefully
hold by my side:
One is benevolence[14]
Second is frugality[15]
Third is not dare to stand in front of people

Benevolence should produce courage
Frugality should produce affluence
Do not dare to stand in front of people, so praised be the
master of the people

Give up benevolence but to be brave
No frugality but to be affluent
Do not stand behind but master the world
One certainly must die!

Take the benevolence to fight, surely win

Take the benevolence to defend, surely secure

Heaven wants to save someone
Then gives benevolence to help him

68

A good fighter does not use aggression in martial arts
A good fighter does not get angry
A smart winner is not fighting directly with the enemy
A smart leader puts himself below

That is called someone with virtue does not contest
That is called someone with virtue that knows how to use the strength of others
So that is completely suitable with the Way

69

Conducting a war has a saying:
One does not dare to be a master
But just want to be a guest
One does not dare to advance one inch
But just wants to take a foot back
That is advancing without contest
Set a battle without having to raise your arm
Capture the enemy without having to use a weapon
Winning the enemy is like going into an empty space[16]

Nothing is more dangerous than the contemptuousness of the enemy

Contemptuousness of the enemy will lose many treasures
like fallen leaves on a branch
So when fighting
The benevolence side will win[17]

70

My words are easy to understand, easy to practice
But people do not understand
Therefore people do not practice

My words have the root
My job is well-structured
Because people do not understand me
So they don't know me

People who understand me are very little
People who follow me are rare
So the sage wears the rough cloth
But the heart embraces precious jewels

71

Knowing the unknown is superior
Not knowing but pretending to know is wrong

Of course, one must not know the wrong thing
Because knowing the wrong thing is a disease
Therefore, one shouldn't get sick

72

When people are not afraid of power
Then the king must be scared of his power

Do not bother with people's lives
Do not bother with the people's work
Not bothered, so people do not bother the king

The sage knows himself, therefore he is not showing off
The sage keeps Virtue himself, therefore he is not proud
So one leaves the latter and keeps the former

73

A brave one who greedily fights must die
A brave one who is calm must live
Those two things:
One births and one dies
Be very careful
Even a sage also thinks it is difficult

Heavenly Way, not contested but winning
Do not say but respond well
Do not call but things come
Quiet but clever plan

The net is sparse
However scatter, it is difficult to pass[18]

74

People are not afraid of death
Why use death to scare?
If it makes people always afraid
And if every criminal is caught and killed
So who left?

Killing is carried out by executioner
Replace that person
Like replacing a woodcutter
Rarely does not cut hands

75

Heavy taxes make people hungry
And the people are hard to rule because the
the law is too strict

People despise death
Because the rulers are harsh

Only people who live are not too extreme
Then precious life

76

Newlyborn humans are pliable
When they are dead, they are stiff
Newly born trees are soft
When they are dead, they are hard and dry

So stiff and hard represent death
Pliable and softness represent life
Strong and violent is the dead
Hard trees are cut

So hard and strong should be put under
Pliable and softness should be put above

77

The Way of heaven is like stretching a bow
High, then lowering the bow
Low, then raising the bow
Abate the surplus
Fill the lack

The Way of people are not so
Abate the lack
Fill the surplus

Who knows how to take the surplus and give it to the world?
Only a Way person can do that!

So sages do without relying on
Success without contesting
Don't show self genius

78

Under the dome of the sky, nothing is softer than water
But the hard-hitting attack is nothing more
So nothing can replace it[19]

Weak wins strong
Soft wins hard
Everyone knows
But no one can follow

So sage:
Withstand the stains of home country
Then he can master the nation
Withstand the disasters of the people
Then he can be the king of the people[20]

Straight words sound like a contradiction

79

Solve big enmity
Yet small enmity
So why is it right?

So sage:
Keep the contract on the left
Without harassment

Those with Virtue keep the terms of the treaty
Non-Virtue person takes it all

Heaven Way is not biased
But always stand by the people with the Virtue[21]

80

A small country has small population
Although there are many means
But still no need

People value death
So they don't move far away

There are boats and carts
But no need to use them
There are armors and weapons
But they are not on display

Make people use the knot style again
Food is simple but delicious
Cloth is rudimentary but beautiful
The house is primitive but peaceful
Tradition is pure but fun

So the neighboring countries see each other
Hear each other's chickens crowing and dogs barking
But when dying in old age
Still not going back and forth to each other[22]

81

The truthful words are not gaudy
The gaudy words are not the true
Good people do not argue
The people that argue are not good
People who know are not broad-mind
The broad-mind people do not know

The sages do not hoard
The more one helps others, the more one has surplus
The more one gives others, the more one has

The Way of Heaven expands without hindering
The Way of sage does without contesting[23]

Notes

THE FIVE SPHERES AND OTHER WRITINGS

A Few Words
1. Source: Wikipedia. If calculating the bordered area of ancient Vietnam in the past, north was contiguous to Động Đình lake located at the 29th parallel, south bordering Hồ Tôn (Chiêm Thành) country located at the 11th parallel, west bordering Ba Thục country at the meridian 105th East and east bordering the Pacific Ocean was located at the meridian of 118 East. The total area of ancient Vietnam had has about 2,900,000 km². But Vietnam's area in 2017 was only 33,212 km².

2. Way: Đạo. Đạo in Vietnamese literally means a Path or a Way, figurative meaning carries an abstract concept of the path, direction, path that leads people to some goal or ideal. However, all these different Paths or Ways have the same basic foundation based on goodness, beauty, pure, healthy nature, and "trueness" in pursuit of happiness and peace for human. When it comes to Đạo, people often think that it is a religious issue that targets Buddhism, Christianity or

other religions that are handed down today. Actually, Đạo is mainly about spirituality, which relies on the beliefs or beliefs of the followers to encourage people to do good and avoid evil. The other paths also teach people how to live, behave, how to love, give, receive, and justice. I use the word "Way" during translation, which means action Way in all things, not alluding to religion. I use the word "Way" for English translation in this meaning.

3. The "Successful Way" series include a set of four books written in the "A few Words" section was also translated by me; temporarily not yet published.

4. Ancient Vietnamese land, north bordered Động Đình Lake, south bordered Hồ Tôn country, west bordered Ba Thục country, and east bordered Pacific Ocean, then ancient Qi land in ancient times lied in the land of ancient Vietnam.

5. The country's outline is between the Hoai Ha and Yangtze. These places lied in the land of ancient Vietnam.

6. This phrase meant nothing can make you move from outside and nothing can bother you from inside. I used this phrase as same meaning in "The Thirty-Five Articles About Sword Strategy" in "On Stone Body" section by Miyamoto Musashi.

7. The old Vietnamese proverb says that four things a true saint needs to do in life: first is to train mental and physical intensively (cultivate oneself). Second is taking great care family (family ruling). Third is to help the nation (nation ruling). After that, make people peaceful "world peace".

8. Viet Cong simply means Vietnamese who follow the Communists. They are not Vietnamese because their purpose is to serve Communism through the model of authoritarian Communist party rule; lurking Vietnamese people with the guise for the people, for the nation.

9. I call anti-nationalist "Marxist-Leninist" dictatorship because this regime has been suffocating all the rights of life, liberty, and right of the Vietnamese people. All authorities are only in a handful of Vietnamese communist party leaders through the control of Chinese Communist Party.

10. Thái thú is the original Vietnamese term. According to the "Đại Từ Điển Tiếng Việt", thái thú means a ruler of a district under Han Dynasty invader.

11. Vietnamese trader here means a Vietnamese who indirectly or directly working for China to seize power and national property for himself under the name of the Vietnamese communist party.

12. The ancestral property left to the current Vietnamese descendants is the Viem Viet civilization and the territory of only three hundred thousand square kilometers. Otherwise, the world will no longer know what Vietnam is because Vietnam might closeout by China few thousand years ago.

About Miyamoto Musashi
1. According to our tradition about age calculation, he is 62 years old. But in the West, it is counting one year old at first birthday while in the East we are one year old at birth. Here I calculate according to the age according to the West.

2. So Miyamoto Musashi wrote all three books under the title: The Thirty Five Articles About Sword Strategy, The Five Spheres and The Way Of Walking Alone.

3. Lucky day: can be on the 4th, 10th, 16th, 22nd or the 28th of the month. Japanese people believe these days are the lucky days in the month.

4. Warrior Way: Michi Hei Ho みち へい ほ.

The Five Spheres

Introduction
1. Warrior Way: Michi Hei Ho.
"Michi" means Way as noted above, "Hei" means soldiers or soldier (In ancient Japanese writing, it does not distinguished noun between singular and plural), and "Ho" means method or form. The word Way here has the same meaning in Vietnam as "people religion". Sometimes Miyamoto Musashi uses the word Way to mean strategy such as a "strategist" or the truth way to do something.
2. Two Heaven Unifications: Ni Ten Ichi Ryu.

"Ni Ten" means the two gods and "Ichi Ryu" is a flow. I think Miyamoto Musashi meant the use of two swords as one path of water flow.

3. The twentieth year of the Kanei era, which is 1643. There is also other book noted in 1645 (?). I think the year 1643 is correct because he finished writing "The Five Spheres" in 1645 before he died.

4. Buddha Guan Yin: The Green Tara (Sanskrit: Shyamatara; Tibetan: Sgrol-ljang) was believed to be incarnated as the Nepali princess. She is considered by some to be the original Tara and is the female consort of Amoghasiddhi (see Dhyani-Buddha), one of the "self-born" Buddhas.

5. Shakyamuni Buddha: whose profound insight penetrated universal truths and the laws, and principles governing life in this world – "Buddha" means "the awakened one" or "the enlightened one" in Sanskrit.

6. Bodhisattva (in Mahayana Buddhism) is a person who is able to reach nirvana but delays doing so out of compassion in order to save suffering beings.

7. It is between 3 am to 5 am.

Scroll 1 – Earth

1. Military strategy or "Strategy" deals with the planning and conduct of campaigns, the movement and disposition of forces, and the deception of the enemy. The father of Western modern strategic studies, Carl von Clausewitz (1780–1831), defined military strategy as «the employment of battles to gain the end of war.»

2. A lord is a leader or a major influence in a career chosen as in bank lords, a high position in feudalism, a nobleman or a caste; a person whose common name contains by courtesy the title of lord or a number of higher titles. The warrior clans have taken control of Japan for most of their history. These families all have lords and control their own army.

3. There are four branches of the Fujiwara clan. This clan dominated Japan during the Heian period. There are also four different tea schools. It is possible here that Miyamoto Musashi referred to the four "houses" belonging to farmers, merchants, warriors and crafts.

4. This is the writing of Japanese people. When they write the word "carpenter", it combines the word "noble" and "talented" together (in Japanese characters writing ofcourse).

5. The warrior clans have taken control of Japan for most of their history. These families all have lords and control their own army.

6. Japanese Samurai wield two swords through the left belt with the cutting edge on them. The shorter sword is called the companion sword. Samurai always carried companion sword with him and carried longer sword just outside the door. There are occasional rules governing the pattern and length of swords. The Samurai class was allowed to carry two swords but the other classes were only allowed to carry one sword to fight the bandits on the way between towns. The Samurai kept the short sword by the bed and had racks for the long swords inside the lobby of each house.

7. Dojo is mostly done indoors. There are many forms and rituals to be observed and to be safe from the curious eyes of rival schools.

8. Ken (間) is a traditional Japanese unit of length, equal to six Japanese feet (shaku). The exact value has varied over time and location but has generally been a little shorter than 2 meters (6 feet 7 in). It is now standardized as 1.8182 meter.

9. According to Wikipedia, musket is a muzzle loaded long gun that appeared as a smoothbore weapon in the early 16th century, at first as a heavier variant of the arquebus, capable of penetrating heavy armor. By mid-16th century, this type of musket went out of use as heavy armor declined, but as the matchlock became standard, the term musket continued as the name given for any long gun with a flintlock, and then its successors, all the way through the mid-1800s. This style of musket was retired in the 19th century when rifled muskets (simply called rifles in modern terminology) became common as a result of cartridged breech-loading firearms introduced by Casimir Lefaucheux in 1835, the invention of the Minié ball by Claude-Étienne Minié in 1849, and the first reliable repeating rifle produced by Volcanic Repeating Arms in 1854. By the time that repeating rifles became common, they were known as simply "rifles", ending the era of the musket.

Scroll 2 – Water

1. In 16th century Japan, sword testing was tested by highly specialized testing experts. The sword will be attached to a special cutting frame to do body-tested cuts, straw bundles, armor and metal plates, etc.

2. Yin - yang in Chinese, "Âm - dương" in Vietnamese or "In - Yo 陰 陽" in Japanese are cosmic dual forces, ie. Moon-sun, female-male, dark-bright, left-right. Musashi favored the "In-Yo" walkway, although he emphasized the importance of the right and left legs as written in the Wind scroll.

3. Path is like a way of life and is the natural path of the sword. There is a natural movement of the sword regarding its natural behavior. This is called the path of the sword.

4. It is hard to understand Musashi's approach and attack because it comes from nothingness. So people usually don't know where it came from. It is essential to study traditional schools and basic cutting practices. Remember that fighting techniques can start from a distance further than at first glance. It is said that when humans face death at the sword point. Understanding is enhanced.

5. Monkey here means short-handed monkey. In Japanese Buddhist legend, a monkey observes the moon reflected in a stream in the fall. This monkey reached out to try to scoop the moon but fell into the water. So then the monkey no longer dared to open its arms so far. This is a famous story in the era of Musashi and the mention of a monkey will allude to this meaning.

6. Lacquer is a liquid made of shellac dissolved in alcohol or of synthetic substances that dries to form a hard protective coating for wood, metal, etc. Japanese used this on furniture, household decorations, architectures, weapons and armors etc.

7. Musashi is considered to be the inventor of the double sword style. His school is sometimes called "Nito Ryu" (Two Sword Schools) and sometimes "Niten Ryu" (Two Heaven). He wrote that the use of two swords is when there are many enemies. But people practice the secret style with a sword in each hand to gain a real advantage in protecting themselves. Musashi uses the word "two swords" which means using all available resources of a person in battle. He never used two swords when he was against a sword despite being skilled.

8. One strike or one win, the Japanese word is "hitotsu gachi".

Scroll 3 – Fire

1. One finger slang is about 3 cm (1 cm = 0.39371 inches).

2. Historically, Japanese hand fans were tools of aristocrats and the samurai class. They were a way to signify social standing, and even communicate messages. In Japan, during the Heian period, these fans became such a hit that laws were created to restrict their use to particular social classes.

3. Shinai (竹刀) means bamboo sword. The word "shinai" is derived from the verb shinau (撓う), meaning "to bend, to flex", and was originally short for shinai-take (flexible bamboo). Shinai is written with the kanji 竹刀, meaning "bamboo sword". According to Wikipedia, the earliest use of a bamboo weapon to train with instead of a sword is credited to Kamiizumi Nobutsuna (1508-1572?) of the Shinkage-ryū. The shinai was developed in an effort to reduce the number of practitioners being seriously injured during practice, making a practice weapon that was less dangerous than bokutō (木刀), the hard wooden swords they were previously using. This is also the motivation behind the development of bōgu (防具), the armour that protects the kendoka. Bamboo swords are usually made of grafted bamboo cloth or leather.

4. Japanese armour was generally constructed from many small irons (tetsu) or leather (nerigawa) scales (kozane) or plates (ita-mono) or combination of these, connected to each other by rivets and macramé cords (odoshi) made from leather or braided silk or chain armour (kusari). The whole armor used to be 6 pieces in the past: front cover, back cover, gloves, sleeves, chest cover and thigh cover.

5. This is often the place to worship ancestors in a Japanese home. The head of the household is usually sleeping closest to this place. Here they often placed the altar rising over the wall; sometimes containing a hanging scroll, armor, or other religious property.

6. Nautical mile is a unit used in measuring distances at sea, equal to approximately 2,025 yards (1,852 m).

7. Release four hands: Yotsu te o hanasu. This means that the condition of grappling with both arms attached to the opponent's two arms.

8. Shade moving: kage wo ugokasu.

9. This is recorded in the chronicles of the Terao family. Once, a lord asked Musashi: What is the body of a rock? Musashi replied: Summon my student Terao Ryuma Suke to come here. When Terao appeared. Musashi ordered him to commit suicide by dissecting his stomach. Just when Terao was about to stab himself. Musashi restrained Terao and said to the lord, "This is the body of a rock".

Scroll 4 – Wind

1. Short sword or companion sword is called wakizashi (脇差) by Japanese and is one of the traditionally worn by the samurai in feudal Japan. The wakizashi has a blade between 12 to 24 inches. The wakizashi being worn together with the katana was the official sign that the wearer was a samurai or swordsman. When worn together the pair of swords is called

daishō, which means "big-little". The katana is the big or long sword and the wakizashi is the «little» or companion sword. Wakizashi are not necessarily just a smaller version of the katana; they could be forged differently and have a different cross section.

2. "Surface" or omote (表) in Japanese. Omote is a concept that applied to almost any aspect of Japan. Omote refers to the image which an individual, a company, or any institution wishes to present to outsiders or the public in general. As with any image, omote is composed of a mixture of reality, myth, and lie.

3. "Interior" or oku (奥) in Japanese. It means depth or inner part in English.

4. Kemari 蹴鞠 is a ball game that was popular in Japan during the Heian period. Kemari has been revived in modern times. The first evidence of kemari is from 644 AD. The sport was introduced to Japan about 600, during the Asuka period. Nowadays, it is played in Shinto shrines for festivals. According to Wikipedia, George H. W. Bush played the game on one of his presidential visits to Japan.

5. The ball, known as "mari" in Japanese, is made of deerskin with the hair facing inside and the hide on the outside. The ball is stuffed with barley grains to give it shape. When the hide has set in this shape, the grains are removed from the ball, and it is then sewn together using the skin of a horse.

6. Express courier: haya michi.

7. The Old Pine: Oimatsu. "The Old Pine" is an old Japanese musical melody for flute or harp.

8. Takasago 高砂 is a traditional Noh play. It is considered a very auspicious story, involving a loving and long-married couple. The play was formerly known as Aioi (相生 Aioi) or Twin Pines (相生松 Aioi Matsu).

Scroll 5 – Emptiness

1. Bugei 武芸 here refers to adjusting or perfecting martial arts in strategy and techniques of other sects to facilitate systematic teaching and dissemination in a formal learning environment.

2. Shin-i futatsu no kokoro (しんーい ふたつ の こころ): two hearts or two minds combined. It might be seen and unseen or heart and soul putting together.

3. Jitsu no kokoro (じつ の こころ): true heart or accurate and clear heart.

The Thirty-Five Articles About Sword Strategy
1. Futatsu no tachi (ふたつ の たち): two swords or two of us.
2. Taishō (大正): general as in military general.
3. Teashi (手足): regard to hands and feet or limbs.
4. Tobu ashi (飛ぶ足): flying feet.
5. Fuyū ashi (浮遊足): floating Feet.
6. Tozan ashi (登山足): climbing feet.
7. Hikkomeru ashi (足を引っ込める): withdrawing feet.

8. Ushiro ashi (後ろ足): back-forth feet.
9. Watashi no tsuke (私のつけ): attachment of the eyes.
10. Metsuke (目付): muscle mass.
11. Me o chikaku suru (目を知覚する): perceiving eyes.
12. Mirume (見る目): seeing eyes.
13. Ken no michi (剣の道): sword path.
14. Kage wo osayuru (影をおさえる): loosen shadow.
15. Kage no oto (影の音): negative shadow or unseen shadow.
16. Kage wo ugokasu (影をうごかす): moving shadow.
17. Kage Pojitibuna (影ポジティブナ): positive shadow.
18. Chīsana kushi (小さな櫛): small comb.
19. Ishi no kokoro 意志の心 the mind of will.
20. Shin no kokoro (新の心): the spirit or the new heart.
21. Kōgeki kikai (攻撃機会): attacking opportunity.
22. Rakkā setchaku (ラッカー接着): lacquer adhesion.
23. Aki no saru no karada (秋の猿の体): autumn monkey's body.
24. Hinji hontai (ヒンジ本体): hinge body.
25. Shōgun to guntai (将軍と軍隊): the general and the troops.
26. Ichi nashi (位置なし なし): defensee not defensive or position without position.
27. Shakutai (石体): stone body or rock body.

The Way Of Walking Alone

1. Dokkōdō (獨行道 道) means the solitary path or the path to progress alone, or the path to travel alone. According to Wikipedia, Dokkōdō is a short work written by Miyamoto Musashi a week before his death in 1645. Dokkōdō consists of 21 precepts. Dokkōdō was largely written on the occasion Musashi gave away his assets in preparation for death and was dedicated to his favorite disciple Terao Magonojō, who

brought these teachings to the heart. Dokkōdō expresses a strict, honest and ascetic view of life .

THE LAW OF WAR

Chapter 1 – Planning 始 計

1. The two words 始 計 (Shǐ jì) in Sino-Vietnamese dictionary mean starting, first or calculating, estimating or planning. I think the word planning is easier to understand and more accurate because people often plan things first and then act (let alone Sun Vu was a person with a deep sharp systematic strategic mind).

2. The ancient versions often translated as heaven or God in the sense of "heavenly time" or God meant the ruler of mankind. But the word 道 (Đạo) means the path or in Lao Tzu's literal sense as the old translations often wrote. However, who understands the Taoist word 道 (Đạo) of Lao Tzu. I think the word righteousness is best used because in ancient Vietnamese, it means "the will of people was the will of God". Besides, we see Sun Vu use this word in that sense throughout the thirteen chapters he wrote. I use the word righteousness in the meaning of Lao Tzu.

3. Flexibly improvably is the use of improvisation to deal with unusual or unexpected events that occur during a war.

4. At the time of Sun Vu in two thousand five hundred years ago, the king and his advisers and generals often divination instead of calculating. They used the method of "yin-yang" or hexagram of bamboo or tortoise shell to ask the god for

the plan and if over sixty percent is won and if under sixty percent is lost. But Sun Vu at that time knew how to calculate based on facts to discuss the plan for win or loss. What a transcendent mind!

5. In the past, the king often had to abstain from the precepts for three days for sacrifice and then discuss the battle plan with the generals at the temple before raising soldiers.

Chapter 2 – Combating 作戰

1. The army here consisted of a hundred thousand soldiers divided into one thousand battalions. Each battalion has one hundred soldiers and is provided with a light chariot wagon and a heavy chariot wagon.

2. A light chariot wagon consists of four fast-moving horses, usually used for attacks. Each light chariot wagon has 75 soldiers to follow.

3. The heavy chariot wagons are often used for defense. Each heavy chariot wagon has 25 soldiers.

4. Ancient armor was usually made of bamboo or animal skin.

5. Li 英里: 1 li = 0.5789 km.

6. During this time, about 400 - 500 BC, people used gold to trade or exchange, not money currency.

7. In the old days people used the word "hundred people" as a number to generally refer to all people in the country, not just one hundred of them in a country.

8. 1 bushel = 40 liters. An old unit of volume measurement.

9. 1 picul of fodder 一 匹 草 = 50 kg. An old unit of weight measurement.

Chapter 3 – Offensive Strategy 謀 攻
1. The word army 師 here meant one division is consisting of 12500 soldiers.
2. One brigade consists of 500 soldiers.
3. One regiment consists of 100 soldiers.
4. One battalion consists of 5 soldiers.
5. Attack the strategic plan of the enemy.
6. Prevent the coalition forces to create more military power for the enemy.
7. Use your military strength to fight.
8. It means fighting at the enemy strong fortifications.
9. For example, making special moving vehicles so soldiers can hide inside while getting close to enemy wall gates.
10. The high mounds for observing enemy movement in the city or for our soldiers to jump over enemy walls and attack.
11. If our army is five times the size of the enemy, we can make enemy pays attention to the front, surprise him in rear, create a stir in the east and attack the west.
12. It is possible to use the tactic of deploying a few of our troops in the east but attacking in the west.
13. Reduce enemy military power.

Chapter 4 – Military Disposition 軍 形
1. This vulnerability may be due to lack of preparation, lack of stratagem. Here, I think Sun Vu referred to weather created by nature such as heavy rain, dry weather, dark clouds etc.,

so people are not in control to plan ahead. Our general Trần Hưng Đạo was very good at this subject, he taught the technique of considering the appearance of stars to accurately forecast weather conditioning in advance in the first part of his book called "The Essential Art of War". But most of our translators did not translate that part because they thought it was vague.

2. In acient Chinese, they believed the earth's gods lived under nine layer of the earth. One of eight gods belongs to the eight trigrams. It is believed that anyone who enters under the ninth layers is easy to hide and defend because this layer is the deepest.

3. Same as above, Chinese people believed there were nine levels of heaven. The nineth layer is supposed to be highest, therefore it is easier to attack if one is staying in this layer. We may think now as using aircrafts to attack ground.

4. Defeating the enemy is very easy because the great general had previously created situations for the enemy to be in a defeated position.

5. 1 "dật" = 500 grams.

6. 1 "thù" = 1 gram.

7. 1 "knobstick" = 6.48 meters.

Chapter 5 – Military Force 兵勢

1. "Indirect" here means attacking enemy force on the side (left or right). Usually, it is a surprise attack using strange moves that the enemy has not thought of.

2. "Direct" here means attacking enemy force head on.
3. The magic of real and unreal is to make enemy confuse of what is real and what is fake from us. Mainly for enemy not able to predict our true intentions.
4. The five based colors are red, blue, yellow, white, and black.
5. The five based flavors are sour, bitter, salty, sweet, and spicy.

Chapter 6 – Real and Unreal 虛實
1. Five elements are metal, wood, water, fire, and earth.
2. Four seasons are spring, summer, autumn, and winter.

Chapter 7 – Maneuvering 軍爭
1. The three generals here meant the general holding three troops is the commander in chief of the front, middle and rear battle troops.
2. Here means the front, middle, and rear enemy troops.

Chapter 8 – Nine Changes 九變
1. Barren land is the place where food and water supplies are scarce.
2. Being surrounded with no way out.
3. In a very dangerous situation, if one doesn't fight back with all ones has, he will die for sure. Fighting back may have a chance to survive.
4. Because there are roads if passing by will destroy your troops.
5. If we are not sure we will win, we will not fight.
6. Besiege the fortresses take times and risk of not taking it.
7. The terrain is not favorable, we do not fight.
8. If according to the king's order we will lose the battle, then we should not follow.

9. I am guessing the five benefits that Sun Vu mentioned here are from the 1st chapter on Planning: righteousness, atmosphere, terrain, general, and martial law.

Chapter 9 – Marching 行 軍
1. Relying on the stream has the advantage of having a source of drinking water for soldiers.
2. It is difficult for soldiers to fighting up because the earth's gravity always pulled down soldiers' weight and weapons. Soldiers have to use more strength to both advance and fight.
3. On contrary, fighting down is easy and takes less effort, especially in the past, soldiers often use spears to fight.
4. The enemy's soldiers in the middle of stream will be in turmoil and can't do much. If the force is the same then it's two against one, we can see that we have double advantage.
5. Same principle as 'Don't climb up to join battle on high ground.'
6. Because it's difficult to move and easy to get ambush. Beside, human don't drink salt water.
7. It is not clear who king Huỳnh Đế is but the old books noted that king Si Vưu of Viêm Việt used the four topographical tactics in this chapter to defeat all four neighbor kings, including Tam Miêu.
8. Because the fear of sudden water rise, the troops will be drown or separate and could not save each other in this situation.
9. The enemy is thristy.

Chapter 10 – Terrain 地形
1. Usually southeast.
2. Exit is difficult because rivers, trenches or strongholds. So it's easy to be surrounded by enemy when withdraw troops.
3. The army entering this terrain is difficult to battle due to the lack of force concentration because of dividing forces.
4. This terrains usually have cliffs on both side and very narrow path in the middle.
5. These terrains are usually pass, bar, hill, mountain, abyss etc. Attack here is easy to trap death.
6. Because it is far and wide, it is difficult to supply weapons, food, and reinforcements.
7. In the past, incompetent kings and general often blame 'heaven and earth' for their mistake.
8. Run before the fight.
9. Run after lost battle.
10. In the past, if general lose a battle, he often get humiliated and guilty before his king.

Chapter 11 – Nine Ground Positions 九地
1. The position to against enemy on dipersed ground is to fight enemy on the lands within one's own country. Therefore soldiers often linger on wife, children, brothers, sisters, and parents. That is why they are easily flee or not risk death against enemy. So they are often broken or failed.
2. On shoal ground, the soldiers are often depressed, wanting to retreat back to their homeland.
3. In a position to compete with the enemy to gain advantage.
4. Hưng Đạo Vương Trần Quốc Tuấn used this tactic perfectly against the Mongols in the 13th century. He didn't directly

attack where the Mongols wanted but keep the important grounds for later suprise attack. He made sure the enemy can't get any food supplies from our land while destroyed enemy food supplies. At first, he didn't engage in battle on our land to peiserved the vigor of the army and people. He waited for enemy to be in mysterious then total attack and win in the end.

5. Camping and linger on shoal ground has many disadvantages. Our soldiers' moral is in a situation of fatique, fear and fustration.
6. Because one doesn't want to lose our troops when enemy prepared. But if one takes it first, there are many advantages.
7. When going deep into enemy territory, food for troops is one of the most critical jobs because it is difficult, expensive and dangerous to transport from thousands of miles.
8. Forest mountains, rugged cliffs, swamps and wetlands are difficult to move as well as reinforcements but easy to be destroyed by ambushes so we must quickly move out of these places.
9. Being surrounded on all sides, it is impossible to use ordinary tactics to break the siege.
10. On death ground, if one decides to fight hard then one might survive and win, but if not, he has no chance to survive.
11. Taking the most advantageous conditions of the enemy in advance, it is imperative that he has to change from being active to passive. The enemy was in a passive position, so he had to follow your control.
12. Legend has it that Chuyên Chư was from Wu country, hid a small sword in grilled fish's belly, and stabbed Vương Liê~u, Wu's prince, to repay prince Quang for nuturing

and taking care of Chuyên Chư old mother. Chuyên Chư was killed by Vương Liễu bodyguards. Thanks to that, prince Quang was crowned king, namely Hạp Lư of the Wu dynasty.
13. Tào Quế is high official from Lỗ dynasty. When Tề Hoàn Công met his vassals in Khá territory, Tào Quế held a sword to inhibit Tề Hoàn Công asking him to repay Lỗ territory.
14. Today people do not know for sure what kind of snake is Suất Thiên in the mountain of Hoành Sơn. But in 'bát trận' said that sometimes 'trận xà bàn' can change to 'Suất Thiên' formation.

Chapter 12 – Fire Attack 火 攻

1. According to lunar calendar, these four days are 7, 14, 27, and 28.
2. Quickly attack from the outside to help our troops in the enemy camp and win.
3. Do not attack immediately because enemy may have prepared.
4. The principle of fire is to burn according to the wind direction. One doesn't want to attack against wind direction because it will burn one's troops. In contrast, attacking with wind direction is to use the wind to burn one's enemy.

Chapter 13 – Using Spy 用 間

1. One 'vạn' = 10000. This is the unit for measuring quantity. Sun Vu wrote 10 vạn so it is 100000 soldiers.
2. The national public fund here is understood as the court (kingdom) members (king family and its relatives). These people must contribute money, armors, weapons, horses, food etc. to the war.

3. During Sun Vu time, the court (kingdom) divided land as follow: 8 houses were entitled to own 9 plots of land. The middle space is used to build houses and dig wells. Each house is given a space around for cultivation and plowing. If any house has a soldier, the other seven houses must provide all expenses such as clothing as well as laborious service to follow to carry the transport. That is why 100,000 soldiers bothered 700,000 houses.
4. In the past, kings and generals used to believe in superstition.
5. Local people knows about their place of living more accurate than foreigners. The issue is whether they accept the work for the other party or not. Often the local spies are lured to work for other party.
6. The officials were dissatisfied with the court or had their own personal gain.
7. These types of spies are often bribed by means or known to be enemy spies, but we pretend to be ignorant and reveal false information so they can misreport us.
8. The suicide spy is our spy against enemy's spy. So when enemy sees things that don't happen right, they will kill that person. Therefore, it should be called suicide.
9. The report spy is our spy lying in the heart of enemy. He is intelligent, high position, and influential person. He scanned the enemy's military openly without fear of being exposed.
10. Y Doãn was the general of the Ân dynasty.
11. Khương Tử Nha was the strategist master general of the Zhou dynasty.

THE PRINCE

1. Francesco Sforza (1401-1466): Duke of Milan, part of Italy today. He came from a mercenary general and became the Duke of Milan in 1450.

2. King of Spain Ferdinand (1452-1516): Originally accepted to divide the kingdom of Naples, Italy by French King Louis XII, but King Ferdinand drove the French army and recaptured Naples in 1503. He was the husband of Isabella, and he was also the financier for Columbus to find a new world (America).

3. Duke of Ferrara: In fact, there were two dukes, Ercole d'Este (1431-1505), who lost territory to the Venetians in 1484 and his successor, Alfonso d'Este (1476-1534), who held power despite the objections of three different popes. The d'Este family ruled Ferrara for nearly 400 years.

4. Pope Julius II: Succession to Pope Alexander XI, attention for his defense of the secular and spiritual powers of the Catholic church.

5. King Louis XII (1462-1515): Invader of Italy and the direct main ruler of foreign countries right before the time when the book of The Prince was written. King Louis XII succeeds King Charles.

6. Lodovico Sforza (1451-1508): Son of Francesco Sforza and was a Duke of Milan. He encouraged King Charles VIII of France to invade Italy.

7. The Aetolian and the Achaean were the competitors of the Greek nations. Around 211 BC, the Aetolian asked the

Romans to help them fight against Macedon's Phillip V. The Romans defeated Phillip, and a few years later, defeating the Aetolian and their ally, the Antiochus III of Syria, proved to be effective in capturing Greece.

8. King Charles VIII: Ruler of France, who conquered Italy at the urging of Ludovico Sforza but was quickly expelled.

9. Pope Alexander VI (Rodrigo Borgia): The corrupt and decadent leader of the church who did not hesitate to put bastards into positions of power.

10. Darius (280-330 BC): King of Persia, one of the territories that Alexander the Great conquered.

11. Alexander the Great (356-323 B.C.E.): King of Macedonia and one of the great conquerors of the ancient world.

12. Girolamo Savonarola (1452-1498): Dominican monk, predestined missionary, and prophet, ruled Florence after the Medici family was stripped of power.

13. Hiero is also known as Hieron II, King of Syracuse (c. 271-216 BC). He commanded the Syracusan army and was so successful that he was chosen as king by the citizens.

14. Cesare Borgia: Son of Alexander VI, Duke Valentinois of France, and conqueror of Romagna region in Italy. Machiavelli's prime example of an ideal prince.

15. Orsini and Colonna confronted families of the Roman aristocracy, both of whom had great powers in Italian

politics. In particular, the Orsini family was a bitter rival to Borgia, and Cesare Borgia ordered at least three members of the Orsini family to be killed.

16. College of Cardinals: A council responsible for electing a successor when the current Pope dies.

17. Agathocles (c. 361-289 B.C.E.) was the King of Syracuse, expelled from Syracuse because of his power and fame. He returned through the intervention of Hamilcar, leader of the allies of Syracuse, the Carthaginians. A military coup follows, in which Agathocles kills or expels the oligarchs that rule the city.

18. Oliverotto da Fermo (c. 1475-1503): Machiavelli describes exactly how he wields power. Soon after, he was involved in a plot by the captains of Cesare Borgia to try to limit Borgia's growing power. This group includes Vitellozzo Vitelli, brother of Oliverotto's advisor, Paolo Vitelli. Pretending to be reconciled with them, Borgia lured the conspirators to a meeting in Senigallia, where he killed them.

19. Nabis, ruler of Spartan (c. 207-192 BC): Machiavelli may have exaggerated Nabis's success, but Nabis introduced many social reforms.

20. Brothers Gracchi Tiberius (166-133 BC) and Gaius Gracchus (154-121 BC): Roman officials instituted many social reforms and were killed by aristocratic opponents.

21. Messer Giorgio Scali was the leader of the Ciompi (woolly workers) rebellion in Florence in 1378. The Wool Workers'

Association held some political power, but its leaders, including Scali, were quickly overthrown and then executed.

22. The cities of Germany were the Holy Roman Empire, a loose coalition of nations that included most of what is now Germany, as well as parts of Italy and France. During the Machiavelli era, the empire consisted of more than 70 royal cities, which enforced greater and fewer levels of obedience to the Emperor, Maximilian I.

23. Pope Leo X (Giovanni de Medici): Pope at the time of The Prince was written. His election resulted in Machiavelli being released from prison. He became Pope in 1513. It was during the general amnesty commemorating his election that Machiavelli was released from prison. Pope Leo then disbanded Martin Luther, the Protestant reformer.

24. The ancient city of Carthage in northern Africa, founded by the Phonecians near the modern site of Tunis and destroyed by the Romans, was rebuilt by the Romans and destroyed by the Arabs.

25. Epaminondas is a famous Theban general. Philip II of Macedonia (382-336 BC) was not a mercenary but an ally of Thebans.

26. Filippo Maria Visconti (1392-1447), Duke of Milan. Francesco Sforza's rise to power in Milan is described in Chapter 2.

27. Queen Giovanna II of Naples (1371-1435): The case relates to a dispute between Giovanna and Muzio Attendolo

Sforza (1369-1424). Sforza supported Anjou's of Louis III as Giovanna's successor while she supported Alfonso V, King of Aragon.

28. Paolo Vitelli (c. 1459-1499) led the mercenaries working for the Florentines. The authorities of Florence became suspicious of his behavior in the war against Pisa and caused him to be executed.

29. Vailà city in which the Cambrai Federation, including the forces of Julius II and Louis XII, defeated the Venezia in 1509.

30. Alberigo da Cunio (1348-1409) was Count Cunio. He founded the St. George group, the first company of Italian mercenaries.

31. Constantinople was an old name for Istanbul. Capital of the Byzantine Empire. During the civil war, the emperor asked the Ottomans to intervene. Constantinople fell into the Ottoman Empire in 1453.

32. David was the great king of the Jews, just a young shepherd boy as he fought for King Saul against the Philistine giant, Goliath. David's rejection of Saul's armor appears in 1 Samuel 17: 38-40.

33. The Goths were Germans, and they invaded and conquered most of the Roman Empire.

34. Philopoemen (253-184 BC): Greek and leader of the Achaea Federation; he defeated Nabis the Spartan several times.

35. Hannibal (247-183 BC): President Carthage - crossed the Alps to invade Italy in 218. He was defeated by Scipio Africanus in 202 BC. Fabius Maximus, more conservative in his tactics than Scipio, also fought against Hannibal.

36. The wisest Chiron of all centaurs (half human and half horse), famous for his knowledge of medicine. He was the teacher of Asclepius, Achilles, and Hercules.

37. The Guelph supports the pope's interests. Their opponents, the Ghibelline, were supporters of the Holy Roman Empire.

38. Niccolò Vitelli (1414-1486) leads the mercenaries, father of Paolo and Vitellozo Vitelli. He became the leader of Città de Castello and destroyed several fortresses built there by his rival, Pope Sixtus IV.

39. Countess of Forli Caterina Sforza Riario (1463-1509): Her husband is Girolamo Riario (1443-1488). Negotiations with Caterina were the subject of Machiavelli's first diplomatic term in July 1499. When her husband was assassinated, she resisted the rebellion at one of her fortresses until she was helped by his uncle, Ludovico Sforza of Milan. When Cesare Borgia invaded at the end of 1499, her people greeted him and once again rebelled against her, and she was forced to surrender despite defending her fortress.

40. The Moors were Muslim inhabitants of Spain. Moors invaded Spain from North Africa at the beginning of the eighth century and controlled much of Spain until Ferdinand kicked them out during the re-occupation, completed in 1500. Ferdinand expelled the Jews at the

same time in a desire to turn Spain into a purely Christian nation. Machiavelli implied that this was a purely political campaign carried out under a religious cause.

41. Bernabò Visconti (1323-1385), the ruler of Milan, famously used bizarre punishment.

42. Antonio Giordani was a lawyer working as a minister of Pandolfo Petrucci, the ruler of Siena.

43. Emperor Maximilian I (1459-1519), ruler of the Holy Roman Empire. Father Luca Raimondi was one of his counselors. Machiavelli had an opportunity to observe Maximillian when they visited Maximillian's court on a diplomatic mission from 1507 to 1508.

44. Philip of Macedon - Philip V (238-179 BC), king of Macedon. He was defeated in 197 BC by Titus Quintus Flaminius, a Roman general at Cynoscephalae.

45. Speaking of Lorenzo Di Piero De Medici. Lorenzo de Medici was the grandson of Lorenzo the Magnificent. Prince's position was exclusive to him. The Medici family was the most powerful citizens of Florence, the leader of Europe's largest bank, and through strategic marriage alliances, has joined many European royal families.

THE BOOK OF ETHICS

Part I: The Way (Chapter 1 to Chapter 37)
1. Way is the path that people follow, sending all things to act but its origin is the mystery. Way is the universal law of the universe, governing all species.

2. Whenever a noun is used to designate something, the specified object has been limited. Since Way is absolute, there is nothing to compare.

3. The body of Way is "non-being", extremely magical. The use of Way is "being", extremely great.

4. These verses use the law of criticism in life, the purpose is only to advise us to be calm before everything. Only then will the mind be quiet.

5. Lao Tzu said that lust is the focal point of the chaos. He thinks that people just need to eat enough, be healthy, pure, and have no desire, by then the society will naturally be autonomous.

6. The application of the Way is both an entity and a void, taking it all, using it, and being extremely flexible. Because Way is naturally infinite, being mystery everywhere. It's body is hard to find and the act is hard to realize.

7. The Way creates all species naturally. The world should behave according to natural reason, then everything is in the right place. The society will be peaceful and happy.

8. Because the body of the Way is nothingness, so it covers, contains, biochemistry and nurture all species without ever running out.

9. A saint reaches to a sublime position because he takes other men's job for his work; put other people things first.

10. "When done, retreat" is synonymous with the folk saying: "Success, the body withdraws."

11. Hold a position without leaving it, behave in a righteous way without changing hearts, see doubts without indiscriminate acceptance, see benefits without taking it indiscriminately, the person with the above conditions is a master.

12. Everything moves in opposite directions: leaving and returning. To return is to go to the source, to be pure and also to be the Way.

13. When all things live by nature, without humans intervening, there is no forced force, there is no reason to practice humanity, manner, intellectual, filial piety, loyaly. These things violate the nature of mankind and arise only in opposition to a dishonest society.

14. There is nothing more enlightened by considering the substance of the matter inside.

15. To do our best to listen to the will of the people, lose the autonomy to obey the will of the people.

16. Those who have the Way never earnestly raise soldiers, use force. If you have to use it, even if you win or lose, many people will die in the battlefield. That is a misfortune for the world.

17. The Way and worldly knowledge are very different, so Lao Tzu uses the first 4 contrasting sentences with the title "Soft wins hard".

18. Even to the Way, I do not want. Not wanting it because I have immersed myself in the Way. Way and I are one. That

is the real Way. If I still desire Way that means Way is different from me and I am outside of Way. That means Way is like an obstacle to me. So neither does Way ever bother.

Part II: The Virtue (Chapter 38 to Chapter 81)
1. This chapter captures Lao Tzu's principles. He took "nameless" as Way and "named" as Virtue, belongs to the being, then the order from virtue down to human, manner, ceremony, wisdom. The lower the worst, the far away. Heaven and earth gave birth to all things, and the earth was very large but heaven and earth have never claimed to be virtuous. All things also do not know the virtue of heaven and earth. That is why there is no need of virtue, no need of accepting virtue, and no need of knowing virtue. So there is perfect, transcendent virtue. Actually, according to Lao Tzu, heaven and earth do nothing, but nothing they won't created. All living creatures that are in heaven and earth never need to intervene or self-acknowledge. It is because of not doing, so there is nothing to do, nor nothing, because nature does it.

2. Virtue is what people have in themselves, embrace everything that they all have their own will (Virtue is the divine power of the saints, so that whatever they do, they can easily succeed).

3. Way can't be seen. One is body, two is yin and yang, and three is yin and yang harmony. When yin and yang are in harmony, they create all things.

4. As human, everyone is greedy to live and fear death. But the greed of life makes people blind, foolish, shorten their

life and dig their own bury. Because outside, we let the matter destroy, inside we let the lust to burn, for our fellow human beings, we are jealous and contested. Isn't that just yourself rushing into swords, tigers, rhinos?

5. Way is the body of virtue. Virtue is the use of Way. So body is Way and the use of Way is Virtue. So the use of Way is very deep and mysterious.

6. The more ones say the more wrongs one gets. The more one does the more wrongs one gets.

7. Tô Triệt discussed that: Lao Tzu, when it comes to morality, often uses children as an example, which is to say that. Oh! Children have foreign objects coming but do not know how to react, so they cannot talk about use. It is inherently silent, quite, and without lust. Its body is very innocent. People have a mind and then they have an image. There must be a collision with other objects that oppose us. The hurt doesn't tell the end. Only a child is heartless, does not confront external things. Ask which way does it hurt? It does not hold, but self-holds firmly. It does not desire but acts on its own, reacts. It's because it's redundant, not because of its mind. If the mind has moved, the qi will be damaged, but screaming must lead to loss of hoarseness. Now it screams all day but is still at ease, just because its mind is not moving and its qi is calm. If you draw, don't let the outside harm the inside. Knowing peace is called normal, so it can keep the root to deal with everything around. On the contrary, it greatly increases life, making it impossible for qi to react according to the natural path. People are getting stronger and stronger, trying their best,

then old age will follow. That is to lose the nature of the red child.

8. Tô Triệt said: things can be close to them, they can be cold, and they can be noble and they can be mean. The human being is in harmony with the Tao, encompassing all things evenly, so that nothing is close or far away. He considers both favorable and unfavorable circumstances, happiness as well as suffering, so there are no problems. I don't know what is honor and what is shame, so there are no people who appreciate convenient people. All relativity is left out of the circle of feeling. Therefore, being in the world is very high and luxurious.

9. Trương Mặc Sinh said: Those who fix the country's affairs, the eyes must see far, see wide, plan eternal things, so they do not use the artificial but use the main. Soldiers are unpredictable and dangerous things, the holy man only temporarily copes with temporary events. That's why it was said, "make country justice and use tricks to control the military affairs." However, to bring justice to the country must be in accordance with the Tao. But it is still a conditioned way of rule, can only keep one country, but taking the whole world is definitely not possible. Therefore, it is said to bring "nothing to get the world." Nothing means empty, no action, no arrangement of work. To hold is to take, here it means to hold to fix, arrange to change. That is to make people naturally act according to the Tao, by the way of unconditioned.

10. This chapter borrows the cooking of baby fish to compare it with the correction of a great nation. Cooking baby fish

should not be contemptuous of stirring. Repairing large countries should not be too much work, too much changes. There is not much to change, that is, only putting one's heart into following the natural transformation, applying the "correction without doing anything". In this way, heaven and earth, ghosts and spirits, all things, and the world will all be in peace, without harming each other. Virtue will join together to make peace and return to One.

11. This chapter is about the natural way of keeping Way naturally. Only those who keep the Way for big, small, few and many can be considered equal. Only those who keep their Way behave of favor or revenge contrary to the common sense of the world. When it comes to plotting difficult things from easy, and doing big things from small, only those who keep the Way, know the roots, can understand the meaning of the easy and the small.

12. People follow the Way just like the water flows down low, flowing smoothly. The leader instructs the people, although the people do not understand it, they can still follow it. When they understand and have enjoyed the true taste of the Way, they will dance and stomp their feet; naturally joyfully enlightened.

13. The king does not self humble, the world will not compete well with him. The king does not boast, the world will not compete with the king. The king must behave in such a way that everyone knows that there is a king above and in front of everyone, then people will happily honor the king to sit on and stand in front.

14. Good heart comes from the mind. That is the use of Way. For example, when a child's life is in danger. Mother dares to sacrifice her life to save the child. What other strength is there than the strength that radiates from the bottom of a mother's heart?

15. Hàn Phi Tử argues that a wise scholar who uses thrift will get rich. A sage who knows how to take care of the spirit will be full of spirit and not be damaged. The master knows that the soldiers' lives are precious, the population will increase day by day and the country will expand more and more, in short, wealth, fullness of spirit, large population, vast country, abundant and full life. All due to one word savings.

16. Owner is against, guest is favorable; tired owners, cavalier guests; forward is arrogance, backward is humility; to move forward is to be impatient and agitated, to retreat is to be gentle and quiet. Take advantage of waiting for tired enemy; take rest, wait for pride; get quiet and wait for impatiently. Such strength is the invincible power. That army went without a battle; twist shirt without using arms; wield weapons like no weapons; capture the enemy without fighting enemy. The above points show us what it is to win without fighting, like bringing troops into an empty place.

17. Because the saint knows pain and suffering, he appreciates everyone, making the whole people eager to rise up. So, definitely defeat the enemy. That is why it is said: so when fighting, the side with sincerity will win.

18. Nguy Nguyên explained that: strong in dare to do will often pay attention to the point of killing and not letting go.

Strong in not daring to do, will often focus on the point of preserving people's lives. In the two lines, both use the strong, but the advantage and the disadvantage, are divided into two. It is impossible not to scrutinize. Why? Because people are strong in the daring to kill and because they are obedient to God's anger and hatred, so they are determined to practice without thinking that it is difficult at all. But God's will is deep, who knows for sure who is really beng hated by God. Therefore, even saints obey God's orders to punish sins, but from the penalty of killing, they do not dare to disdain. God gives birth to all things like parents give birth to children, born without ever having the heart to destroy. Timely until an object rushes to find its way to death, even if it wants to save it, it can't be done, so the net is tilted upside down. It proves that the net of the heaven is thin, though it is sparse, but it does not let any hairs out. Why does heaven need to borrow people from the world to keep their blessings?

19. Breaking hard is nothing better than hammer and fire. Although hard as iron, stone can't stand it. But hammer and fire alone are no better than water. On the contrary, it is also eroded, crushed and extinguished by water.

20. King Câu Tiễn suffered disgrace for his country. King Lê Lợi during the reign of the Ming Dynasty, for the sake of his country, suffered disasters and tribulations when he lost the battle, his family was separated, Lê Lai had to die for him instead.

21. Trương Mặc Sinh argued that: having great resentment, only worrying about reconciliation to dissolve, of course,

it is inevitable that there will be some residual resentment, so is that not a good solution? Therefore, saints often keep the piece on the left side of the contract without asking or demanding from others. Saying this means that the saint corrects the world, the owner is in "doing nothing but ruling", so he only holds the piece on the left side of the contract, prays that it is enough to be consistent with the faith, does not bear harsh demands and demands on humanity people. Then there will be peace between the top and bottom, right from the start, resentment has no reason to arise, let alone resentment and wait for resolution. Therefore, the virtuous king often held the left side of the contract, determined not to disturb the masses. The new ungodly king advocated setting up many laws, using many methods of destruction and killing at will to show his will to the nation. But the way of heaven does not only love people, but only always helps virtuous people, unscrupulous people should examine themselves and be alert.

22. Hà Giám Tôn said that a small country with few people, in the middle of a large country with many people, although it is difficult to govern, if one can follow the use of the Way and strive to keep the nation from being disturbed because of skillful occupations, strange, profanity, then even though many sharp tools, ten times more powerful than human strength, still can not use for anything. The things that need to be used are only plows, harrows, and hoes, which make people satisfied with their lives, their possessions are usually full. Therefore, they naturally value death and do not want to leave their dwelling place; respecting death for the sake of living and not relocating because of a peaceful

business; born in any land where it is enough to live in that land, although having boats and vehicles, they do not have to ride or sit on. There are no fighting comics, no theft inside, no resentment against neighbors outside. Armor and military equipments are purchased enough but not worn, use, and displayed. The goverment doesn't push taxes for many, the people doesn't file a lawsuit. Simple rustic customs, almost nothing to do. People can just tie the rope to record the job is enough. Eating their own chestnut, barley is delicious because of their own transplant. Wearing a raw cotton fabric, beautiful because of their own weaving. Not asking for the five scents and colors to cause confusion, so the people live in peace and quiet, enjoying the customs, although the neighboring countries can be seen and heard by each other clearly of the sound of roosters crowing and dogs barking, but no one intends to move. In the country, there is no practice of soldiers wearing armor, hunting animals, or stationing posts. People do not interact with each other until old age and death. It is not forbidden by anyone, but because of the need for daily communication, the story of wandering in the battlefield or fleeing from the war is even more absent. Everyone who has tools that they don't use, has boats and ships that don't go, has armor that they don't wear, all because of their beliefs, naturally become like this, not because of the law. Rusticism has turned into a routine, people will find that they eat well, dress well, stay still, and be happy with their lifestyle. The sage corrects, the effect is clearly visible. When the old way of life has become familiar, the story of "hanging clothes, clasping hands, everyone is at peace" is no longer a myth or a fantasy.

23. Tiêu Hanh explained that: people can enjoy Lao Tzu's books and see beauty; seeing that in the end, there is nothing wrong with the logic of all things, as if it were close to the rebuttal and the vast understanding. However, they do not know that there is something else - true faith but not beauty, good without refuting, knowing but not learning widely - lies within. What does it mean? That's because what is said in five thousand words is the Way that is not contained, stored, or empty. By not contained, stored or empty then the heart is not bound, imprisoned. One speaks without saying so! However, it's not that we don't work for people but we don't compete, so we never separate of what we "have"; not without giving it to others, but never making to self that we already have much to be consumed. Then why hate rebuttal, hate studying widely? Just because you keep holding on to your opinions to compete with the rest of the world, you are in the category of "the more you talk, the more its consumed you" - not the way of heaven. If the scholar who understands the above in his heart to forget the five thousand words in this book, then Tao Te Ching already understood more than half.

Further Readings

THE FIVE SPHERES AND OTHER WRITTINGS

1. Balstasar Gracián, *The Art of Worldly Wisdom*, Translated by Christopher Maurer, MJF Books, 1992.

2. Ban Hoằng Pháp, *Chú Nghĩa: Loạt Bài Huấn Luyện Đạo Đức Nơi Ngôi Tây An Cổ Tự*, Ấn Quán Thương Binh, 1963.

3. Bhaktivedanta Swami Prabhupada, *Srimad Bhagavatam*, The Bhaktivedant Book Trust, 1978.

4. Bruce Lee, *Tao of Jeet Kune Do*, Black Belt Books, 1975.

5. Carl von Clausewitz, *On War*, Translated by J.J. Graham, Barnes & Noble Book, 2004.

6. David Scott & Tony Doubleday, *The Elements of Zen*, Barns & Noble, Inc., 1997.

7. Dương Diên Hồng, *Mưu Lược Hưng Đạo Vương*, Mũi Cà Mau, 2000.

8. Eckhart Tolle, *The Power of Now*, Namaste Publishing and New World Library, 1999.

9. Erich Fromm, *Phân Tâm Học Về Tình Yêu*, Translated by Thụ Nhân, (Không thấy NXB và năm ấn loát).

10. F.X. Tân Yên Nguyễn Hùng Oánh, *Thần Học Giáo Dân*, NSTTĐM, 1981.

11. Felicien Challaye, *Nietzche Cuộc Đời và Triết Lý*, Translated by Mạnh Tường, Xuân Thu, 1990.

12. Hàn Phi, *Hàn Phi Tử*, Translated Phan Ngọc, Văn Học, 2001.

13. Hiroshi Moriya, *The 36 Strategies of the Martial Arts*, Translated by William Scott Wilson, Shambhala, 2013.

14. Hoàng Cơ Thụy, *Việt Sử Khảo Luận*, Book 1, 2, 3, 4, 5, 6, Nam Á, Paris, 2002.

15. Inazo Nitoba, *Code of the Samurai*, Chartwell Books, 2013.

16. Jean Jacques Chevallier, *Những Danh Tác Chánh Trị*, Translated by Lê Thanh Hoàng Dân, Trẻ, 1971.

17. Kim Định, *Việt Lý Tố Nguyên*, An Tiêm, 2001.

18. Lão Tử, *Đạo Đức Kinh*, Translated by Hạo Nhiên Nghiêm Toản, Thiệu Văn Thị, Đại Nam.

19. Lê Xuân Mai, Nguyễn Ngọc Tỉnh, Đỗ Mộng Khương, *Thập Nhị Binh Thư*, Văn Hóa Thông Tin, 2002.

20. Linh Giang, *Thuật Chính Trị Cổ Kim*, Đại Nam.

21. Miyamoto Mushashi, *A Book of Five Rings*, Translated by Victor Harris, The Overlook Press, 1974.

22. Miyamoto Mushashi, *Ngũ Luân Thư*, Translated by Bùi Thế Cần, Thế Giới, 2013.

23. Miyamoto Mushashi, *The Book of Five Rings*, Nihon Services Corporation: Bradford J. Brown, Yuko Kashiwagi, William H. Barrett and Eisuke Sasagawa, Bantam Books, 1982.

24. Miyamoto Mushashi, *The Book of Five Rings*, Source: http://www.holybooks.com, 1664.

25. Nguyễn Hiến Lê, *Khổng Tử*, Văn Hóa, 1992.

26. Nguyễn Hữu Liêm, *Tự Do Và Đạo Lý*, Biển Mới, 1993

27. Nguyễn Như Ý, Đại Từ Điển Tiếng Việt, Văn Hóa Thông Tin, 1999.

28. Nguyễn Tử Quang, *Chính Trị Cổ Nhân*, Đại Nam, 1957.

29. Phillip Novak, *The World's Wisdom*, HarperSanFrancisco, 1994.

30. Noah Webster, *Webster's New Universal Unabridged Dictionary*, Deluxe 2nd Edition, Dorset & Baber, 1983.

31. Ralph D. Sawyer, *The Seven Military Classics of Ancient China*, Westview Press, 1993.

32. Ray Pawlett, *The Handbook of Tai Chi*, Barnes & Noble Books, 2005.

33. Robert Greene, *The 48 Laws of Power*, Penguin Books, 1998.

34. Shelton B. Kopp, *If You Meet The Buddha on the Road, Kill Him!*, Bantam Books, 1972.

35. Thomas Cleary, *The Japanese Art of War*, Shambhala, 1992.

36. Trần Gia Phụng, *Việt Sử Đại Cương*, Book 1, Non Nước Toronto, 2004.

37. Trần Hưng Đạo, *Binh Thư Yếu Lược*, Translated by Nguyễn Ngọc Tỉnh, Quê Mẹ Paris, 1988.

38. Tư Mã Thiên, *Sử Ký*, Translated by Phan Ngọc, Văn Hóa Thông Tin, 1999.

39. Zhuge Liang & Liu Ji, *Mastering the Art of War*, Translated by Thomas Cleary, Shambhala, 1989.

THE LAW OF WAR

1. Carl von Clausewitz, *On War*, Translated by J.J. Graham, Barnes & Noble Book, 2004.

2. Dương Diên Hồng, *Mưu Lược Hưng Đạo Vương*, Mũi Cà Mau, 2000.

3. Karl von Clausewitz, *War, Politics, and Power*, Translated by Edward M. Collins, Regnery Gateway, Inc., 1962.

4. Gerald A. Michaelson and Steven Michaelson, *Sun Tzu – The Art Of War For Managers*, Adams Media, 2010.

5. James Trapp, *Sun Tzu – The Art Of War*, Chartwell Books, Inc., 2012.

6. Khương Lữ Vọng, *Thái Công Binh Pháp*, Translated by Lê Xuân Mai, Thanh Hóa, 1996.

7. Khương Lữ Vọng, Hoàng Thạch Công, *Thái Công Binh Pháp & Tố Thư*, Translated by Mã Nguyên Lương & Lê Xuân Mai, Xuân Thu 1990,

8. Lưu Minh Sơn, *Thập Nhị Binh Thư*, Văn Hóa Thông Tin, 2002.

9. Mã Anh Kiệt, *Tôn Ngô Binh Pháp Toàn Thư*, Đại Nam.

10. Ngô Như Tung, Hoàng Phác Dân, *Binh Pháp Tôn Tử*, Mũi Cà Mau, 1998.

11. Nguyễn Hiến Lê, *Hàn Phi Tử*, Văn Hóa, 1995.

12. Ralph D. Sawyer, *Sun Tzu - The Art Of War*, Barnes & Noble, Inc., 1994.

13. Ralph D. Sawyer, *The Seven Military Classics Of Ancient China*, Westview Press, Inc., 1993.

14. Samual B. Griffith, *Sun Tzu – The Art Of War*, Oxford University Press, 1963.

15. Sun Tzu, *The Art of War*, Translated by Nigel Cawthorne, Arcturus Publishing Limited, 2011.

16. Trần Hưng Đạo, *Binh Thư Yếu Lược*, Translated by Nguyễn Ngọc Tỉnh, Quê Mẹ Paris, 1988.

THE PRINCE
1. Baldesar Castiglione, *The Book of the Courtier*, Penguin Classics, 1976.

2. Ban Hoằng Pháp, *Chú Nghĩa: Loạt Bài Huấn Luyện Đạo Đức Nơi Ngôi Tây An Cổ Tự*, Ấn Quán Thương Binh, 1963.

3. F.X. Tân Yên Nguyễn Hùng Oánh, *Thần Học Giáo Dân*, NSTTĐM, 1981.

4. Jackques Bergier, *Tình Báo Khoa Học*, Translated by Bùi Nguyên Hiếu & Nguyễn Chi Phương, 1992.

5. Khương Lữ Vọng, *Thái Công Binh Pháp*, Translated by Lê Xuân Mai, Thanh Hóa, 1996.

6. Lê Xuân Mai, *Tư Mã Binh Pháp*, Thanh Hóa, 1997.

7. Linh Giang, *Thuật Chính Trị Cổ* Kim, Đại Nam.

8. Lưu Minh Sơn, *Thập Nhị Binh Thư*, Văn Hóa Thông Tin, 2002.

9. Ma Trọng Thẩm, *Binh Luật*, 2021.

10. Ma Trọng Thẩm, *Ngũ Luận và Những Ghi Chép Khác*, 2021.

11. Ma Trọng Thẩm, *On The Soldier's Path*, 2020.

12. Ma Trọng Thẩm, *The Five Spheres and Other Writings*, 2020.

13. Mã Anh Kiệt, *Tôn Ngô Binh Pháp Toàn Thư*, Đại Nam.

14. Nghiêm Xuân Hồng, *Lịch Trình Diễn Tiến Của Phong Trào Quốc Gia Việt Nam*, Đại Nam.

15. Nguyễn Hiến Lê, *Hàn Phi Tử*, Văn Hóa, 1995.

16. Nguyễn Tử Quang, *Chính Trị Cổ Nhân*, Đại Nam, 1957.

17. Niccolo Machiavelli, *The Art of war*, Translated by Arte Della Guerra, Da Capo Press, Inc., Original printed in 1521.

18. Niccolo Machiavelli, *The Prince And Other Translated by* W.K. Marriott, Fall River Press, 2008.

19. Niccolo Machiavelli, *The Prince And The Discourses*, Random House, Inc., 1950.

20. Roger Fisher, *Beyond Machiavelli*, Elizabeth Kopelman & Andrea Kupper Scheider, Penguin Books, 1994.

21. Sài Vũ Cầu, *Mưu Lược Gia Tinh Tuyển*, Book 1, 2, 3, 4, 5, 6, 7, Công An Nhân Dân, 1999.

22. Stanley Bing, *What Would Machiavelli Do?*, MJF Books, 2000.

23. Trần Hưng Đạo, *Binh Thư Yếu Lược*, Translated by Nguyễn Ngọc Tỉnh, Quê Mẹ Paris, 1988.

24. Tùng Châu Ngô Đình Nhu, *Chính Đề Việt Nam*, Đồng Nai, 1964.

25. William J. Duiker, *The Communist Road to Power in Vietnam*, 2nd Edition, Westview Press, 1996.

THE BOOK OF ETHICS
1. Bukkyo Dendo kyokai, *The Teaching Of Budda*, Society For Promotion Of Buddhism, 1995.

2. Chang Chung Yuan, *Original Teachings Of Ch'an Buddhism*, Grove Press, Inc., 1969.

3. David Scott, Tony Doubleday, *The Elements Of Zen*, Barns & Noble, Inc., 1997.

4. Đào Duy Anh, *Việt Nam Văn Hóa Sử Cương*, T.P. Hồ Chí Minh, 1992.

5. Eckhart Tolle, *The Power of Now*, New World Library and Namaste Publishing, 1999.

6. Ellen M. Chen, *The Tao Te Ching*, Paragon House, 1989.

7. Giáp Văn Cường, *Lão Tử: Đạo Đức Huyền Bí*, Đồng Nai, 1995.

8. John Heider, *The Tao Of Leadership*, Batam Books, 1988.

9. Kim Định, *Việt Lý Tố Nguyên*, An Tiêm, 2001.

10. Lý Tế Xuyên, *Việt Điện U Linh Tập,* Translated by Lê Hữu Mục, Khai Trí, 1960.

11. Man-Ho Kwok, Martin Palmer, Jay Ramsay, *Tao Te Ching*, Barns & Noble Books, 1993.

12. Michael Reagan, *The Holy Bible*, Illuminated Family Edition, Skyhorse Publishing, 2000.

13. Nghiêm Toản, *Lão Tử Đạo Đức Kinh*, Khai Trí, 1971.

14. Nguyễn Duy Cần, *Lão Tử Tinh Hoa*, Đại Nam.

15. Nguyễn Hiến Lê, *Luận Ngữ*, Văn Học, 1994.

16. Nguyễn Hiến Lê, *Mặc Học*, Văn Hóa, 1995.

17. Nguyễn Hiến Lê, *Trang Tử Và Nam Hoa Kinh*, Văn Hóa – Thông Tin, 1994.

18. Nguyễn Hiến Lê, *Tuân Tử*, Văn Hóa, 1994.

19. Nguyễn Hồng Trang, *Trang Tử: Trí Tuệ Của Tự Nhiên*, Đồng Nai, 1995.

20. Nguyễn Hữu Liêm, *Tự Do Và Đạo Lý*, Biển Mới, 1993.

21. Phạm Văn Sơn, *Việt Sử Toàn Thư*, Khai Trí, 1972.

22. Nguyễn Văn Trương, Đinh Kim Quốc Bảo, *Từ Điển Anh-Anh-Việt*, Văn Hóa Thông Tin, 2008.

23. Phanxicôxavie Nguyễn Văn Thuận TGM, *Đường Hy Vọng*, Spes-Divine Compassion Publications, 1991.

24. Phùng Quý Sơn, *Mạnh Tử*, Đồng Nai, 1995.

25. Ralph Alan Dale, *Tao Te Ching*, Fall River Press, 2002.

26. Ray Grigg, *The Tao Of Relationships*, Batam Books, 1988.

27. Tư Mã Thiên, *Sử Ký*, Translated by Phan Ngọc, Văn Hóa Thông Tin, 1999.

28. Vũ Kim Biên, *Văn Hiến Làng Xã Vùng Đất Tổ Hùng Vương*, Trung Tâm UNESCO Thông Tin Tư Liệu Lịch Sử Và Văn Hóa Việt Nam và Cơ Sở Văn Hóa Thông Tin Thể Thao Phú Thọ, 1999.

29. William Scott Wilson, *Tao Te Ching*, Shambhala Publicattions, Inc., 2012.

www.ingramcontent.com/pod-product-compliance
Lightning Source LLC
Chambersburg PA
CBHW071940220426
43662CB00009B/924